PLAYMAKING WITH CHILDREN

Playmaking

from KINDERGARTEN

SECOND

By WINIFRED WARD

Assistant Professor Emeritus

NORTHWESTERN
UNIVERSITY

WITH *Children*

through JUNIOR HIGH SCHOOL

EDITION

APPLETON-CENTURY-CROFTS, Inc.

New York

To

HUGHES MEARNS

In some small measure this dedication is my "thank you" to a great teacher and writer. I owe him much. No other person has had so great an influence on my philosophy in teaching young people. Even when not quoted directly, he is on page after page of this book. I am glad to have had the privilege of introducing to so many teachers and students those three fine books of his: *Creative Power, Creative Youth,* and *The Creative Adult.*

Preface

THIS NEW VERSION OF *Playmaking With Children* HAS GROWN
out of fresh experiences with classroom teachers, camp and recreation directors, and religious education leaders all over the
country. Until the last six years my students in creative dramatics,
at the Northwestern University School of Speech, had largely
been specialists, many of whom would go out to teach creative
drama in universities or teachers' colleges.

With the realization, however, that most of the playmaking in
the schools was being guided by elementary teachers, and that
comparatively few of these people had had any special training
for this work, I came to the conclusion that my book would be
most helpful if it were directed more definitely toward the classroom teacher.

For this reason I have not taken for granted that the reader
is a speech-trained person. I have tried to give techniques in a
step-by-step manner which will be easy for a beginner to follow,
knowing that as soon as she gains confidence from successful experience she will develop techniques of her own. (Since so large
a proportion of elementary teachers are women, I reluctantly continue to use the feminine gender even though, I am glad to say,
a larger number of men each year are teaching creative drama.)
I have also included several lessons recorded directly in classrooms and camps. For these I am deeply indebted to Beverly
Nygreen, Ann Heekin, Wilma McNess, Nahum Shoobs, and
George New.

Since playgrounds and camps make wide use of playmaking, there is a chapter on recreation which concerns their activities and those of the Boy and Girl Scouts. The book in general, however, is for them as well as for classroom teachers, specialists in speech education, and leaders in religious education.

Playmaking is still in the future in most church schools, but many leaders in religious education believe that a creative approach would have a much greater appeal to young people than does the present way of teaching. The chapter on the dramatization of Bible stories may open the door to a few of the possibilities, especially for vacation Bible schools.

It will be noted that playmaking is not the only art with which this book is concerned. Creative arts belong together. We create a play and find that music intensifies its mood and helps us to express its ideas rhythmically; that dance-pantomime is sometimes better than words; that, having experienced a creative play, children are often inspired to express their ideas also in poetry or paint and clay. I believe that more and more in the future, they will be exposed to all the arts, and encouraged to say what they think and feel through the medium of whichever arts are most natural to them.

I am grateful to many people in addition to the teachers whose recorded sessions appear in the book. Kenneth Graham, of the University of Minnesota, has made suggestions for the revision which were most valuable. Harold Ehrensperger, of Boston University, gave me ideas for the chapter on religious education. Rita Criste, my successor at Northwestern University and at the Children's Theatre; Elinor Rice, of the Dramatic Department; Ruth Hadden, fourth-grade teacher at Haven School; Margaret Woods, of the University of Washington; Marcella Bellmar, of the Barbereux School; Madeline Bowers, of the Pasadena public schools; and Mabel Wright Henry, of the Wilmington (Delaware) High School, have all enriched my book by the contribution of ideas, concrete illustrations, or photographs. Hazel Easton has, as always, been a valuable critic, as well as a help with my manuscript.

In sending forth this new *Playmaking*, my earnest hope is that it may encourage a stronger faith in children and their creative abilities—the kind of faith by which Natalie Cole has released the creative spirit in the children she has taught, and achieved amazing results in art and in writing; the kind of faith which brought about the remarkable creative writing by the students of Hughes Mearns.

The philosophy of both these teachers is expressed in these words from *Creative Power:**

. . . deliberately I plant in likely souls a faith in the possibilities of creative ability even when they give no outward evidence of having any. Many may conceive this procedure to be immoral; that it works, miraculously almost, is my simple utilitarian defence.

In effect I tell them, not all of it, of course, at any one time: "You have something to say. . . . Something of your very own. Try to say it. Don't be ashamed of any real thought or feeling you have. Don't undervalue it. Don't let the fear of what others may think of it prevent you from saying it. Perhaps not aloud, but to yourself. You have something to say, something that no one else in the world has ever said in just your way of saying it. . .

"You have something to say, something important, but the thing itself is not half so important to you as what the saying will be to you. If you can teach yourself to find that unique and valuable possession inside of you and succeed in getting some of it out of you, you yourself will grow astonishingly in personal power. So search for it early. Get it started in order that you may begin to grow.

"You have something to say. Find out what it is. That is the beginning. Once really started, it will carry you through life; for you will be doing for yourself all that education can ever do for anybody, encouraging that deeper and powerful self to rise within you and take possession."

W. W.

* Hughes Mearns (Doubleday & Co., 1929). By permission of the author.

Contents

xii

Appendix

Illustrations

CHAPTER 1

The Art of Playmaking

WHAT CHILDREN DO IS MORE SIGNIFICANT TO THEM THAN WHAT they see and hear. Most boys and girls would rather get into the thick of a game than to be spectators. They would choose to play in an orchestra instead of listening to one, or act in a dramatization instead of sitting in the audience. They glory in action. As one boy expressed it, "It was *exciting* being a pioneer. They had adventures instead of just walking to school chewing bubble-gum the way we do!"

Modern life with all its inventions tends to smother this love of activity and initiative in children. Elaborate toys that offer no chance for ingenuity, comic books that have slight reading text, television programs that require little thinking take the place of all manner of activities requiring imagination: exciting games involving the whole neighborhood; the building of tree-houses and elaborate wagons out of left-over boards and wheels; shows complete with strong man, clowns, a talking horse, and ending with a lurid melodrama—activities that were a part of the life of yesterday's children.

It is fortunate that a child's natural interests persist in spite of devices that threaten to stifle them. Give him the chance to use his excess energy in real, live action, and he will usually forsake them for something he likes to do; and what the little child likes to do a large share of his time is make-believe play.

1

He may come down to breakfast as a puppy, change into a robber with a pistol in each hand as he goes stealthily out the door, play store with the little girl across the street, or, when no real children are around, with an imaginary companion; and when bedtime comes go up to bed as an airplane zooming off from the living-room airport.

DRAMATIC PLAY

This is the aspect of playmaking called *dramatic play*. It is the play-living in which a child "tries on life" by putting himself in the place of any grownup who catches his interest, to say nothing of all the animals and inanimate objects he is quite as likely to become when he is four. He is entirely unselective! When he makes-believe at kindergarten, his interpretation of the adult world around him, and especially of his parents, gives his teachers a revealing picture of his home life and an understanding of his general behavior.

Much research has been done by psychologists concerning the meanings and the functions of dramatic play in a child's life. Most of them agree that "in addition to its general utility in relieving tensions and externalizing inner experience it helps the child set the boundaries between reality and unreality." [1] While he is reliving experiences he has had or doing what he has seen grownups do—the powerful grownups who can drive trucks or buses, who can operate on tonsils or put out fires—he is exploring (not consciously, of course) what it feels like to be these people. It is one of his best ways of forming concepts of his environment and his relation to it.

PLAYMAKING OR CREATIVE DRAMATICS

Playmaking, the term used interchangeably with *creative dra-*

---

[1] Ruth E. Hartley, Lawrence K. Frank, and Robert M. Goldenson, *Understanding Children's Play* (Columbia University Press, 1952).

matics, is an inclusive expression designating all forms of improvised drama: dramatic play, story dramatization, impromptu work in pantomime, shadow and puppet plays, and all other extemporaneous drama. It is the activity in which informal drama is created by the players themselves. Such drama may be original as to idea, plot, and character, or it may be based on a story written by someone else. Indeed, in dramatic play it is often as simple as one child's reliving of a situation from past experience or a fragment from a current event, motion picture, or television program.

OBJECTIVES OF PLAYMAKING

The purpose of this informal drama when used in education is not the training of actors, not the production of plays for audiences, and not primarily the developing of appreciation for a great art. Its objectives are these:

1. To PROVIDE FOR A CONTROLLED EMOTIONAL OUTLET. It is the belief of many that the most vital use of creative dramatics and the other arts, whether for normal or exceptional children, is for emotional release. We all have strong feelings and an urge to express them. Yet there are few times or places when such expression is legitimate. Instead, we are constantly having to suppress our emotions, and this suppression in many cases results in an unhealthy mental condition. J. S. Plant, in his book *The Envelope,*[2] cites the fact that practically none of the children (from six to eleven years) referred by school or court to his psychiatric clinic comes from an area where there is adequate emotional outlet.

The craving for emotional experience is strong and universal. Life to most people is inexpressibly dull without it. It is the search for excitement that causes most of the juvenile delinquency in the country. Fires are set, cars are stolen, sometimes

[2] (The Commonwealth Fund, 1950).

even murders are committed for the sake of thrill. Monotony is resisted by children and adults alike, many of whom feel that they are merely existing unless they live from one high point to another. When they cannot have excitement in real life, they seek it vicariously in the mass-entertainment media. The problem that this fact poses for education is what kind of experiences to offer that will not suppress emotions but rather help children to grow toward emotional maturity.

Emotional Release Offered by the Arts

Better than any other school experience, *the arts offer opportunities for channeling emotions into constructive uses*. Music, the graphic and plastic arts, writing, dance, and drama all direct them into channels that bring aesthetic and spiritual satisfaction to the individual. This satisfaction is not for the moment only, for when a child discovers the art through which he can best express his feelings and ideas, he usually enjoys it throughout his life. It contributes to the building of inner resources that make him independent of passing excitement, and stimulates creative thinking which gives him a never-ending zest for living.

Drama is unique among the arts in its concrete use of people and social living as material. "It is the art of all dimensions, of which life itself consists." In it a child has many vicarious experiences in conflict situations which can help him to meet real ones. Playing the part of Joseph in that dramatic scene in which he forgives the brothers who have sold him into Egypt makes a far deeper impression on a child than merely reading about Joseph. Being many kinds of characters gives him not only outlets for emotion but the chance to understand and discriminate among various ways of meeting situations. And long after he ceases to express himself actively in drama his experiences in theatre are many and delightful, for he has developed a lasting interest which brings great satisfaction.

2. TO PROVIDE EACH CHILD WITH AN AVENUE OF SELF-EXPRESSION IN ONE OF THE ARTS. According to May Hill Arbuthnot,[3] one of the needs of children is "to achieve—to do or be something worthy." Every one of us is hungry to express himself in some way and to gain recognition for what he does. Some people find their greatest satisfaction outside of the arts. But sooner or later very many men and women, with careers remote, perhaps, from any art, feel the urge to express themselves in painting or modeling, in music, literature, drama, or in some other form of art. Choruses, little theatre groups, classes in art, handicrafts, and creative writing filled with middle-aged men and women are evidence to the need felt by many people for some kind of creative expression.

Because the arts add immeasurably to the richness and enjoyment of living, and because some people express themselves best in one art, some in another, we need to expose children, not to one or two only but to a variety of them. At present our schools provide boys and girls with many opportunities in music, art, and writing, but fewer in creative dance and drama.

An illustration of how a child finds himself in one or another of the arts came in a recent letter from a young mother telling how as a little girl she felt painfully inadequate in her association with other children. "It seemed as if I could never quite measure up," she wrote. In sports, so important to children of the middle grades, she was hopeless. "In running games I was always the first one caught, or if I were 'it' I could never catch anyone else. When our gym class played baseball I couldn't hit the ball nor throw it properly. I was the last one chosen on any team."

Then when she was in the sixth grade her family moved to a town where she was exposed to creative dramatics. "Here was something I could do!!" she wrote. "Not only that but when in

[3] *Children and Books* (Scott, Foresman and Co., 1947).

eighth grade our class was to do a demonstration of a creative scene from *The Taming of the Shrew* I was actually chosen— *me*—not by the teacher but by the students—to be Katherine. *It was one of the most important things that ever happened to me.*"

The sequel to the story was that in the School of Speech where she later chose to study because "that was the place where the demonstration had been," she made an outstanding record in theatre. Now, years later, with her littlest boy in school, she plans to go back to college and learn to be an elementary teacher. "I'm happy," she wrote, "to be armed with creative dramatics and am just waiting for a chance to help somebody else over the hump."

3. To ENCOURAGE AND GUIDE THE CHILD'S CREATIVE IMAGI-NATION. The wonderful imagination with which little children are endowed dies out or becomes dormant unless it is exercised. Like the muscles it *must* have exercise if the individual is to become a creative thinker. The kindergarten encourages imaginative thinking, but less and less as the child progresses in school does he have use for creativity. Indeed, in many schools it is not only not cultivated but it is actually discouraged.

"Most adults lose their creativeness and only a few can save it," writes Viktor Lowenfeld in the book *Creative and Mental Growth*.[4] "To preserve it and unite it with the mature mind of man is, indeed, one of the highest privileges of art education."

In the strong emphasis now being placed on social understanding, so vital in the world today, we have been neglecting another crucial responsibility: the developing of the unique personality of every child. The result of constantly influencing children to adjust to the group, to conform to the accepted pattern, has been general mediocrity. There has been too little encouragement of the individual child. Always there should be a balance between

[4] (The Macmillan Co., rev., 1952).

the two. We wonder why we do not have great leaders, outstand-ing statesmen, preachers, composers, scientists. Education is in need of a recipe for distinction.

It is an interesting fact that though the progress of civiliza-tion is dependent upon creative imagination, its importance is only beginning to be recognized. Competition in business and industry has forced employers to realize that *ideas* are what count most in economic supremacy, and that their most valuable em-ployees are men and women with imagination. So great an awak-ening is now taking place that industries generally are offering rewards to employees who turn in usable ideas to better their products. In time, perhaps, a comparable creative effort will be made by our nation to solve "people-problems," as Alex Osborn[5] calls them. A beginning has been made in courses called "Cre-ative Imagination," which are being offered in a growing num-ber of universities. It is the first admission by higher education that creative power *can* be developed.

Since most adults today have come up through schools where imagination was largely ignored, it is better that something is being done about it than that the lack is simply deplored. The time to develop creative imagination, however, is not in adult life after it has been dormant for many years. Childhood, when imagination is fresh and strong, is the time to begin cultivating it; and there is no school experience which gives better oppor-tunity for creativity than playmaking.

4. TO GIVE YOUNG PEOPLE OPPORTUNITIES TO GROW IN SOCIAL UNDERSTANDING AND CO-OPERATION. In order to live successfully with other human beings we must understand them; and the wider, deeper, and more sympathetic our understanding is, the richer will be our own life. To understand another person, to know how he feels, we must put ourself in the other's place and try to feel as he does. It requires sensitivity to make one aware of

[5] *Applied Imagination* (Charles Scribner's Sons, 1953).

what another is thinking and feeling by the way he looks and speaks and acts, and it necessitates imagination to interpret the meaning of these outward expressions of inner feelings.

Experience in drama makes a child more sensitive to the thoughts and feelings of others because these are the very essence of his study. Human beings with their many points of view, their deeds and misdeeds, their aspirations and reflections are the material with which he works when he dramatizes a story and plays various parts in it. And though his understanding is limited to the simplest terms when he is young, he grows steadily in his comprehension of emotional conflicts and their manifestations in conduct.

Along with the interest in and sympathy for the characters in the story comes an ability to adjust himself socially to the group of boys and girls who are co-operating with him in creating the play. Few incentives for working together toward a common end are stronger than this. The discipline of having to subordinate his own ideas when the others do not agree with them, the sustained effort of carrying the project through to completion, the joy of contributing his part to it—all these things mean that he is learning to co-operate while he is enjoying himself. For "in team-work he learns the pleasure of being necessary to others. This is the ideal way to learn to get along with people." [6]

5. To GIVE CHILDREN EXPERIENCE IN THINKING ON THEIR FEET AND EXPRESSING IDEAS FEARLESSLY. When older children are asked what playmaking is worth to them besides being enjoyable they often think first of this objective because they feel so strongly the need both for the poise which comes from being articulate and the power it gives them among their fellows.

Ability in oral communication is greatly needed by the citizens of a democracy whether they are leaders in high places giving

[6] J. J. B. Morgan, *The Psychology of the Unadjusted School Child* (The Macmillan Co., 1936).

radio addresses for millions to hear or humble folk talking with their fellow townsmen about the social and educational needs of the community. Language arts courses give children considerable experience in speaking, but to elementary children dramatics is more immediately interesting than public speaking, the need for which they seldom feel until later. While they are learning to respect their own thoughts and feelings and to stand before the group with ideas that are their own, they are also becoming more sensitive to the thoughts and feelings of others, a requisite for real communication.

Along with these objectives are others which are usually realized if playmaking is well guided: _initiative,_ resulting from encouragement to think independently and to express oneself; _resourcefulness,_ from the experience with classmates in creating a play which is their own; the freedom in _bodily expression_ that comes from much exercise in expressing ideas through pantomime; growth in the _enjoyment of good literature;_ and the beginning of _appreciation for the drama._

DEFINITION OF TERMS

Because _playmaking_ and _creative dramatics_ are inclusive expressions, it may be well to define the terms which will be used in this book to designate the various aspects of this informal drama. Later chapters will amplify these meanings and tell of materials and techniques for each.

INFORMAL DRAMA is not conventional. That is, its dialogue and action are extemporized rather than written and memorized. As a rule, it is not presented for any audience except the members of the group not playing at the moment. When it _is_ given for an audience, it is likely to be in the nature of a demonstration.

DRAMATIC PLAY, which has already been described in this chapter, is the make-believe of young children. There is no plot in dramatic play nor is there any thought of audience. It is a spontaneous activity full of adventure and discovery.

Johan Huizinga, in his study of the play element in culture, *Homo Ludens*,[7] says that it is voluntary, that it is free, that it is not "ordinary" or "real life." It is rather a stepping out of real life with a disposition all its own. He was describing play in general, but he might as well have referred to dramatic play.

IMPROVISATION, according to its dictionary meaning, is impromptu invention; something done offhand. As used in playmaking, it refers to extemporaneous drama. General plans are made in advance, but detailed action and dialogue are left to the players.

STORY DRAMATIZATION is the activity most often implied by the terms *playmaking* and *creative dramatics*. When a group of children make a story come alive by playing it spontaneously, whether it is original or taken from literature, history, or current happening, they are having an experience in story dramatization. *Plot* distinguishes it from dramatic play. It has a definite beginning, a climax, and a culmination. Since the play is improvised it is never twice the same.

If a dramatization is *written,* the people who collaborate have an experience in playwriting. Lines are memorized, action directed, and the play in all probability is performed for an audience. This is formal, or conventional, dramatization; and though it is a creative experience, it is not what is known as creative dramatics.

"PANTOMIME is the expression of thoughts, feelings, and emotions through bodily action."[8] Early pantomime was a gesture language which the pantomimist learned as he would learn a foreign language. Certain set gestures symbolized particular ideas, and though the performer often expressed emotion in

---

[7] (Beacon Press, Inc., 1950).
[8] Madame Eva Alberti, *A Handbook of Acting* (Samuel French, Inc., 1932).

his miming, he was so limited by the conventional methods that he became more concerned with style than with feeling.

The modern use of pantomime is not limited to certain techniques but is entirely free and natural. It is understood by children before they know the meaning of words. It is a language comprehended by ignorant as well as cultured; and it is the only means of communication between people who speak different languages.

Pantomime is the really vital part of all drama, and most especially drama with and for young people. The first pantomime of little children follows closely the imitative. They do what they see others do, and their imitation of people is the beginning of sympathetic understanding. As children grow to realize what causes the expressive movements they observe in people, they begin their characterization not with the outward movement but with the thought and feeling. In other words, they begin at the center—the heart—and work outwards to the extremities.

Both *hand puppets* and *marionettes* worked by strings are a part of creative drama when they are designed and made by the children who use them. If, in addition, the dialogue of the plays they perform is improvised, the whole project is considered creative drama. *Shadow plays,* too, whether performed by puppets or human beings, may be creative dramatics. Since puppetry is a whole field of art and much has been written about it, it is not dealt with in this book but a listing of books on the subject will be found in the Bibliography.

INTEGRATED PROJECTS. In modern schools drama is often the meeting-place, not only for all the arts, but for academic subjects as well. What children learn about the culture of ancient China, for example, or pioneer life in this country, or Christmas customs in many lands, or great musicians and their works may be brought together as rich background material for a creative play. Social science, arts and crafts, music, physical education, home

economics, and other subjects may all be integrated into one
dramatic project. At the center, tying them all together, is a
story. Sometimes the story is original; sometimes it comes from
literature or history.

One of the best ways to understand other civilizations and
cultures is through such projects. When children re-enact the
life of the ancient Egyptians or Greeks or Persians, and when
they dramatize modern stories of, say, Russia or Sweden or Den-
mark, they have experiences which lead outward by creating
respect for other peoples and civilizations, and onward by arousing interest which stimulates further study of their history and
their relationship to modern living.

THERAPEUTIC DRAMA. All well-guided creative drama has
therapeutic value both to normal and handicapped children. In
recent years, however, psychiatrists have been using *psychodrama,* which is psychiatric treatment through a type of creative
drama that directly concerns an individual's emotional difficulties; and *sociodrama,* which has to do with group problems. *Role-
playing,* an aspect of sociodrama, is now widely used in classrooms, in human-relations clinics, and in business and industry,
to make clear to people on both sides the issues in a controversial
question.

THE RELATION OF CHILDREN'S THEATRE
TO CREATIVE DRAMATICS

Children's theatre and *creative dramatics* are two different aspects of child drama, the first formal, the second informal. There
is no conflict in ideology between them; rather, they complement
each other. Children's theatre is primarily for child audiences;
creative dramatics is primarily for the children who participate.

It is possible for children's theatre to be primarily for child
players and still give excellent performances for an audience but
it does not happen unless the children are talented and have a

superior director. More often than not, the performance suffers if the object of the play is to give children experience in acting.

A theatre has an obligation to its audience even if no admission is charged, for it is important that performances both entertain and set high artistic standards for the children of the community. It is a question whether it is justifiable to give hundreds of children anything but the best one can offer even if a group of players—whether children or adults—might profit from the experience of acting in the theatre.

In creative dramatics, talent is not a requisite, for no audience has to be considered. This is the place to give children a glorious chance to act all kinds of characters, from Titania to Caddie Woodlawn, from the Knave of Hearts to Johnny Tremain. There is no reason why this experience cannot have great value and real satisfaction for a child. And if one proves that he is ready for a part in a children's theatre production, he has a chance to play with greater thrill because he is skillful enough to make his character convincingly real to the audience.

The *purpose* of children's theatre is to provide dramatic productions for child audiences which will offer them the joy of watching stories come alive; develop in them standards of taste; give them an understanding of life values drawn from the human experiences they see on the stage; and open the way for an appreciation of the art of the theatre. In addition, children's theatre plays, if well done, inspire children to achieve higher standards in their creative dramatics classes.

Plays written by playwrights serve as *material* for children's theatre, lines being learned by the players, action planned by the director. In creative drama, ideas, experiences, and stories from literature and history are the material out of which children create plays. There are no set lines to learn, and the teacher acts as a guide, not director.

As to *standards,* the children's theatre aspires to perfection in order to create the illusion of reality for the audience. Perfection is not the object in creative drama, though children are encouraged to do the best creative work of which they are capable.

Results are obtained more quickly in formal plays than in informal. The language is better, and the director can count on what the children will do for an audience. A creative play develops much more slowly because it is the work of a group, and there must be much discussion and trying out of suggestions. If the play should be presented before an audience, the outcome will be uncertain because one cannot predict creativity. Nevertheless, if a group has worked on a dramatization for some time, it will become partially set as to dialogue and so entirely familiar to the whole cast that there is never the tension that is felt in a memorized play. Language may be crude and grammar faulty, but there is a childlike sincerity about the improvised play which often makes it more charming than the carefully worded play of the playwright.

In *effect on the children,* formal plays are conducive to poise and confidence. If well directed, they may contribute to a child's skill and to his understanding of character. Informal drama gives a child a sense of responsibility and much exercise in independent thinking. His creative ability grows from helping in the development of the play and improvising his speeches. His vicarious life-experience is much broader because of the chance to interpret many roles.

To quote from the "Interpretation of Terms" of the committee appointed from the Children's Theatre Conference,[9]

Participation in informal drama is a more natural expression for young children than is formal drama. Since it is spontaneous, creative dramatics comes from their own thoughts and imagining so that they form a habit of thinking what they say rather than reciting it from memory. Older children, with a background of creative dramat-

[9] Ann Viola, chairman, 1955.

ics, are capable of playing naturally in either formal or informal drama.

ANTIQUITY OF CREATIVE DRAMA

Though creative drama is a late comer in education, historical records leave no room for doubt about its antiquity. From the times when primitive tribesmen gave pantomimic representations of the deeds of their gods and heroes, and dramatic dances of their ideas of life, death, and eternity, down through centuries of improvised drama in Dionysian festivals, in medieval interludes, in Italian *Commedia dell' Arte*, we have evidence which leads us to believe that the impulse to create drama has been strong since the beginning of time.

Even without such evidence from the past, we have only to watch our children in their dramatic play to realize that here is something spontaneous, untaught. Who tells them about imaginary companions? Who suggests the thousand-and-one bits of make-believe which seem to be as natural to them as breathing? When one notes the eagerness with which children greet both creative and formal drama, he wonders how it can be that education has not long since made use of so deep rooted an impulse. To ignore it seems a tremendous waste of power.

ATTITUDES TOWARD CREATIVE DRAMATICS

At the present time there are several widely different attitudes toward the use of dramatics in education. Many teachers use it as a *tool*—a tool for learning facts. Because they know that drama has a strong interest for children, some educators recommend that dramatic play be used in social studies by allowing the children to act out such things as occupations in various countries, life in Colonial days, the western movement in the United States, life on a farm, etc. Some even take the position that by having children pantomime facts they have learned, or put historical events in dialogue form, the teacher can check on the accuracy of the children's learning! This is what is commonly known as "making a cart-horse of drama."

A second attitude is that creative drama is purely recreation, not at all concerned with education. Certainly, drama, like every other art, should be recreational. It should always be a joyful experience in its purest sense. If it is cheapened, however, by using it without standards, making no effort in creative thinking, reducing it to mere slapstick-playing of original skits, it can scarcely be dignified by the name of "creative drama."

Third of the attitudes is that which designates it entirely as therapy. That it is therapeutic is generally acknowledged, and this is a significant aspect of playmaking. Those who value it for this purpose alone, however, ignore its value for normal children.

Lastly, there are those who regard it as an *art* with such unquestioned value that they believe it should be a part of every elementary school curriculum, on equal footing with music and the graphic and plastic arts. They are concerned that its use should not be left to the chance that the classroom teacher will be prepared to teach it, but that a trained supervisor or consultant should be a member of the staff to teach the classroom teachers in its use, help them in special projects, and give it the standing it deserves in the school program and the community.

By adding together all these attitudes toward playmaking or creative dramatics, one sees it as an art that can bring richness and enjoyment to life, make unforgettable great stories from literature and dramatic events in history, and cause healthy response and release.

CREATIVE DRAMATICS IN EDUCATION

It has often been said that from the time any good idea is proposed in education, at least fifty years elapse before it is in general use. During the past twenty-five years a recognition of the value of playmaking has slowly been spreading over the country. Now it would seem that its time for general use is near at hand.

Because creative dramatics is based on sound educational principles it is being more and more widely used in elementary schools each year. Many teachers' colleges and universities are offering courses in its philosophy and techniques. Workshops are being held for teachers-in-service. That it has potentialities which are unique for a child's development is recognized by many leading authorities in child development, as well as by psychiatrists who use it for its therapeutic value.

Specifically, creative dramatics is based on the following principles. How they are applied is illustrated both in the "objectives" set forth in this chapter, and more completely in all the chapters which follow.

1. Most modern educationists—those who are neither extremists in the narrow "three R" kind of education nor in the so-called "progressive" methods—agree with John Dewey that education is not merely preparing a child for his future life. It is giving him the chance to live richly *now* in the belief that this is the best preparation for the future. They believe that the whole child should be educated, not just his mind; that he should be developed to his highest potentialities both as an individual and as a social being; that he grows, not from having knowledge poured in by the teacher but rather from participating in activities that challenge his deepest interest and highest powers.

2. Those who make the curriculum should take into consideration the child's natural interests. They should use these interests, guiding and directing them so as to bring growth, and steadily widen them by exposing him to new interests.

3. A child learns best what he experiences. Whether one

reads the educational theories of Rousseau or Pestalozzi, Froebel or William James, Dewey, Kilpatrick, or any one of the contemporary educationists, he finds an insistence on the importance of experience. In fact, though we still may see in too many classrooms a dependence on verbal symbols, it is safe to say that leaders in the elementary field have long since accepted the idea that book-learning means little unless it can be related to the child's experience.

Classroom experiences need to be planned carefully to give the child new understandings. The school should "seek to provide children with experience in sensing and attacking problems, appropriate to their age and maturity, so that their actions are based on creative thinking, on enlightened self-interest, and on a scientific approach to problem-solving." [10]

4. What children learn should have real meaning for *them.* Most children promptly forget facts which do not seem important to them. When they can use what they learn they are more likely to retain it. This is the basis of learning a thing when the need arises. Purpose is a powerful factor in education, and purpose is present when children understand the reason for what they are expected to learn.

5. Children should be given the chance to help plan what they do, to practice choosing, to originate. Dewey, however, strongly criticizes the feeling on the part of some teachers that they should never initiate experiences for the children. "The fear of adult imposition has become a phobia," he writes in *Education Today.*[11] "It means preference for an immature and underdeveloped experience over a ripened and thoughtful one."

6. Every child should be given a sense of adequacy based on self-confidence. Even the most limited child has something to

[10] A statement prepared by the staff of the Winnetka (Illinois) public schools.
[11] (G. P. Putnam's Sons, 1940)

offer. It is the school's business to help him find it and by encouragement to see to it that he develops a sense of adequacy. Along with many of the more gifted children, he probably is in need also of the development in emotional and social maturity that will help him in working with other children.

7. Attitudes and appreciations should be valued above skills and facts. Important as the latter may be, they cannot compare in significance with attitudes, which are the moving force of life.

8. Children should be educated not for the status quo but for a civilization that changes so rapidly that their best preparation is living democratically in the classroom, growing constantly in resourcefulness, taking part in the planning and carrying out of worthy projects, and developing their power of creative thinking to understand their country and their world.

9. Our children should be educated for democracy. Since we believe that democracy is the highest form of government yet devised by man, an active loyalty to it should be fostered in every child. This means developing a sense of responsibility along with the freedom that belongs to democracy. It means creative thinking, courage to speak out for one's convictions, concern for the welfare of others, a respect for their rights, and an effort to keep free from prejudice. Shane and McSwain[12] strongly emphasize this need, and then go on to say, "Last, and decidedly not least in importance, the development of an awareness of the deeper meanings of democracy should prompt in each boy and girl the desire to extend an outreaching hand of friendship to others in building a more humane, friendly, and international culture than preceding generations have achieved."

[12] Harold G. Shane, and E. T. McSwain, *Evaluation and the Elementary Curriculum* (Henry Holt & Co., 1951).

CHAPTER 2

Dramatic Experiences of Little Children

(Five, Six, and Seven)

ON A BEAUTIFULLY WARM OCTOBER AFTERNOON SEVENTEEN kindergarteners with their teacher[1] were spreading their rugs to rest out-of-doors on the campus lawn:

"What about music?" asked Don. "We don't have music."

The teacher replied that she would sing to them if they liked. So she sang some little folk songs; and when a gentle wind ruffled the leaves around them she chanted Christina Rossetti's "Who Has Seen the Wind?"

Then she asked, "What does the wind sound like?"

"It was a thrilling moment," she said afterward. "As fast as I could transcribe, they poured out their ideas, some imaginative, some literal . . . the poetry of five-year-olds in the third week of school.

"One child's phrase influenced another's. The boys likened the wind to some mechanical apparatus. The minister's daughter thought of God. We hectographed their 'poem' to send home in their parents' letter exactly in the order it blossomed forth. Here it is."

---

[1] Beverly Nygreen, Kent (Ohio) State University School.

What Does the Wind Sound Like?

Like a steam engine and a lake, (BOB K.)
Like a big tree blowing, (BOBBY L.)
Like it's going "Whooo" bringing lots of fresh air, (B.G.)
Like a bus going by, (DON)
Like a motor boat, (DICK)
Like a falls, (WARREN)
Yes, Niagara Falls, (MIKE)
It sounds like wind. (MARTY)

Like a tree shaking, (BRUCE)
Like a lake just waiting, (DEBBIE)
Like a wave going by, (BARBARA)
We were out at the ocean once and it's like a wave going over.
  (SUZY)

It sounds like cars going past, (MINDY)
Like someone on a tree shaking a tree, (MIKE)
Like a road-scraper going by (DICK)
Like somebody way up in the trees, shaking the leaves, (ERNIE)
Like God shaking the trees. (BARBARA)

Like a squirrel up a tree, (DON)
Like people stepping on leaves, (B.G.)
Like a bicycle running on the grass over leaves, (SUZY)
Like a car going over some leaves, (JEANIE)
Like pine trees shaking, (MIKE)
The wind sounds like wind. (SARA)

The next afternoon, in the classroom, a tape-recording was made without the children's knowledge of what follows.

TEACHER: Yesterday we were talking about the wind. There are some other sounds that we hear outdoors in the fall that we never hear at any other time of the year.

CHILDREN: I know, I know. I do!

MIKE: I know . . . leaves falling down.

DICKIE: I hear a big, big . . . a big black bus.

T. That's a sound you can hear any time of the year, isn't it? I want to know just the things you can hear in the fall.

BRUCE: Walking on leaves.

BARBARA (*so shyly you can barely hear her*): Thunder.

T. Yes, a good one, Barbara. Sometimes there *is* thunder in the fall. (*Though* BARBABA *has misunderstood the question,* T. *gives her support for her contribution because she has been so withdrawn*)

MIKE: We hear noises on Hallowe'en.

T. (*happily*) Yes! What are some of the noises you hear on Hallowe'en?

CHILD: You know . . . bells ringing.

(ONE CHILD *whistles, presumably to illustrate a Hallowe'en sound*)

SUZY: On Hallowe'en I heard some squirrels going up trees.

T. Oh, good! I was hoping someone would think about the squirrels because that's the only time of the year, isn't it, that the squirrels are busy. What are they busy doing?

ALL: Gathering nuts! Gathering acorns!

T. And when they gather the nuts do you suppose there's another sound you could hear if you had very, very good ears?

BOBBY: Cracking them!

(SOME CHILDREN *make sounds of cracking nuts—crunch, crunch— with their teeth*)

T. Yes! Bobby knows! Every time the little squirrel cracks a nut, it sounds just like that. Now we've thought of the wind and the squirrels and the leaves falling. Is there anything else we can hear in the fall?

WARREN: A man shaking a tree.

T. (*dubiously*) What would the man be shaking the tree for?

SEVERAL CHILDREN: To get some apples down.

T. That *would* be a nice sound to hear, wouldn't it? How would those apples sound falling on the ground?

CHILDREN: Bang! Bang!

(ONE CHILD *thumps with her feet on the rug to indicate*)

MIKE: We could hear . . . uh . . . the squirrels tramping through the leaves.

T. Yes, and what are the leaves going to sound like?

PAM: They crackle.

T. Yes, they crackle! That's good, Pammy. I think sometimes they sound like walking on toast.

CHILD: I think it sounds like walking on crackers.

CHILD: I think it sounds like walking on popcorn.

т. Let's all be squirrels tramping through the leaves. Let's hear how you would sound if you were squirrels tramping through the leaves.

(*The* CHILDREN *respond in a variety of ways. Some hop on hands and knees. Some bend over and scamper. Then the teacher has them return to the rug.*)

т. Mike, I knew you would say "squirrels tramping through the leaves" so I found a little poem-story about a squirrel.

DICKIE: Here's a squirrel. (*He points to a bulletin board picture*)

т. Yes, that's one of our squirrels on the bulletin board. *This* squirrel's name (*holding up picture in book*) is Whisky Frisky.[2]

(CHILDREN *murmur, "Whisky Frisky."* JEANIE *chuckles*)

(т. *says poem with vivacity, suggesting with her arms and hands the height of the tree, the twirling, and—by a sharp clap—the cracking of the nut*)

> Whisky, frisky,
> Hippity hop,
> Up he goes
> To the tree top!
>
> Whirly, twirly,
> Round and round,
> Down he scampers
> To the ground.
>
> Furly, curly,
> What a tail!
> Tall as a feather,
> Broad as a sail!
>
> Where's his supper?
> In the shell,
> Snappity, crackity,
> Out it fell!

(CHILDREN *react with delight*)

т. Do you think we could have three little squirrels go hippity-hop while we say it?

[2] Anonymous, "The Squirrel," in Barbara P. Geismer, and Antoinette B. Suter, *Very Young Verses* (Houghton Mifflin Co., 1945).

(TEN CHILDREN *raise their hands for a turn.* T. *names three little girls.*)

T. We'll say it while they are the little squirrels. (SHE *chants with strong rhythm, the* CHILDREN *joining in on some words*)

> Whisky, frisky,
> Hippity hop,
> Up he goes
> To the tree top!

(ONE CHILD *has a little running step, one is jumping, one spinning*)

T. Can you climb, little squirrels? That's fine! (*Then* ALL *chant*)

> Whirly, twirly,
> Round and round,
> Down he scampers
> To the ground.

T. That was very good. What did Suzy do that really looked like "whirly, twirly"?

CHILD: She went around.

T. Now, Dickie, Don, and Mike.

(T. *repeats the first two stanzas.* DICK *innovates by climbing the jungle gym*)

CHILD: Dickie's goin' up a tree!

ANOTHER: He's goin' up a tree!

T. When we say, "Down he scampers," I think you should come down, Dickie.

(THREE MORE BOYS *play while* TEACHER *and* CHILDREN *repeat the chanting.* ONE *follows* DICKIE'S *example and climbs the gym.*)

T. Look at Bobby scamper to the ground! That's a long tail, Bobby! (BOBBY *is deep in characterization, unaware of the others, admiring his tail*)

T. Let's all be squirrels cracking our nuts and eating our suppers. He has to really chew hard to get those nuts, doesn't he? What else does he do with nuts besides eat them?

TERRY: Puts butter on them.

(*Surprise! Of course* T. *expected* "Hides them.")

T. Does he eat butter?

SOME CHILDREN: No.

SOME: Yes, they eat butter.

T. Well, maybe so. I'm going to play the music now. The people who feel like it can be squirrels here on the rug.

(SHE *improvises music*[3] *on the piano and sings "Whisky, frisky" to its accompaniment, while* CHILDREN *admire tails, crack nuts, and dance. All but two participate. Squealing "Wheee" on the words "To the ground," the* CHILDREN *drop down on the rug in evident enjoyment.*)

T. That was *nice!* Was it fun to be squirrels?

CHILDREN CHORUS: "Yes!"

What Came After

The children's natural dramatic play was stimulated by the Whisky, Frisky poem. The next day they played squirrels out-of-doors on the hill. A huge stump was a wonderful "tree" for the squirrels to climb on. The teacher chanted while they hopped, rolled down the hill for "whirly, twirly," and searched for acorns. At poem's end they were still in character. Sarah noticed that Bobby B., who was rather shy, was being a squirrel on the way back to the room.

"Bobby *is* a squirrel!" she said. Whereupon she hopped along with Bobby, entering into the dramatic play completely.

ANALYSIS OF THE LESSON

A synthesis of sense training, dramatic play, and rhythm characterized this delightfully natural and enjoyable experience which the teacher, Mrs. Nygreen, planned for her kindergarten children.

Though it might have been worked out entirely inside the schoolroom, the fine weather helped to make it more effective by providing a natural environment for setting the mood. It is always well to take advantage of circumstances which will make a richer experience for the children.

[3] Any spirited music could be used.

In this case it will be noted that not only did the teacher take the children outside for their rest period, but she was ready with some little songs when Don reminded her that they were without their usual music. This was, of course, relaxing. And when the breeze ruffled the leaves, she was ready to chant the very appropriate poem "Who Has Seen the Wind?" A teacher who has many lovely poems *in her mind* can reach for the right one without the delay of going to the bookshelf to look it up. Furthermore, it is an advantage to be able to *say* it rather than read it.

Now, with relaxed bodies, and spirits filled with the loveliness of nature and poetry, the children were ready for her question, "What does the wind sound like?"

She had not hurried that question. She knew that creative thoughts do not come out unless something has first gone in! As a result, she got the best ideas from them that they had to give. True, their imaginations would grow with added experiences. They were only five years old, after all, and they had had relatively few experiences to feed their imaginations; so some children came forth with nothing better than "a road-scraper going by." By the end of the year, with this kind of teaching, they would have more imaginative ideas. Already she had several promising ones: "like a lake just waiting," "like pine trees shaking," "like God shaking the trees."

In this session, in which she made the children aware of sense impressions, it will be noted that she concentrated on sound alone. Later she would call attention to things they saw or smelled or tasted or touched.

Recorded Experience with Poem

One of the most uncertain things in the world is creativity! Regardless of how skillful a teacher is, neither she nor anyone else can predict what will come out. Who could anticipate that a question about fall sounds would bring forth "a man shaking down apples"? Or that the response to a question designed to bring out the fact that squirrels are busy hiding nuts in the fall would, instead, get the reply, "Puts butter on them!" However, one thing is sure—a skillful, imaginative teacher will get much more than will one who is inexperienced or matter-of-fact. Creative ideas do not just pour forth!

On the second afternoon, Mrs. Nygreen made a smooth transition from the experience of the previous day by referring to the conversation about the wind. She led from this to other sounds that we hear in the fall—sounds that we do not hear at any other time of the year.

Naturally, she hoped to lead to squirrels in the leaves, scurrying up trees, and cracking nuts, as an introduction to the poem she wanted to use. In a few minutes they reached this point. Then it would seem that she might have introduced the poem rather than asking for more sounds. But she did get some interesting ideas by pursuing it a little further. Note that she used Mike's expression, "tramping through the leaves" rather than substituting the better action word, "scurrying," which is much more typical of a squirrel.

This was a fairly long discussion for little children, and she would doubtless have cut it short if there had been restlessness. Experience teaches one what to expect; and if the discussion is meaningful to the children and it follows an active period, there is a chance to help them grow in the power to concentrate on an idea. Too often young children are not even given a chance to think. Everything is planned for them. If we are to have people who are inventive, who think independently, we need to begin when children are very young. In this case, the period of discussion was followed by a chance for plenty of action. Everybody could be a squirrel! (They had to imagine the sound, of course. This would have been more effective outside.)

Then it was time to introduce the poem with its strong

rhythm, and after choosing three children to be squirrels, she and most of the group chanted it with a pronounced beat, the children saying with the teacher whatever words they could remember. By the time three groups had played it, all the children had come to sense the rhythm very strongly. Finally, all had a chance to play the poem again while the teacher sang the words to improvised music on the piano.

The fact that a feeling for the dramatic play carried over to the following day out-of-doors was evidence that the children liked it and felt the urge to prolong their enjoyment. There is no doubt that their sensitivity to sounds had been sharpened as well as their feeling of rhythm. The whole experience was new and enriching to these boys and girls in their third week of school, and many further experiences would grow out of it. How interesting it would be to know what they would be able to do with a similar lesson by June!

DRAMATIC PLAY

Long before they go to school, children have many experiences in dramatic play. Half their lives, it seems, is spent in make-believe. "Ricky a puppy; scratch Ricky's neck," says the two-year-old, laying his head in his mother's lap. "This is my muscle-builder," asserts four-year-old Billy, pouring it into his glass of milk from an empty tin box. "It comes up to here"— pointing with serious intentness to an exact, if imaginary, line on the glass.

How does it happen that without so much as a suggestion from an adult, a child will play that he is something or somebody else all day? Why is it that he invents an imaginary playmate who is so real to him that he sometimes keeps him around as a friend for several years?

Psychologists who have made a study of children's spontaneous dramatic play say it is "a means by which the child works out his difficulties for himself so that he can meet the challenge of his world with confidence. He also uses it to make up for defeats, sufferings, and frustrations." [4]

Though dramatic play undoubtedly does have therapeutic value for disturbed children, it has so much else that is significant for the normal boy and girl that it is worthy of far more than the amused tolerance commonly given it by parents. Besides all the delightful fun it provides, it is a child's way of learning about the world about him—about parents, tradespeople, circus clowns, airplane pilots. One day he will spend all his money to ride on a merry-go-round, the next he will rig up a make-believe merry-go-round and be the man who runs it. His little sister will call up the grocer on her toy telephone, and in her mother's grownup manner will give an order for supplies. Both are feeling to some small extent what it is like to be a grownup.

While a child is reliving familiar experiences and exploring new ones, he is learning things about himself and where he fits into his environment. It is easier for him to manipulate this small world of play; the real one is pretty big and strange. "Under cover of dramatic play," writes Madeleine Dixon, in that fine book *High, Wide, and Deep*,[5] "social adjustments of the highest order are going on all the time." And she tells how four-year-old Sam, in the children's train-play, lost all his passengers because he "squtched" Rachel in the wicket gate. "Here he was," she writes, "the whole train ready and exciting . . . and now he had gummed his own play." For the little girls had taken refuge back in the sand-box because he had bullied Rachel, and no amount of persuasion could bring them back. It was pretty certain that Sam had learned something that morning because the next day he was positively engaging!

⁴ Ruth E. Hartley, Lawrence K. Frank, and Robert M. Goldenson, *Understanding Children's Play* (Columbia University Press, 1952).
⁵ (The John Day Co., Inc., 1938).

Parents and Dramatic Play

If parents laugh at or rebuff children in their imaginary play, it lasts for a very short time, and the children miss all they might have enjoyed, all they might have learned from it. When a mother tells her friends in a child's presence about the "cuteness" of what he said or did, he is made self-conscious or inclined to show off. Parents should not make him feel that imaginary play is silly or babyish in the effort to hurry him along to maturity faster than he naturally goes. He has a right to be himself and to be respected as a two-, three-, or four-year-old.

When parents do enter into his dramatic play they not only build a delightful relationship with their child (one mother said, "A different look comes into my children's eyes every time I make-believe with them"), but they can use it most effectively in many everyday problems that arise. When anything needs to be done, use a bit of make-believe and it gets done. One young mother wanted her five-year-old daughter to help her make the beds. "I don't like to make beds," pouted Marjorie.

"But I am a new chambermaid in this hotel," said her mother anxiously. "And if I don't learn to make beds well, I'll lose my job. I thought, since you are experienced, you could help me."

So that was it—make-believe! That was different. Immediately Marjorie came running to help, giving her mother pointers about good bedmaking as she worked.

"How do you happen to be a chambermaid?" asked her mother as they finished the second bed.

"Well," replied the child with a grown-up air but a little twinkle in her eyes, "you see, I'm a widow with three small children and we've got to live!"

Preparation for Experiences

A difficult time at home is when mother and the new baby

come from the hospital, and three-year-old Michael sees to his dismay that he no longer is the center of all the love and care of the family. What a heartache this experience has caused count-less Michaels and Janes! This is why some mothers prepare the children for the baby who is coming by not only telling them about it but also by playing out with them some things that will be fun to do for it. If the child next older is prepared for all the care that a tiny baby requires, and has a part in it himself, he may not have to go through the sad time which so many chil-dren experience; and he will have a different feeling for the baby.

Many other experiences, too, can be prepared for by dramati-zation: a first visit to the dentist or the doctor, the first day at school, a visit to relatives the child has never seen. One small girl had to have a serious operation; so she and her mother played hospital and operation over and over again. When the time came she went into the operation with no fear, and afterwards said to her mother, "It was just like we played!"

Are we making children "soft" by taking the fear away from some difficult experiences? Should they not be taught to meet and go through with hard things since there will be so many problems in life? If make-believe weakened or softened a child, there would be reason for not using it to prepare him for certain problems. But a parent is not shielding him from difficulties. The child has to go through with the experience just the same. What the parent does is to help him build an attitude that will make him ready to meet it.

Play-Living in School

The kindergarten room is full of equipment that stirs the imagination. The playhouse, blocks, sand table, pictures, and the very atmosphere of the room with its sunshine and space— all make dramatic play inevitable. The classrooms of the older children have fewer material things to stimulate the imagination. They must depend more on the feeling we as teachers create.

A good deal of imaginary play comes about from the children's experiences. They see the birds flying south in great flocks, and they respond to the poem which we say:

> Fly away, fly away over the sea,
>   Sun-loving swallow, for summer is done;
> Come again, come again, come back to me,
>   Bringing the summer and bringing the sun.[6]

Since it was written by an English poet, the swallows fly south "over the sea." But this makes little difference to American children who think of the birds merely as flying south.

Perhaps, after they are familiar with the poem, all the children will be swallows flying south as we say it, and return as we tell them to "come again." Some Chicago children playing the poem had been divided into two groups, one group being the swallows, the other saying the poem. The cloakroom was the southland "over the sea" where the birds flew for the winter. On the line "Come again—" no birds returned. Again the children said the line, more insistently than before. Still nothing happened. When it required three calls to bring them back, the children in their seats demanded, "Why didn't you come before?" "Because," replied the birds, "we knew it would still be cold in Chicago!"

A trip to a fire station, a post office, a farm, a museum, a children's theatre play can motivate dramatic play in any of the primary grades. So can the making of puppets and the construction of boats and trains from blocks. For it is unthinkable to construct them unless the children play with or on them.

Oiling Machinery

Every good primary teacher has secrets of handling her chil-

[6] Christina Rossetti, *Sing-Song* (The Macmillan Co., 1942).

dren and getting things done without friction. She keeps her machinery oiled!

"Where are my vacuum sweepers?" she asks when there is a litter on the floor. Immediately some of the children who would not ordinarily have the slightest interest in cleaning the floor run eagerly to her to get "turned on." In a few minutes the litter has disappeared and the little vacuum sweepers come to be "turned off."

One teacher[7] who had a hard time keeping beginners in their chairs long enough to hear some instructions had the inspiration to exclaim to a child who had popped up for the third time, "Look out, your magic cushion has flown away!" The little girl, startled, turned to look at her chair, while the others, responding instantly to the teacher's make-believe, said triumphantly, "I have mine! I have mine!"

"What is your pillow made of?" asked the teacher. "Mine is like a rainbow-tinted cloud."

"Mine is . . . blue with stars on it!" "Mine is . . ." and ideas ran riot on pillows, so that the original plan for the hour disappeared and, instead, a peddler sold magic pillows "that would fly away if you left your chair when you weren't supposed to!"

Children who put on their "velvet shoes" before going down the hall to the drinking fountain, don "magic cloaks" which make them invisible (and thus not heard!) as they go out of the building, enjoy the fun of doing it even after they realize the teacher's purpose.

They also delight in "magic spectacles" which help them to see imaginary gifts provided for some child's birthday—gifts enough to go around after the birthday child has had her first choice. And "magic wands" by which the teacher can turn them into whatever she wants them to be are always a source of fun.

[7] Rita Criste, Orrington School, Evanston, Illinois.

Introductions

As in the home, the preparation for new experiences and the assimilation of what they learn are effective uses of dramatic play. A visiting day with children unprepared is not nearly so valuable an experience as it is when they play out what will happen. A dramatization in which some of the children play they are parents, and all are given experience in the correct way to introduce and acknowledge introductions makes the children feel at ease on the real occasion.

"Miss Gray, this is my mother, Mrs. Lyman," says the child. "Mother, this is my teacher, Miss Gray."

By much experience in introductions in make-believe situations, children grow more poised in meeting people both in school and out than are many grownups, who seem never to have learned which person is the one who should be introduced to the other. For the youngest children it would be confusing if, at the same time they were dramatizing visiting day, they were taught that the introduction would be reversed if the teacher went to their home; in which case they would say, "Mother, this is Miss Gray; Miss Gray, this is my mother." Older children, however, can play out and thus remember the gracious way to introduce people in any situation. All of them, in their dramatic play, can get experience in greeting visitors, seating them, and performing other thoughtful acts.

As to assimilating experiences, which Dr. Arnold Gesell considers one of the valuable aspects of dramatic play, children who see a motion picture devoted to safety measures and play it out afterwards assimilate it more effectively than would be possible in any other way. So, too, a trip to a farm or the fire station would be impressed on a child's mind by dramatizing what he saw. Pleasurable re-enactments of any such experiences help to clarify meanings and give them lasting value.

Emotions Are Always Involved

What children enjoy in dramatics is the *emotion* aroused by what they play. Mere action is not drama, nor is it really of any special interest. The safety dramatization should have something of suspense, of danger, if it is to appeal to them. A trip to a farm means fun as they feed the pigs or ride the horse, and this needs to come into the playing. Excitement a-plenty will be characteristic of the dramatic play which follows a visit to the fire station. Make-believe that concerned crossing the street on signal, gathering eggs at the farm, or polishing the engines at the fire station would require something more than the action itself to appeal to children. A leader should always remember that it is the *feeling* that *motivates the action which counts*.

Poems and stories always concern the emotions. When they are short and simple, they are usually played completely, but there is no reason why they need to be. If some bit of dramatic action from a story is especially pleasing to the children, just that bit may be played. When Miss Muffet is a very little child, she will be entirely satisfied to eat her curds and whey, see the spider, scream, and run off. On the other hand, the children often devise a complete play, sometimes with a whole family of spiders, sometimes with a mother and other creatures besides the spider, and a build-up to the central action.

In "Sing a Song of Sixpence," all that is dramatized by most young children is the pie—made by a circle of children—with "birds" inside. All sing the rhyme, and when the teacher cuts the pie, there is great fun as the birds fly out and away! After they have enjoyed this bit, they sometimes go on with the rest of the action: the maid who gets her nose snipped off, the queen eating bread and honey, and the king who is called from his counting-house to enjoy a birthday party.

When they play the riddle

Hand in hand they dance in a row,
Hither and thither, to and fro,
Flip, flap, flop, and away they go,
Fluttering creatures, as white as snow,

and the children, after guessing feathers, fairies, dandelion fluff, and other things, finally get the answer, "clothes on a line," they may do all kinds of things with it. First, they are likely to be various garments hanging on a line. A wind comes up and blows them off, some whirling around, others dropping limply to the ground. Later, they may or may not add characters and details: a laundress and her daughter and neighbors, the washing of the clothes and hanging them on the line, the conversation of the clothes-creatures after the human beings are gone, the disappearance of one or two who have blown away, etc. As in the nursery rhyme, it may be just a delightful bit of dramatic play or a complete dramatization, and the wise teacher will leave the children free to play whichever part of it appeals to them most. But one can be sure it will involve emotion.

Dramatic Play Should Never Be Commonplace

Many activities in school will have no need for dramatic play. It would be a mistake for a teacher to make it commonplace by motivating everything in this way. Because the dramatic is so fascinating to children there is a temptation to overuse it—as, for instance, allowing a child to wear his fine cloak all the time. If it is saved as something very special and delightful for appropriate occasions, it will keep the magic which from time immemorial it has held for children.

RHYTHM

Rhythm is the more or less regular recurrence of emphasis. It may be a very obvious alternation of strong and weak, or so subtle a pattern that we cannot easily sense it. Rhythm is basic in all the arts: in the graphic arts as well as in music, dance, and drama.

We are all rhythmic creatures. Our heartbeat, our breathing, our bodily activities—walking, running, skating, swimming, and practically all other movement—are rhythmical; and they so accustom us to rhythm that we respond to it naturally and pleasurably. This is particularly evident in our motor response to music.

The earlier a child's rhythmic sense is developed, the better will be his foundation both for participation in the arts, and for appreciation of them. He needs first to experience it in bodily activity and in the more obvious patterns. There is great opportunity for this in the many dramatic rhythms which will be a part of his early experiences in drama.

Music is of high importance in developing a child's sense of rhythm because its beat is so pronounced. But poetry can be used with almost equal effectiveness if well presented by the teacher. It is highly desirable to use both music and verse, not forgetting the percussion instruments which can be used alone or combined with music or speech.

For the music, nothing is quite so satisfactory as the piano, granted that the pianist is skilled. If she can improvise or play by ear, so much the better. A pianist who must watch her music is not of great help for either rhythm or dramatic play. The ideal musician for this purpose is one who is sensitive to the feeling of the activity, who can both play and see what the children are doing, who fits her music to their ideas. She may also initiate activities by suggesting in her music ideas for the children to carry out in movement. Bears, horses, ducks, frogs, birds, and all manner of creatures may be suggested by the music, as well as mechanical objects such as clocks, see-saws, swings, airplanes, and trains.

She can suggest what happens in "Three Little Mice"—

> Three little mice went out to see
> What they could find to eat for tea,
> For they were dainty, saucy mice,
> And liked to nibble something nice;
> But Pussy's eyes, so big and bright,
> Soon sent them scampering out of sight.

Sound procedures in rhythmic action may be found in Gladys Andrews' very excellent book *Creative Rhythmic Movement*.[8] All kinds of movement are explored: the movement of machines, interpretations of sounds, activities on Hallowe'en, Christmas, and other holidays; and many, many more. Some of the rhythmic projects grow out of classroom subjects; and a good deal of simple, original music is included for those who use a piano. A creative teacher, whether classroom, music, dramatic, or physical education, will find it a rich source for ideas.

Lacking piano accompaniment, recorded music may be used. Many available records are quite satisfactory if carefully chosen. At the present time there are piano records[9] available for the simplest basic rhythms—such as walking, skipping, swinging— and it is advisable to give the children opportunity to feel at home with them before using dramatic rhythms.

There are also several volumes of records called "Rhythmic Activities," [9] for dramatic expression, such as dwarfs, giants, elephants, trains, etc. These are orchestra records but simple enough to use with young children.

A great number of records made for children are songs. Many of these are good, but they need to be chosen very carefully or they will limit children to certain actions to be done at exact moments. The annotated list of records in the Appendix will, it

---

[8] (Prentice-Hall, Inc., 1952).
[9] See Record List in the Appendix.

is hoped, be of some help to teachers who are searching for appropriate music to use for various purposes.

Movement and Voice

In place of using music, reading of a poem may serve as accompaniment for the children's rhythmic activity, in the manner of Mrs. Nygreen's use of "The Squirrel." In her case, only a few of the children at a time played squirrel while the others said the poem with her. Very often the children clap, tap their desks, walk, run, hop, skip, etc., as we say or read the poem. If we should use the charming little poem "Galoshes," by Rhoda Bacmeister,[10] we would doubtless do so on a slushy day, when the children themselves have been "sloshing" around. We will comment on this in introducing the poem, and ask them how it sounded. They may give us some of the very words in the poem.

"Someone else must have been listening to the sounds that galoshes make," we may say. "Just listen to this poem!"

> Susie's galoshes
> Make splishes and sploshes
> And slooshes and sloshes,
> As Susie steps slowly
> Along in the slush.
>
> They stamp and they tramp
> On the ice and concrete,
> They get stuck in the muck and the mud;
> But Susie likes much best to hear
>
> The slippery slush
> As it slooshes and sloshes,
> And splishes and sploshes,
> All round her galoshes!

[10] From the book *Stories to Begin On*, by Rhoda W. Bacmeister (Copyright, 1940 by E. P. Dutton & Co., Inc.).

When we read it we make the descriptive words very realistic. The children will love to repeat them, both the "sploshy" words and, to a lesser degree, the ones which tell how galoshes sound on ice, on concrete, and in mud.

Now it will be fun for all the children to *walk* it as we say it again, timing it carefully for the various walks. Later, a few at a time walk it while most of the group say it with us. For it is very easy to learn, and fun both to play and to say rhythmically.

Sometimes when a teacher says the poems for the purpose of helping the children feel the rhythm, she may be tempted to distort the words or stress the wrong ones in order to make the rhythm stronger—as saying *wa-ter* in "Jack and Jill" and emphasizing the preposition "to" in "To the ground," in "The Squirrel." This should never be done. Meaning should come first, and the important words should be the ones stressed even when the beat is weakened by so doing. A mechanically even rhythm is uninteresting to the point of sounding like singsong. *Sense should always come first.*

The action should go on, of course, on the silent beats. In "Galoshes" there are silent beats after both *mud* and *hear*. Therefore, we will pause long enough for a step before beginning the following line. This poem is especially easy for the children's action; but in the first use of rhythmical movement children are almost always a little slow. One should not be too insistent on the exact following of the beat at first, for with experience they will come to feel the rhythm more and more definitely.

Mother Goose rhymes are wonderful little jingles to use because not only are they very rhythmical but they are familiar friends to the children. When they are used in this way they seldom can be acted out as they would be in dramatic play. To get the kinesthetic sense of the rhythm, action which will stress this most strongly is used—as walking, marching, skipping, swaying, and the like.

Beginning with "Ride a Cock-Horse," with which a baby has a bouncy ride on daddy's foot, there are such rhymes as "Jack Sprat," "Baa, Baa, Black Sheep," and "Jack and Jill" for marching; "A Dillar, A Dollar" and "Hippity Hop to the Barber Shop" for skipping; "I Saw a Ship a-Sailing" for swaying, and many, many more for various actions.

Some other poems especially good for rhythms are A. A. Milne's "Buckingham Palace" [11] and "Happiness" [11] (John and his great big waterproof boots) for marching; Milne's "Hoppity," and Dorothy Baruch's "Merry-Go-Round," [12] for hopping and skipping; Stevenson's "The Swing," [13] and Dorothy Aldis' "Brooms" [14] for swaying. Others are suggested in Chapter 13.

SENSE TRAINING

Live experiences, plus a parent or teacher who knows their potentialities, are the best means of making young children sensitive to what they see, hear, smell, taste, and touch. Because the senses bring about the enjoyment of so much in life, and because they so often become weak with increasing years, the adult who can help children to become habitually aware of sense impressions will make a lasting contribution to his life.

One teacher took her six-year-olds to visit a farm, and on the next day played out with them the whole delightful experience. They fed corn to the chickens and cobs to the pigs, noting the difference in the weight of the feed; felt the warm softness of the baby turkeys they held in their hands; snorted like the mother

[11] When We Were Very Young (E. P. Dutton and Co., Inc., 1924).
[12] Very Young Verses (Houghton Mifflin Co., 1945).
[13] R. L. Stevenson, A Child's Garden of Verses (Charles Scribner's Sons, 1905).
[14] Everything and Anything (G. P. Putnam's Sons, 1925).

pig, squealed like the baby pigs; slid down the hay in the barn; drank the warm milk; and by doing all these things immediately after the visit, prolonged their enjoyment of the experience as well as gained in their ability to recall sense impressions.

The days are filled with appeals to the senses, and if we from time to time call to the children's notice such things as pleasing voices, interesting cloud formations, the feel of smooth pebbles, the spicy fragrance of a nasturtium and the taste of its stem, they will build up many sense impressions that they can later recall at will.

"What sounds do you like to hear?" asked of a group of children will bring out all kinds of recalled impressions, from the little sounds baby sister makes when she tries to talk, to the sound of a jet plane speeding across the sky. When one teacher asked, "What sounds *don't* you like to hear?" a boy said, "I don't like to hear the voices of grownup people who are cross!" "I don't either," said another child feelingly. "They make me want to hide behind the piano!"

Mrs. Nygreen's question to the children, "What does the wind sound like?" may suggest other questions which may or may not be asked at the time of the experience. If the children are watching a storm, the question, "What does the lightning make you think of?" may bring such replies as "a sharp sword" or "a gold zigzag like on some sweaters." Watching cloud formations may suggest castles, bears, birds, fluffy pillows; the sound in a seashell, fairies whispering secrets; frost on the window pane, fairies, Christmas tree ornaments, Jack Frost painting.

Nursery school children are made aware, when asked to touch the hands of other children, of their delicacy and softness—to the extent, sometimes, of feeling new respect for hands and less inclination to slap them! And most children love the rosy softness of a baby's hands and feet.

Next to actual experiences, there is perhaps nothing better to build awareness of the senses than poems. Christina Rossetti's poems have unusually beautiful pictures, especially this one:

> What is pink? A rose is pink
> By the fountain's brink.
> What is red? A poppy's red
> In its barley bed.
> What is blue? The sky is blue
> Where the clouds float thro'.
> What is white? A swan is white
> Sailing in the light.
>
> What is yellow? Pears are yellow,
> Rich and ripe and mellow.
> What is green? The grass is green,
> With small flowers between.
> What is violet? Clouds are violet
> In the summer twilight.
> What is orange? Why, an orange,
> Just an orange![15]

The loveliest images in the poem are not in what is named to represent each color but rather in its setting: "by the fountain's brink," "where the clouds float thro'," "sailing in the light," "with small flowers between."

Walter de la Mare's "Some One" [16] arouses wonder concerning the mysterious knocking "at my wee, small door." Every child can hear it! And the "tap-tapping of the busy beetle," "the screech-owl's call," "the cricket's whistling," too!

When children are watching unusual clouds it would be a good time to read Rowena Bennett's "Under the Tent of the Sky," which describes a procession of animal clouds marching along as the wind cracks his whip. And if someone brings a red

[15] *Sing-Song* (The Macmillan Co., 1942).
[16] *Peacock Pie* (Henry Holt & Co., Inc., 1928).

balloon to school, the children would greatly enjoy her "Crimson Balloon." [17]

> The crimson balloon was a headstrong young thing;
> He jostled his brothers and tugged at his string
> And said to his master, "Let go of my tail,
> And over the tops of the houses I'll sail.
>
> I'll ride on a cloud and I'll visit the moon
> (He is nothing himself but a silver balloon).
> I'll bump him down into this crookedy street
> And shine in his place with the world at my feet."
>
> Just then came the wind with a cough and a sneeze
> That blew him up into the pin-cushion trees
> Where, BANG! he collapsed with a terrible sound
> And wizened and shriveled, he sank to the ground.

We shall find many other poems and a number of stories that will fit into occasions when the time is exactly right for intensifying certain sense impressions—poems such as Stevenson's "Where Go the Boats?",[18] Marion Webb's "Fancy Dress," [19] Elizabeth Madox Roberts' "Firefly":[20]

Firefly

> A little light is going by,
> Is going up to see the sky,
> A little light with wings.
>
> I never could have thought of it,
> To have a little bug all lit
> And made to go on wings.

[17] *Songs from around a Toadstool Table,* by Rowena Bastin Bennett. (Copyright 1930, 1937, by Follett Publishing Company, Chicago, Illinois).

[18] R. L. Stevenson, *A Child's Garden of Verses* (Charles Scribner's Sons, 1905).

[19] *Stories to Dramatize* (Children's Theatre Press, Anchorage, Kentucky, 1952).

[20] *Under the Tree* (Copyright 1922, by B. W. Huebsch, Inc., 1950, by Ivor S. Roberts).

and stories such as "The Little Pink Rose," "Little Duckling Tries His Voice," and "The Adventure of Three Little Rabbits." [21]

Finally, we may use the charming musical-action stories of Kay Ortmans' *Let's Play Series* on records (described in the Record List in the Appendix), which are admirable not only for deepening sense impressions but also for giving happy experiences in rhythm and dramatic play. They are a boon to teachers untrained in guiding such activities because the leader is on the records, and a most engaging leader she is!

What do we expect such experiences—in dramatic play, rhythm, and sense impressions—to do for the child? We have taught few facts. It is impossible to make accurate tests. Many of the values of experiences such as these are intangibles that are not immediately apparent. We know this: the only teaching which really counts is that which gets over into the lives of children to the extent of making them better people—people of finer sensitivities, attitudes, and appreciations. This is our great objective.

[21] See Story List in the Appendix for the three stories.

CHAPTER 3

Dramatic Play in the Middle Grades

(Children of Eight, Nine, and Ten)

Imaginings[1]

Imagine!
A tiny red door that leads under a hill,
Beneath roots and bright stones
And pebbly rill.

Imagine!
A quaint little knocker and shoe-scraper too,
A curious carved key
Waiting for you.

Imagine!
Tiptoe on doormat, you're turning the key,
The red door would open
And there you'd be.

Imagine!
Shut the door tightly so no one should see
And no one would know then
Where you would be.

Imagine, if you can!

---

[1] J. Paget-Fredericks, *Green Pipes* (The Macmillan Co., 1929).

THIS IS A POEM TO STIR CREATIVE THINKING IN THE MOST matter-of-fact child in the group! Beautiful, curious, and sometimes frightening things are waiting on the other side of the red door, and there are few children who are not eager to show in pantomime what they see when you say the poem for them. No child need fear being wrong, for who knows what is *really* there?

Often, of course, there is a shining treasure; but sometimes there is a cosy little shop where lost things go, dwarfs hammering away at "flying saucers," a terrifying witch standing over a captive princess who is being made to scrub the floor, or a long passage leading to a glittering palace. The person who discovers the door may be anyone from a child wandering away from camp to a scientist searching for uranium.

Whatever the children do with the poem, in art, in creative writing, in dance, or in drama, it is the kind of thing to put them in a creative mood. The use of such a poem is one of many ways to foster and challenge the imagination, and it seems to appeal to the ten-year-old as strongly as to the child of eight.

For those who have had little or no experience in dramatics there will be small attempt at characterization when playing the poem. It will be merely a pantomime for others to guess. But whether dramatics is new to the children or not, imaginative play—make-believe with little or no pattern—will still be an important part of their experience. Beginners will have the simplest of pantomimic activities, growing gradually into characterization and story dramatization, while children who have long expressed themselves through this art will be capable of going at once into its less simple phases. Pantomime, or expressive body movement, however, should be stressed at every age level. Large, free action is alway motivated in the beginning, until an increasingly finer co-ordination warrants the use of smaller muscles in detailed movement.

CREATIVE DANCE

There probably is no better way to attain freedom in pantomime than through creative dance. The body speaks as well as
the voice; and when children have an opportunity to work under
the guidance of a sensitive teacher of dance, they gain not only
grace and poise but the means of expressing beautifully their
thoughts and feelings through bodily action. Dance of this kind
is truly drama, and it needs just one more step—miming with
words—to make it complete.

Ideally, the same teacher should guide the children in creative
dance and drama. But practically it more often works out that
the teacher of physical education, with her special training and
the space of a gymnasium, can better give children the experience
of creative rhythmic movement.

In such classes the children explore space, rhythm, music, and
percussion, as well as movement, and experiment with a great
number of ideas. For "movement should be an automatic tool," [2]
writes Gladys Andrews, "leaving the children free to concentrate
on the idea."

The effects of various colors and sounds on the feelings are
expressed by the children in movement, as are also many childhood experiences in school and out: with the gay mobiles they
have made and hung in their room; a zoo with its monkeys and
kangaroos, its birds, deer, elephants, and bears; the farm with its
work and its animals; a fair with its balloon man, its ice-cream
cones, and its merry-go-round. Seasons and holidays suggest
many creative movements; and the rhythmic beat of percussion
instruments stimulates ideas of traffic, industry, and, best of all,
Indian pow-wows.

The need for piano music and much space makes all this difficult for the classroom teacher even if her training and natural

[2] *Creative Rhythmic Movement for Children* (Prentice-Hall, Inc., 1954).

ability fit her to guide such movement; but whenever it is possible, either in the home room or in the gymnasium, it will add greatly both to the creative arts program and to the children's freedom in playmaking.

PANTOMIME WITH RECORDED MUSIC

Next best to creative dance is pantomime with music on records to set the mood and suggest the action. Many children respond to music more than to any other stimulus; and they will walk with the grace and dignity of royalty to the stately measures of the minuet, and take on the eerie shapes and actions of Hallowe'en witches, ghosts, and goblins to the music of Moussorgsky's "A Night on Bald Mountain."

MacDowell's "Of a Tailor and a Bear" [3] can launch a third- or fourth-grade group into an exciting and comical bit of dramatic play, the music adding much to the story. Before using it for pantomime, the children will have the chance to listen to the record and detect the tuning of a fiddle and the clumsy dancing of the bear—though they may not guess at first that it *is* a bear.

Then, very likely, we will tell them the story as it is given in the album: of the happy tailor sitting cross-legged in his shop, whistling and sewing; the sudden appearance of the huge, shaggy bear, growling and glaring about him; the fear of the tailor, allayed to some extent when he notices the broken strand of rope hanging from the bear's collar and realizes that it must be a tame bear that has escaped from its master. His quick thought of taking his fiddle and playing a dance, the bear's growling when it is too fast, followed by the slowing down of the music, the gathering of the townsfolk at the window, and at last the appearance of the bear's master to save the day, is all very dramatic and full of good action.

It is better not to attempt to fit the pantomime to the record

[3] See Record List in the Appendix.

because so much effort is required for the exact timing that there
is little creativity. But aside from establishing the feeling for the
story, the record can be played during the quiet beginning and
ending and, if timed carefully, during the dancing of the bear.

Many other records add greatly to the feeling for characters
and stories: for the princess who slept for a hundred years, Cinderella at the ball, for the goblin who became an elf, the "Hurdy-
Gurdy Man";[4] for Indians, people of various countries, the man
in the circus who walks so precariously on the tightrope.

When playmaking is an extracurricular program, leaders often
play a record as the boys and girls come in for their class—music
that will evoke the feeling and stir the imagination for what they
are about to play. Music can add beauty and glamour as well as
rhythm to almost any kind of imaginary play, so that a leader
in creative dramatics searches constantly for suitable records.

EXPERIENCES WITH SENSE IMPRESSIONS

Though children of eight, nine, and ten have had so many
experiences in hearing, tasting, smelling, touching, and seeing
that they are able to recall them without difficulty, the senses
become dull as they grow older unless they are kept sharpened
by exercise. This means that some adult must appreciate the
need of keeping children conscious of the beauty and interest in
sights and sounds, tastes, smells, and touch. For not only are
the senses basic in playmaking, but they contribute immensely
to the joy of living. Therefore, beginning pantomimes may well
concern sense reactions.

If creative dramatics is new to children of these age levels, we
shall perhaps first make them aware of the senses by actual
rather than recalled experiences as we do with the younger boys
and girls. The sound of a tiny bell, the fragrance of a flower
compared with perfume, the taste of a certain spice in cookies,

---

[4] See Story List in the Appendix.

"You stop shaking my tree!"

BARBEREUX SCHOOL
Evanston, Illinois
(*Marcella Bellmar, Teacher*)

Kindergarteners "trying on" the character of the
cross little gnome in "Fancy Dress"

Children being the
squirrel in
"Whisky Frisky"

KENT (Ohio) STATE
UNIVERSITY SCHOOL
(*Beverly Nygreen, Teacher*)

James A. Fos

KEITH COUNTRY DAY SCHOOL
ROCKFORD (Illinois) COLLEGE
(*Wilma McNess, Teacher*)

The "Hurdy-Gurdy Man" plays the second tune in the poem by that name

Herzog Photograp

The Nutcracker of Nuremberg

MILLER SCHOOL, Evanston, Illinois

(Ann Heekin, Teacher)

Children building a space ship to fly to "The Dark Side of the Moon"
An Integrated Project on "Space"

MILLER SCHOOL, Evanston, Illinois
(*Ann Heekin, Teacher*)

Courtiers stare at a blank wall on which Tyll Ulenspiegel says he has painted
their portraits in colors invisible to any who are not of noble birth

the feel of silk and sandpaper, and the comparison of two illustrators of the same book, as Rackham and Shepard for *The Wind in the Willows*—all such things are conducive to sensitivity. And even better than bringing special objects to the classroom for the purpose is the calling attention from day to day to such things as the pungent smell of a fall bonfire, the sound of a lovely speaking voice, the beauty of sunshine and shadow through the trees.

Recalled sense impressions can often be developed into interesting situations for pantomime. When this is done strong concentration on the part of the children is needed to make the sensation real and vivid, and for that reason we place much emphasis on it. The following are suggestions of types of situations for pantomimes to give children experience both in sense awareness and in body movement.

HEARING

1. Hear a sound early in the morning that rouses you to some kind of action.
2. Be startled by an unexpected crash.
3. Listen to a band in a distant circus parade.
4. Hear a sound like a far-off voice while you are exploring a mysterious cave.
5. Hear a call for help.

For example, all the children may be sleeping. A robin lights on the window sill, waking them with his song. Startled, they listen for a moment, then go back to sleep, glad that it is too early to get up. In a few seconds the milkman makes an unusual amount of noise with his bottles at the door below, and the children are partially wakened. The next sound rouses them wide awake, for it is mother calling that breakfast is nearly ready and Uncle John has come to take them out to the farm for the day. They jump out of bed in a hurry, not even pausing to stretch and yawn. They wash their faces and hands, brush their teeth, dress, comb their hair, and run down to breakfast.

The important thing is *really to hear* these imaginary sounds. If everybody is playing we may wish to say softly, "A robin lights on the window sill and begins a lively song." . . . "The milkman makes a clatter with his bottles." . . . "Your mother calls." These are merely signals so that the reactions may come all at once. *How* the children react is left to them. And in most of the pantomimes, signals will be unnecessary.

Touch

1. Walk barefoot on a pebbly beach, then in soft, cool grass, and finally in shoes that hurt.
2. Pull taffy and get some stuck on your fingers.
3. Pick up a baby rabbit.
4. Sew and stick yourself with a needle.
5. Feel your way through a strange room in the darkness.

Example: "Why have you come into this room?" "Is it large or small?" "What are the things you touch?" "How do they feel?" "How cautious are you?" "Are you looking for anything?" "If so, do you find it?" "How do you get out?" Such questions as these, asked, perhaps, before the pantomime begins, stir the children's imaginations and help them to get vivid sense impressions.

Taste

1. Try a new dish and discover that you like it very much.
2. Compare the taste of two kinds of pop.
3. Drink chocolate that is too hot.
4. Choose your favorite fruit from an imaginary basket and eat it.
5. Eat what is left of the chocolate cake icing in the bowl.

Example: "Don't you like the looks of the new dish?" "Do you decide not to eat it?" "Are you expected to *try* it?" "Do you like to admit that the first taste is surprisingly good?" "Just how *does* it taste?" "Do you eat it all and want more?"

SMELL

1. Walk into the house and smell your favorite cookies.
2. Try to decide which perfume to buy for your mother on Mother's Day.
3. Come dangerously near a skunk.
4. Go into a rose garden.
5. Smell a bonfire of leaves.

Example: "You go into a store and show the saleswoman your money for perfume. She lets you smell one kind and you think it is good. But you don't want to buy the first kind so you go on smelling others with the result that you soon can't tell one from another. What do you do?"

SIGHT

1. Come upon the witch's house in "Hansel and Gretel."
2. See a baby bird that has fallen from its nest.
3. See a building on fire before anyone else discovers it.
4. See in a store window just the shoes you want, and go in and try them on.
5. Meet a favorite aunt at the airport. Watch the plane land.

Example: "You are walking to school when your attention is attracted to the roof of a house where you see smoke coming out. You stop to make sure that it is not from a natural cause. Just then you see tiny flames and you run up to the door, knock loudly, and show the flames to the owner."

LEARNING TO CHARACTERIZE

Having had experience with many pantomimes in their own character, the children are ready to concentrate on learning to

"be" other people; so we may say, "What do we have to do when
we play we are someone else?"

"Act like him," replies Susie glibly, sure that she is right.

"Are you sure?" we ask. "Isn't there something that must
come before action?"

The children think for a little while, then get the idea and
someone volunteers, "We have to think like him and feel like
him."

And from beginning to end, this is what we stress. All playing
in creative dramatics must come from the *inside*. The thoughts
and imaginations of the children create the characters in their
plays; and though boys and girls are guided both by what the
story says about the people and by the influence of the teacher,
the characters come out according to the children's understanding of them. It matters not that a leader thinks of a hero as far
more fine and subtle than do her pupils. Unless words are put
into their mouths, the children create him as *they* understand
him, and he is meaningless if an adult conception is forced upon
them. The knowledge of people matures slowly; and it is our
privilege as teachers or leaders to stand ready to guide by indirection. This is one of the important contributions we can make to
a child's development.

The first step in characterization will logically concern people
very familiar to the children. They may be at a ball game, in a
park, at a circus, in a railway station, or waiting for a bus. Or
they may be various folk engaged in activities common in the
fall, winter, spring, or summer, depending on what time of year
it happens to be. Whatever the children do, they will need to
be reminded to observe people most carefully in order to help
themselves to *be* these people.

Suppose it is decided to be men and women on a fine fall day.
Every child can choose some person to be and decide what he
will be doing. If there are many children it is well to let perhaps

ten "try on" their characters at one time all over the room. This has the double purpose of giving all the children the chance to play in a short time, and making no child the center of attention at first. Then, after they have had a chance to get the feel of their characters, we may say, "Do you recognize some of these people? I see some interesting ones."

If any of the children in their seats pick out someone who seems to be more than ordinarily convincing, we may ask all the children except him to get out of character for the present. Otherwise, we ourselves may choose someone.

Suppose Tom is chosen first. We ask him to assume his character again and we watch what he is doing.

"He's raking leaves and he's tired—maybe old," offers Jim.

"I think he's just lazy," says Nancy.

"Try to make it plain enough so we can really tell," we suggest.

Tom tries again, and this time it is clear that he is lazy rather than old because he seems to hear a reprimand that makes him suddenly begin raking in a very lively and youthful manner.

This brings a laugh which makes everyone feel more confident, and one after another of the children assumes his character again while the others guess. This is done quickly so that the other children may have a turn also, as it is important to give everyone his chance. If some child is too reserved or shy to be a part of the playing, it is better not to urge him but to try to make him so interested that he will want to play next time.

The degree of characterization is sure to be very slight this first time. A few children do well with it even when they are very young, but others will never appear to be anyone but themselves no matter how much experience they have. All of them will find it easier to individualize their characters if they are very different from themselves, and especially if they are such extreme personages as funny old men, shrewish women, fat, jolly cooks, or strange, eerie beings. As they come to understand and appreciate what the people are thinking and feeling, what they look like, how they speak, many children develop the ability to give some illusion of reality. The important thing, however, is not the outward characterization but the inner feeling; and unless they play for a formal audience, *skill* in characterization is not a necessary aspect of playmaking.

Situations Involving a Variety of Characters

As soon as more than one character is involved, there is an impulse to speak as well as to act. It is entirely possible to play out whole stories without words, and indeed highly desirable to do so. But while pantomime will always be basic in playmaking, there is no reason why speech should not be added as soon as the need is felt. So now there may be original scenes with several characters, bits of stories from readers, situations from social studies, and even an occasional current happening.

Some time ago, for instance, there was a story in the news about a truck-driver who was taking a heavily loaded truck on a long trip across country. As he came near Canton, Ohio, he had to pass under a viaduct which was slightly lower than any of the others he had passed. Though he saw the sign giving the amount of clearance, he thought it would allow room for the truck, and he started to drive under. Suddenly he found that he was wedged tight under the viaduct. Try as he might, he could go neither forward nor back. What could he do?

A farmer working in a field near by offered to add the strength of his tractor to the big truck motor. But to no avail! And by this time a good deal of traffic was stopped on each side of the viaduct. A clean-cut, well-dressed man got out of the nearest car and spoke impatiently.

"Please get your truck out of my way. I'm going to a wedding and I shall be late."

A farmer with a load of squealing pigs called out, "What goes on here? My pigs need to be fed!" Then he got out to see if he could help, and like all the others who had gathered around began suggesting ways to move the big truck.

After all ideas had proved useless, it was agreed that the only possible thing to do was to send to the city and have a welder bring his torch and cut the top off the truck. Poor driver! His load would be held up, his truck ruined.

About this time a little boy came riding down the street on his tricycle. Wriggling through the crowd he looked at the tightly wedged truck, thought a moment, and then came forth with an idea.

"I know what you could do. You could let some air out of the tires."

Every man looked at his neighbor. Then they began, somewhat sheepishly, to help the driver carry out what the little boy had suggested. By the time the tires were half down the truck could be moved; and to the great relief of everyone, especially the driver, traffic soon moved along as if nothing had happened. And the little boy? He went pedaling off to play cops and robbers with the boy in the next block.

Here is fine material for a study in characters, and the ten-year-olds, especially, will think of all the familiar people who are sure to gather when an emergency such as this occurs. It is an illustration of how contemporary events sometimes offer excellent material for playing.

But even though modern situations are understandable to children, there is no reason to believe that they cannot also play the characters in folk tales. For children who have reached the age of eight have considerable background in folklore. In readers, in library books, in their home story books, and occasionally on television, they have met such characters as cobblers, woodcutters, dwarfs, kings, queens, princesses, lords, ladies, millers' sons, and many other people of "once upon a time." Therefore, they feel almost as much at home with them as with modern people.

Such situations as that in "The Old Market Woman," "The Shepherd Boy and the Wolf," and the villagers' scene in "The Peddler and His Caps," are very good as the next step in characterization. So also is the following incident in the story called "The Mysterious Box." [5] Opportunity for many and varied characters in a situation easy for children to understand, with enough suspense to provide fun in the playing, and a warmth of feeling toward the good-hearted little cobbler make it very usable for children with small experience in characterizing. We might introduce it in some such way as this:

"When you need a pair of shoes, what do you do about it? Yes, of course, you go with your mother to the shoe store and choose a pair that fit, look well, and seem to be stout and well made. You have a choice of many kinds, don't you? Wouldn't it seem queer if we had to have every pair specially made for us? We'd have to plan a long way ahead if we didn't want to go barefoot!

"Well, that is just what people had to do at the time of this story; and, as you will see, most of them had to wait a long, long time for them." Then we tell the story of

The Mysterious Box

Once upon a time, right here in our very own land, there lived a kind old cobbler. He was a very good cobbler, so good that everyone wanted the shoes that he made. People came from far and near to have him make their shoes for there was no other cobbler half so good for miles around. The kind old man wanted to make shoes for everybody, but he had so many orders that he couldn't possibly fill them all. He would have liked to make shoes for the butcher down the street, the baker next door and the candlestick-maker in

[5] F. Edward Harris, Kent (Ohio) State University School.

the next block, but he could not find time for these because he had so many orders from the officials; and of course they had to have shoes. There was the mayor, his wife, the governor, the chief of police, and all the councilmen and their wives. Even though he got up early in the morning and worked all day and far into the night, he could not seem to get all his orders filled. He could not make shoes for all the village people, his friends, and all the officials.

One day he received a letter. It was a strange letter from a far away place. He opened the envelope and took out the paper inside. At first a puzzled look came across his face, and then a smile crept underneath his nose until it almost reached his ears. That night some of the townsfolk noticed that there wasn't any light in the cobbler's workshop. They thought that he was tired and had gone to bed early for a change. The next morning when the door to the shop wasn't open and they didn't hear the cobbler's merry whistle, they began to wonder what had happened. All of the doors and windows were locked and the cobbler was gone.

The days grew into weeks and still the cobbler did not return. Then, early one morning a big wagon came rumbling into town and stopped in front of the cobbler's shop. Much to the amazement of all the townsfolk, the men from the wagon left a big box in front of the cobbler's shop. Everyone was curious as to what was in the box. It was so high that Mr. Barker, the schoolteacher, could just look over it when he stood on his tiptoes. It took two or three people standing in a ring holding hands to get all the way around it. As the day grew older, more and more people came to look at the mysterious box in front of the cobbler's shop. The mayor came and all the officials came. They looked and looked, and they put their heads together; and they whispered and whispered.

The baker came with dough all over his hands. The butcher came, wearing a big white apron, and he even rapped on the box with his meat-cleaver and listened—but nothing happened. Some children came by and climbed all over it. One of them found a knothole and poked his finger through. He had to stand on his tiptoes to peek in, and when he did, he saw what everybody else saw when they peeked—nothing at all, because it was too dark in the big box!

That evening the cobbler returned to the village. Everybody crowded around him asking where he had been and what was in the box. "Tell us! Tell us!" they cried. Finally, in front of his shop, he stood up on the little three-legged stool where he used to sit to make the fine shoes that everybody wanted but only a few of the officials could get.

"In this box," he said, "is something wonderful for all my friends." Then he got a hammer and opened the big box. Everyone gasped, for they had never seen such a beautiful—such a strange—machine. "This fine machine," the cobbler explained, "will help me make shoes for everyone. Now the butcher, the baker, and the candlestick-maker, and everybody who wants shoes can have them and not just the officials."

"Wonderful!" shouted the people. And the stoutest of the men carried the machine into the shop and helped the cobbler put it together. And from that day forth the kind old cobbler whistled even more merrily than in the past. For now he was able to keep the whole village in fine, well-made shoes.

The children seem to enjoy listening to it, so we ask, "Would it be a good story to play?" They are always eager to dramatize a story that is as suitable for playing as this one, and if they seem enthusiastic we ask, "What sort of a cobbler did you see as I told about him?"

"Kind of small and bent," says Larry.

"Yes, from bending over his shoemaking all the time," adds Dan.

"How do you think he is dressed?"

"Oh, in old clothes, with a big apron—not a white apron, but clean," says Ellen.

"And he has bushy gray hair—," Peter begins. But several children object.

"No—no! It's thin. He's almost bald."

"Peter's cobbler can have bushy hair if he sees him that way," we say. "It is more important that we agree on what he is like inside."

Barbara thinks he is kind and honest and hard-working, and he feels very sorry that he cannot make shoes for all who need them. Everybody agrees as the story has stated this clearly.

"Let's see if we can *be* the cobbler as he sits at his bench and works on the shoes. Let's feel as he feels all the way through. And let's feel that we *look* the way he does.

The children, in their seats, then become the cobbler, and some busy themselves at once cutting out leather while others stitch or hammer at their work. In this way they begin to get the feeling of the gentle little man without the self-consciousness which is likely to come if others are watching.

"Now who are some of the people who will be coming to the shop?" we ask, and they enumerate many people, both official and humble.

"Whoever plays the parts this first time may make their characters just the way they think they should be. Make them *real people* so that we know one from the other. Who would like to be the mayor?" Several hands go up and someone is chosen. Others volunteer for the rest of the people, and a child is chosen for the cobbler—very likely one who has caught his spirit better than most.

After the children have decided on the place for the shop, the cobbler goes to work and the customers begin coming. Some come to order shoes, others to get those which are ready, while those who are not officials are put off sorrowfully by the cobbler.

Conversation the first time will be scanty and unnatural, and both cast and observers will note its lack. Perhaps several of the customers are haughty and demanding, threatening to take their business "to the cobbler down the street" if this cobbler does not do better work.

"Did you get the idea from my telling of the story that the people felt this way about the cobbler?" we ask.

"No!" several assure us. "And the story says that he is the best cobbler for miles around so they would be thankful to get his shoes." "And the cobbler is kind and hard-working and the people like him."

"But one or two of the officials might be hard to please just the same," insists one of the "complainers." "They might be fussy even if they didn't threaten to go to another cobbler."

All agree to this, though they believe that most of the people would like the cobbler and be kind to him. And of course one or two unpleasant people would both make the scene interesting and build more sympathy for the cobbler.

The next cast, then, has one or two dissatisfied people and much more variety in the dialogue. Some describe the kind of shoes they want and even bring their own velvet or leather. The cobbler takes the measurement of the people who order, and most of those whose shoes are ready are pleased. When the dissatisfied woman criticizes hers, her husband tells her that she ought to be glad to have such fine shoes! When the butcher, the baker, and the candlestick-maker come hopefully, the cobbler is very sad that he cannot promise them for a long, long time.

Most enjoyment will come from the second scene of the story —the main incident, which concerns the bringing of the big box, the curiosity of the townsfolk, the feeling and peeking and measuring—and speculating! And then the satisfying climax when the cobbler appears and shows them the fine machine which is to help him make shoes for everybody!

As the children play the various characters in this and later stories they are slowly growing in understanding of people. In life we rarely know the motives behind the actions of people so that we cannot understand why they think and act as they do. But in a story the author gives us "a long, clear, view," as May Hill Arbuthnot puts it; and by discussing, playing, evaluating, and replaying the parts, we get to know the people much better than by merely reading about them. In "The Mysterious Box" only the cobbler is characterized by the author; all the other people must be built up out of what the children have observed and read in folk tales.

This is the beginning of story dramatization, the experience of creating plays based on stories. By this time the children should feel more free in expressing ideas through bodily action, sense impressions should be sharper, and their feeling for rhythm intensified. They have made a beginning in characterization—in understanding and expressing character traits.

How long has it taken to progress thus far? That is impossible to say, since children, teachers, and circumstances differ so greatly. As in any other art, each step depends on readiness. The process should not be hurried, but neither should it be held back when the children are ready for something more challenging. Whatever their progress in playmaking, they will seldom outgrow the need for exercise in the *elements* of creative dramatics which they have learned by dramatic play.

CHAPTER 4

Improvisations of Older Children

(Eleven, Twelve, and Thirteen)

BOYS AND GIRLS OF ELEVEN YEARS ARE VERY FREE AND NATURAL in their playing. If they have been expressing their ideas and their feelings through creative drama for several years they have acquired some skill in pantomime, improvisation, and characterization, they are more fluent in speech, and they have a strong feeling for communication.

In many ways this is an ideal age for playmaking. Children of eleven have a tremendous store of energy and enthusiasm, a lively curiosity about people and events; and if they have been creating plays with the guidance of a teacher who really knows drama they have some understanding of the structure of a good play.

Eleven is also a good age for beginning creative dramatics. The majority of eleven-year old children have not reached the self-conscious stage as yet, and they respond with zest when given material that challenges their interest.

Less free than eleven-year-olds but far more so than most eighth-graders are children of twelve—the age when they usually

64

enter seventh grade. This is not the ideal time for beginning creative dramatics but it is far better than the eighth grade, when the fear of what their classmates will think causes young people to be reluctant to express any emotion. A teacher who thoroughly understands them, however, and establishes a feeling of friendliness and confidence in the group, can be successful even with this difficult in-between age.

On the other hand, eighth-graders who for several years have been made to feel that the drama class was a legitimate place to express their feelings often do quite remarkable work in plays of their own making. It is a good indication that if children from their early years could grow up with a controlled emotional outlet such as this, there would be fewer adolescent problems. If, in addition, they could have experience in creative dance, it would mean control of fast-growing bodies which make so many of them awkward and self-conscious.

BEGINNING IMPROVISATIONS

Suppose we consider a group of older children who have had no experience in creative dramatics. Where shall we begin? Will it be better to explain the difference between this informal, improvised drama and the formal kind they are more likely to expect? Or plunge into the playing without any preliminaries?

There is, of course, no *one* best way, and the approach will depend on (a) the teacher's feeling as to how she personally can do it most naturally, (b) the children's general attitude and interests, and (c) the circumstances under which she is working. Following are some approaches to improvised drama which teachers have used successfully for beginning classes of older children. Such groups differ so widely in degree of maturity that the teacher must be the one to decide which kinds of improvisations are most suitable for her sixth-, seventh-, or eighth-grade group.

If children are on the sixth-grade age level, they are usually eager to begin activity at once. Therefore, after a short period of getting acquainted, we may want to introduce pantomime by asking, "How many things can you say without using your voice?" Such an introduction brings out how much we all talk in pantomime, saying such things as "yes," "no," "come here," "go away," "I don't know," "hello," "goodbye," "I won't listen to you," "shame on you," "good for you," etc., without making a sound.

After they have demonstrated the everyday use of pantomime, a term which we may then define,[1] we might say, "Let's imagine we had no language except pantomime. That is, we not only do not use our voice but we do not even use our lips. We express our thoughts entirely through our body. How would you say, 'My little sister broke her arm'? Or, 'Come over on your bike and see my airplane model'? Or, 'If you want to see something funny, come with me. But be quiet!'"

The Teacher's Playing

"Now this is a guessing game," we may say next. And this procedure is as effective for the seventh grade as the sixth. "I'm going to pantomime something, and if I do it well you should be able to guess exactly what each movement means. Then you may have turns." Our own participation has the effect of making the activity important and may do much in breaking down any barriers between us and the children if we enter into the play whole-heartedly. There is a certain advantage in not being too good at pantomime—a fact that should reassure the unskilled leader! If the children think you are too wonderful, some of them may be held back by the fear of being awkward in comparison.

[1] See Chapter 1.

We might, for instance, be searching for something (which must be definite in our own mind). Are we searching in a room, in a whole house, out-of-doors, in the woods—or where? Are we sure we shall find it or are we very anxious? Do we find it? Can the children tell by the way we react and handle it what it is and how we feel?

Or, we might make some soup, putting in certain ingredients, cooking and tasting it. Is it good? Or is something wrong? Do we know what to do to improve it? *Do* we improve it or not?

Such pantomime will lead to the children's participation; and it is advisable, when giving them the chance to take part, to suggest some definite or categorical types of activities they themselves have done or might do: things they have done at camp or at a picnic, sports they enjoy, adventures they have had. By giving them ideas for pantomimes, we preclude imitation of movie or television thrillers which, if once begun in a class, are very difficult to cope with. Specifically, in any of these upper grades the following suggestions might be tried:

1. You smell smoke in your house. Trace the smell to its source. What is causing it?
2. You receive a gift which you can hardly believe is for you. Unwrap it. What is it? Does it please you?
3. On April Fool's Day you see a purse on the sidewalk. You do not know whether to pick it up or not. What happens?
4. Walk stealthily through the woods trying to see a deer, but suddenly come upon—what?

Though we may have made the general assignment, the guessing part of the game depends on the end of the pantomime, which we have left to their imagination. In a large class several children may pantomime at once. And if it is not made a guessing game, as many children may play as there is space. In this case we shall be looking for children who should be asked to repeat their pantomime for all to see. These will not be show-offs but more timid children who will gain confidence by being chosen to pantomime for the others.

Pantomimes Motivated by Some Emotion

In these first pantomimes no attention has been called to the feeling or mood, even though it is inevitable that the children feel something of joy or excitement or fear in the make-believe which concerns sports and adventures. Now they should be ready for pantomimes *motivated* by some emotion. Since it is not easy for most boys and girls of this age to express their feelings, it is a good thing to begin with situations that excite just *one* strong emotion. The following may suggest a few, and the children will think of others. These situations should, of course, be built up to be more complete:

1. You find a letter in your mail-box from a favorite uncle who invites you to go with him and your aunt on a wonderful western automobile trip. After thinking for a few moments of all the fun you will have and of how grand it is for them to take you, hurry off to tell your mother the good news!
2. You walk down the street on your way home from school. Notice a little child dart out in the street after a ball. You have just had time to think how dangerous it is to do it when a car comes rapidly around the corner toward the child. What will you do?
3. You see a boy mistreating a small dog which you know is not his own. You become so angry that you risk interfering with what he is doing. You run between the boy and the dog and rescue the frightened puppy. Then you let the boy know what you think of him.

A transition from one emotion to another goes a step further and makes for more flexibility as well as deeper insights. Such exercises as the following may be a beginning for the better ones the children can devise:

1. You are watching a football game. You are anxious and fearful, for the odds are against your team. Suddenly you are thrilled by a spectacular run down the field, followed by the first scoring for your team.

2. You get off the train in a strange city, and after it has pulled out, realize that you have left your purse on it. No one seems to be at the station to meet you as you had expected. You wander around, uncertain and fearful, having no money even to telephone, until all of a sudden you are gladdened by the sight of your aunt running to meet you.

3. You hurry into the house bursting with the news that you have been given the leading part in the school play! No one in the living room, no one in the kitchen, no one in the house at all! What a disappointment! A note on the table says that your mother will be late in getting home. Your spirits get lower and lower as you realize that you will have to wait a long time to tell your news. Finally you decide to go over and tell a neighbor. You start off.

CHARACTERIZATION

As in the younger age level we shall follow these beginning pantomimes with others in which the players become various characters. Always stressing naturalness—seeing, feeling, and thinking the character from the inside—we urge observation, awareness of the people around them. "If they are cross or ill-natured, what makes them that way?" "Is it ill-health, perhaps, or has their life been hard and unpleasant?" "Why is it that old people often move more slowly or stiffly?" We ask the children how it changes their own walk if they are happy or angry, ill or in wonderful health. We need to consider, too, what is the immediate cause of behavior. "Has something just happened that causes them to be elated, discouraged, fearful?"

Sometimes each pupil may be a different kind of character but all reacting to the same situation, as:

1. A lively child, a domineering woman, a tired old man—entering a room and sitting in a chair by a table. Why do they come to sit there? How do they feel? What do they do?

2. A robber, a naturalist, a camper who is lost—walking along a path in the woods. Make their purpose evident.

3. A farmer driving sheep, a poet dreaming of the poem he wants to write, a haughty woman—discovering a big stone in the middle of the highway. (As in the tale "The Stone in the Road.")

4. A vain emperor, an attractive young girl, a small boy—going to a mirror and looking into it.

Using the same situation for several different kinds of people has the advantage of pointing up individuality in characterization. Each player wants to differentiate his character from the others, and it is more evident when several react to the same situation.

People children know in books are good subjects for these pantomimes, also, and if they choose well-known books and show their character in a familiar action, the others should be able to guess who they are: Tom Sawyer, for instance; Robin Hood, Cinderella's sisters, Aladdin. An especially thrilling pantomime from this last story is that which takes place in the underground cave into which Aladdin descends with such mixed emotions: fear because of the magician's warnings, delight inspired by the trees loaded with colorful fruits made of precious stones, terror when he finds himself shut in—made even stronger when the genie appears. In fact, this story, like most of the other *Arabian Nights* tales, is full of fascinating possibilities for pantomime.

One group to whom the teacher[2] had read the story of Oscar Wilde's "The Birthday of the Infanta" did some very touching pantomime as the little hunchback when he is summoned to the

[2] Elinor Rice, Noyes School, Evanston, Illinois.

palace to dance for the Infanta. As he waits for her to appear, happy that the beautiful little Infanta who had thrown a rose to him when he danced in the garden wishes to see him again, he looks around the room and discovers a big mirror. What a grotesque creature he sees looking at him! Never having seen a mirror, he does not know that this horrible little monster is himself. He laughs at it, and it laughs back. He stretches out his hand to touch it and feels only the hard glass. When he sees that it does everything that he does, a terror slowly grows upon him as he realizes that it may be a kind of echo such as he has experienced in his forest home. Then he makes the supreme test by taking the precious white rose from his breast and kissing it; and seeing that the monster does the same, he gives a wild cry of despair, according to the story, and falls sobbing to the floor.

Though the intensity of the emotion was far beyond anything these children had ever experienced, they sensed enough of the feeling of the dwarf to put a great deal of meaning into their pantomime. One at a time they played the scene, some of the class taking other parts if they did not quite dare to play the dwarf. They could imagine the situation and it seemed to give a number of them great satisfaction to attempt to feel the emotions he experienced. This pantomime, even more than most, required time and thought on the part of the teacher to give it deep meaning for the children who played the part of the little dwarf. All pantomime is empty, however, without real thought. We must never forget this.

MIMING WITH MUSIC

Mechanical ideas often motivate pantomime carried out with music, especially in creative dance movement. Gladys Andrews[3] suggests such ideas as a typewriter, an escalator, a pencil sharp-

[3] *Creative Rhythmic Movement* (Prentice-Hall, Inc., 1954).

ener, an egg-beater, a television set, a traffic light, a clock. Beginning with the *idea* of a typewriter, say, a child tries out some movement expressions of the idea until he finds those which seem right to him. These are then worked into a composition.

Both for creative thinking and experience in rhythm these expressions are excellent, especially if the teacher is able to help the group compose music for them. It is not difficult to think of movement for any of the above ideas, though it is harder if they try to create people with the characteristics of machines.

One girl who had just returned from a summer camp was asked whether she had had dramatics there. She replied without enthusiasm, "Some. I was an earring." A dramatic counselor, wishing to try something novel, evidently had been unwise in the use of an idea for which the girl was not ready. Furthermore, she had assigned something that ordinarily has no movement and so made no appeal to the imagination.

Boats, airplanes, and other transportation ideas, animals, sports, occupations, and many more pantomime and dance possibilities can be used successfully by a trained teacher.

The use of music is without doubt the best way to induce certain *moods*: sadness, gaiety, a feeling of grandeur, awe, apprehension. The children who pantomimed the scene from "The Birthday of the Infanta" found it easier to experience something of what the dwarf was feeling because of the soft, appropriate music supplied by a pianist. The "Aladdin" pantomime would be heightened emotionally by Oriental music.

Next to an accompanist who can improvise are well-chosen recordings. "The Sorcerer's Apprentice," [4] for instance, played before a class begins a dramatization of the story, gives them a strong feeling for it. "Danse Macabre" will create a perfect mood for a Hallowe'en story. A good minuet works wonders in secur-

---

[4] See Record List in the Appendix for this and all other records mentioned.

ing grace in the walk of overgrown boys and girls; and the impressive march in *Aïda* assures dignity in the marching of young people in a royal procession.

"The Dance of the Hours," from *La Gioconda*, has many uses because of its variety. One group of young people tried out for the roles of the Dog, Cat, Fire, Milk, the Hours, and others, to this one record for a children's theatre production of *The Blue Bird*. "Morning," from the *Peer Gynt Suite*, parts of Morton Gould's *The Fall River Legend Ballet*, Debussy's "Clouds," and numerous other records referred to in the Appendix are being used for children in this age range.

Whether played softly for relaxation, for mood during pantomimes, for direct rhythmical movement, or for dances, suitable records contribute immensely to any class in playmaking.

ADDING DIALOGUE

How soon does the time come for using dialogue? How long are children content with pantomime? No stated time can possibly be set for the adding of speech to action. There is no rule. The leader has to determine when the time is right, and more often than not the impulse will come from the children's feeling that they need it.

Though most classes do a good deal of pantomime first so that the children may come to realize that the body can talk as well as the voice, some groups feel the need of speech much sooner than others. The material used makes a great deal of difference; so does the leader's competence in teaching pantomime. By the third or fourth session many classes are ready for dialogue, though pantomime can and should continue to be used without speech a part of the time throughout a child's experience in playmaking—usually in the beginning stages of every story they dramatize.

Simple group situations—sometimes the very ones they have used as pantomime—are natural beginnings for dialogue. Situations dependent on language, as telephone conversations, interviews, shopping excursions with various kinds of shoppers and salespeople, lost-and-found offices, and the like, cannot be done satisfactorily without dialogue. One such situation that depends much more on dialogue than action is

An Afternoon in a Travel Agency

If most of the children take trips occasionally, they will enjoy a travel agency. One person is the agent, the scene is his or her office, and a succession of people come to arrange for trips. It is the business of the agent to tell the prospective travelers about the fine tours he can arrange for them. Those who come to the office should, in the conversation, make clear who they are and what their families are like, and they should have ideas as to where they would like to go.

One seventh-grade girl who came into the office provided the teacher[5] and class with amusing variety when instead of inquiring about a trip for herself she informed the agent that she had come to check on a certain acquaintance who *said* she had taken a trip arranged by him; and she simply wanted to find out whether or not the woman had made it up! After some conversation, when the agent looked in his files and found a record of a Canadian tour he had arranged for the friend, the woman thanked him, saying, "That's all I wanted to know," and went out. She had achieved a characterization as real and as individualized as anyone in the class.

Dialogue will no doubt be a part of whatever dramatic use is made of the following charming little poem. It could, of course, be a dance pantomime or just a bit of dramatic play, though it has possibilities for a complete creative dramatization.

[5] Polly Lowndes, Nichols School, Evanston, Illinois.

The Visitor[6]

My great-great-grandmother, Phipps by name,
Tiptoed out of her picture frame.
Stepped from the lowboy, down to a chair,
Then to the carpet and curtsied there.

Grandmother's hair was powdered white,
And her shoulders gleamed in the softened light.
Her ivory fan moved to and fro,
Wafting a perfume of long ago.

"My dear, please don't be afraid," she said.
"There's a boy upstairs in the Blue Room bed.
I've heard him laugh and I've heard him fret,
But nobody's brought him to see me yet!

"Why, only this morning I heard them say,
He was five months old this very day.
So now when he's sure to be fast asleep,
Please won't you take me for just one peep?"

I said I was charmed—it was only fair,
And I led the way up the darkened stair,
Which is rather a shivery thing to do,
With a great-great-grandmother following you.

She knelt by the baby's blanket nest,
And she touched his hand to her fair young breast.
And I heard her laugh as she smoothed the clothes,
"Thank heaven, he has the family nose!"

Then she tiptoed back the way she came,
And settled down in her picture frame.
There's the happiest smile on the canvas lips
Of great-great-grandmother Charity Phipps!

Today's young people seem worlds away from that period of
graceful manners and courtly minuet, of spacious homes and

[6] Mary Rooney, *Recital Readings* (Walter H. Baker Co.).

family portraits. But there is a romantic charm about it which appeals to most girls of twelve, thirteen, and fourteen, and it isn't difficult for them to imagine themselves in an eighteenth-century setting.

What might a group of seventh- or eighth-grade girls like to do with this poem? Use it as a pantomime with stately music? As a dream? As a complete play? Might they perhaps imagine a group of young moderns in a final dress rehearsal for a minuet to be danced at a Washington's Birthday entertainment the next day? Perhaps dress rehearsing in simple Colonial costumes—or in a suggestion of such costumes?

Might they think of the baby upstairs and hope to see it? Might they ask if the nurse couldn't bring him down to show them? Might the daughter of the house who is rehearsing with them see to it that he is *not* brought down because she perhaps resents the baby and the devotion lavished upon him? Will she later dream what she acts out with the lady of the portrait?

Very likely they will think of possibilities very different from this and develop one into a play. Whatever they evolve, it can be a happy and an unusual experience which should build in them some appreciation for a kind of beauty not often to be found today.

THE USE OF PROPERTIES

For a group with plenty of imagination, a curious or interesting property such as an unusual jewel-box which has, perhaps, been made for one of the three kings in a Nativity play; or an ornate mirror of the type Snow White's jealous stepmother might have used; a strange-looking necklace; or perhaps an old sword, may be the starting-point of an improvisation.

The children look at it from every angle, handle it, consider who might own it; and then proceed to build a story or incident around it. It may be a modern story or a "once-upon-a-time" tale.

It may take place in America or in a foreign country. Sometimes it is only fragmentary; again it is a complete tale. But the experience of creating and playing it is a valuable co-operative project, requiring serious thought.

Another kind of dramatic play—one that can be more generally used if good properties are assembled—is done with the use of enough properties or bits of costume for all the young people in the group. Either the teacher or the class—or both—may bring such articles as a cane, an old shawl, a quaint hat or headdress, a pair of mitts, a "bag of gold," Indian moccasins, an ostrich plume, a fur boa, a heavy gold chain, a scroll.

To begin with, we might choose one of the most interesting properties and hold it up, asking, "What kind of a person might wear (or use) this?" All manner of ideas will come forth concerning the character, his likes and dislikes, his habits, and what he might be doing with the property. A child who has offered the best ideas will doubtless be given the property to use in a pantomime. And later, others may use whatever properties are suggestive to them of some other particular character and action.

This playing will in all likelihood lead to the giving out of all the properties, one to a child. The class may then be divided—perhaps by numbering to five—and each group will be given time to plan a short scene centered around the properties they have.

In one such playing, the clothesbasket (in which the properties had been kept) became a canoe in which an Indian maiden, with hair quickly combed into two braids, paddled swiftly along, turning frightened glances back to her imaginary pursuers. Soon a stalwart pioneer in a Daniel Boone hat (his property) appeared on the shore toward which she was racing, and beckoned the maiden on. Faster and faster went her paddle, and at last—just in time—she reached the shore and was rescued by her valiant woodsman!

Another group had drawn, among other things, a bag of gold and a crown which was much too large for any of them to wear. This suggested that the king offer the gold to whatever person could make his crown fit. It was only after a succession of the proud court people had tried in all sorts of absurd ways to make it fit that a humble servant in the palace showed the king that the crown was adjustable, and so won the bag of gold.

Until children have had the chance to use properties once or twice, they are not likely to be so inventive as was this older group. But once arouse their imaginations, and many of them will be so full of ingenious ideas that they will forget themselves as they work out their plans. It is a wonderful game for cultivating the imagination, and it is good fun besides.

FOR SPONTANEITY IN LANGUAGE

More difficult than the properties game, and worthy of the most experienced players, is this exercise which depends upon language. The leader or one of the children suggests a sentence which the first player uses at the opening of a scene. Two or three other children in the scene respond to it in any way they choose. Each one may change the meaning which the first player intended. No one knows, therefore, how the scene will come out; and sometimes it has a hard time coming out at all!

For instance, the first player might say, "The fire is almost out." His meaning might be that a building has burned down. The second player, not knowing what the sentence is to be (for those who are to play may have been sent out of the room while it was being decided), makes a quick judgment and then runs to look, saying, perhaps, "And we're all out of matches!" Whether the first player accepts the interpretation of the second or vice versa is left entirely to the children who are playing. If the first player is fond of his own idea and sees a good way to work it out, he may decide to explain to player number two that the second idea was not what he meant. On the other hand, he is just as likely to fall in with it. What the first two will do with the third interpretation is anybody's guess! For the third might think that they had been on a picnic and say, "We won't need it any more. I'll get some water. We don't want to start any forest fire!"

If the children are alert and intelligent, they can develop a complete scene which may really make good sense! It is possible that the players will accept the interpretation of the last one to come in, or, if one of the others has an especially good idea he may re-direct the playing back to the meaning he has given to it. Such a game requires concentration on the part of the players in the scene and is usually very entertaining for the others to watch. Much depends on the possibilities in the sentence chosen.

GAME OF PHRASES

Children in the class may contribute to a list of words or phrases, from which three are chosen by vote as the starting-point of an improvisation. The interest lies in selecting phrases so widely different that it requires much ingenuity to weave them together into one scene.

In order to avoid expressions so commonplace that they will not stir anyone's imagination, we may want to lead off with a phrase of our own. If we suggested "a flaming bush," "tiny as a leprechaun," "a bed of yellow pansies," or "the sound of bells in the distance," we would be sure to get many unusual and widely different expressions. If each one is written on the board, the children will delight in choosing the three hardest to weave together.

After they have voted, the class is divided into groups and given time to plan a scene built around the same three phrases. At the end of about ten minutes, each group, in succession, plays the scene it has devised. Occasionally, after the words have been chosen, the children are given until the next day to think up ideas, since many children with good imaginations cannot come forth with plans instantly. Each then submits his ideas to his group, one, or a combination of several, is chosen, and they decide on a part for each player.

One older group thought out and played the following humorous scenes. The phrases the class had chosen from the complete list were: "a haunted castle," "a joyous clown," and "dainty as a feather."

FIRST SCENE: A king and queen on their thrones in the haunted castle, talking about how poorly the servants kept the castle. Of course they hadn't been able to pay them for years, so that all the king's guards and all the queen's attendants had left, and only two maids remained. And now these maids came in and gave notice: they would not go on any longer working without pay, especially in a haunted castle. They left, and the king said that there was nothing for it but that the queen must do the cleaning.

"All 354 rooms!?" exclaimed the queen. "Then you will have to help."

"A *king* clean a castle?" he answered. "Ridiculous!"

But she thrust a mop into his hands and they went to work with great zest. The cobwebs were dreadful—and here the players who had been maids returned as cobwebs, their fingers outspread, and the royal pair were trying to get rid of them as the first scene ended.

SECOND SCENE: A circus train engineered by "a joyous clown," with the cars (chairs) filled with animals. As they "sped" along, the clown seemed to see some little object out of the window which looked "dainty as a feather." He reached for it repeatedly, failed to get it, so stopped the train and jumped out to follow it. In and out among the trees he wandered, and finally caught it. It looked exactly like a feather except that it seemed, somehow, to be magic.

FINAL SCENE: The joyous clown came upon the castle as he vainly tried to find his way back to the circus train. Here he discovered the king and queen completely worn out and discouraged in their efforts to keep the castle clean and free from ghosts. By this time the clown decided to see whether this thing he had found was magic, as he suspected. He asked it whether it could make the castle clean and beautiful again. And, lo, it was done! So the clown gave the magic thing that was dainty as a feather to the hard-pressed king and queen and went joyously on his way to find the circus!

And what did the players get from the experience? Great exercise for the imagination and for facility in expressing ideas while they were having a delightful adventure in group co-operation. Little in the way of characterization or meaning, but a feeling of success in what they had undertaken, and consequently greater freedom in their next assignment.

A JUNIOR HIGH SCHOOL CLASS

Most of the foregoing improvisations are quite as suitable for an eighth-grade class as for a sixth or seventh. But whenever we are faced with the launching of dramatics with one of these older groups to whom the subject is new, we need to study the situation very carefully in order to make sure that our approach is effective. What in their past experience will affect their attitude toward dramatics? Have they taken part in formal drama, and was it of good quality? Does their experience consist in skits hurriedly prepared for camp or "Y" recreation? Are they likely to welcome playmaking, consider it inconsequential or "sissy," or regard it with actual distaste?

When dramatics is an elective, one knows that most of the children come into the class because they expect to like it, or at least think it will be "fun." Even in this case, however, pressure from parents who think it would be good for them, or the influence of friends who are to be in the class, brings some students whose interest is hard to win. If there is no choice of electives some children may be actually antagonistic. So at best we want to plan our first meeting with especial care.

Because this particular introduction was used with great success with a difficult group of junior high school students—sev-

enth, eighth, and ninth grades together in a class of forty-five
—some of whom came with a hostile attitude, it is given here
as a suggestion of one type of approach which is as sure, perhaps, as anything a person could use to secure instant absorption.

The teacher[7] had arranged her room with a park bench in
the front with a few leaves scattered around it. Under some of
the leaves she concealed a small purse with a supposedly valuable stickpin in it. Without any preliminaries she began, speaking slowly as if to impress each fact on their memory: "I have a
problem I'd like to have you help me solve. Will you imagine
that this bench is in Grant Park in Chicago? (*They all knew
Grant Park.*) It stands fifty feet south of the Art Institute, facing east. The Illinois Central tracks are below and the lake beyond. There is a low hedge along this side. It is three o'clock in
the afternoon of a gloomy fall day. People occasionally sit for a
time on the bench—sometimes Art Institute students to eat a
lunch or talk for a few minutes before their next class, sometimes loiterers who just sit, or commuters who have a little time
before their trains. About twenty feet to the north and nearer the
street, an art student is sketching the big fountain south of the
building. Occasionally the caretaker passes, spearing bits of paper
and rubbish to put in his basket.

"Under these leaves is a purse which someone has dropped."
(*She stooped and picked it up and the students saw it for the first
time. She opened it and showed them the pin.*) "This looks like
a very valuable pin. I am not sure whether this is a real diamond
with the little emeralds around it or not, but it looks real. . . . I
wonder who lost this purse—what kind of a person it was . . .
and why he or she carried only the pin in the purse. It could
belong to either a man or a woman, as you see. I wonder how
this person happened to lose the purse . . . why he or she sat

[7] Wilma McNess, Keith Country Day School of Rockford (Illinois) College.

on this bench . . . whether it could have been an immigrant recently come to this country, bringing a precious heirloom, . . . a housewife who had brought it down town thinking to sell it so that she could pay a certain debt . . . whether it was a man from one of those little shops out on West Madison Street. . . . And I wonder, too, who will come to this bench without finding the purse . . . someone who perhaps longs for something he hasn't the money to buy . . . or some people who would never try to find the owner and would hurry to sell it. Of course, I wonder, too, who *will* find it. Will it be the caretaker . . . or a discouraged art student . . . or some young boys or girls who think it is worthless . . . or someone who will give it to the caretaker or take it to the Art Institute. . . . Everyone's opinion will be welcomed and respected. Each one of you may have a turn at suggesting who lost the purse . . . who found it . . . who else sat on the bench today. What do you think?"

For a few moments there was silence; then one hand after another went up, and many students had ideas they wanted to propose—so many, in fact, that the rest of the forty-five minutes sped by before all had had a chance to tell what they thought. In fact, it required another period to get the various characters discussed.

For the third class meeting, Mrs. McNess divided the class into four groups. Each group built one character to put in the scene as a result of the two previous discussions. The four characters were named and given qualities of personality and physical appearance. Each group cast the character it created from its own members. These four played the scene through once.

In the fourth and final class, volunteers played the scene twice, the playing being interspersed by a great deal of discussion as to what the scene needed. During the last few minutes the teacher gave her introductory talk about creative drama and praised their first project.

What It Is Worth

First and most important, this kind of an introduction to playmaking instantly captured the interest of a frankly skeptical
group of teenage boys and girls. Not only was it absorbing for
the moment but it provoked so much thought that the ideas
aroused held them for four sessions and impelled them to use
the bench again in the Christmas play they later created.

The element of mystery and suspense in the teacher's objective presentation of the situation was a dramatic way of arousing
the thoughts and feelings of the young people. Picking up the
purse which they had not seen before was a surprise element
which heightened the suspense. In a few words she described
the scene in such detail that it was absolutely clear to all; and
she suggested several specific people who might have lost the
purse, might have missed discovering it, might have found it.
This set fire to their imaginations and stimulated them to think
of many other possibilities.

A problem like this drew them at once into the heart of creative
dramatics. It was a study of people—people they could easily
imagine—in a situation which might be very dramatic. Without
any self-consciousness they could explore the thoughts, the feelings, the actions of many people. They could study motives, conflicts within people, patterns of behavior—the very essence of
drama.

It was an especially good plan to choose a locale which they
had all seen, yet one that was in a great city where anything
might happen. Knowing the tremendous variety of people who
throng the streets of Chicago, there was no limit to the possibilities of characterizations they might use.

The teacher's serious presentation of the situation, and her
absorption in it broke down the teacher-pupil relationship which
so often stands in the way of natural work. Yet the whole proc-

ess of discussing, planning, and playing still required much from her. Strong guidance, especially the ability to ask good questions, was needed to insure an orderliness of procedure, the weighing of suggestions, and the satisfying solutions.

Finally they were ready to hear about creative drama and the course. Having had an exciting experience which had won them all over to whatever kind of dramatics this might be, they listened with interest to what the teacher had to say. It illustrated beautifully the value of beginning with an experience that gave meaning to an explanation. "Learning alone can be an empty cup. It can be the travel guide-book without the trip. Associated with experiences . . . it sends one on further journeys." [8]

What followed this experience? An entirely original play created by the class from a title given them by the teacher. It was called "The Rush and Hush of Christmas." As indicated by the name, it dealt with the problem of making Christmas a time of rushing about, with concern for material things instead of spiritual. Because of their first experience, the students were unified and ready to build something really impressive out of the idea which had been given them.

From here the teacher might turn to literature as material, using something at first that had a challenging problem so that the transition from modern life situations would not be too abrupt. Now and then, if a conflict situation in the school lent itself to dramatic treatment, they might well do some role-playing.[9] Having built a strong rapport with her class, the teacher would now be able to win them over to almost anything she wished to use, whether it was one of the projects given earlier in this chapter, a problem in role-playing, or a classic from literature.

[8] Hughes Mearns, *The Creative Adult* (Doubleday & Co., Inc., 1940).
[9] Role-playing, since its purpose is therapy, is discussed in Chapter 12.

CHAPTER 5

Literature for Playmaking

"WHEN CHILDREN ENJOY A BOOK LET THEM *do* SOMETHING ABOUT it," says May Hill Arbuthnot.[1] To prolong their enjoyment of it, deepen its impression on them, and make it a part of their cultural wealth, we as teachers need often to use it as a motivation for creative writing, arts, crafts, and playmaking.

Suppose we finish reading to them that most beautifully written of all books for children *The Wind in the Willows*.[2] It has been a real experience. Few of the children would have read it for themselves because it is not easy reading even for fifth- or sixth-graders. It is a book that needs to be read to them at just the right time by a grownup who loves it so much that she can make them care for it, too.

By the time the end comes, the lovable Water Rat, eager little Mole, the friendly Otter and Badger, and the preposterous Mr. Toad are old friends, and it is sad to give them up. This is the time to "do something about it"—not forcing expression but offering an opportunity of keeping these friends about a little longer. Some of the children may want to model the characters out of clay, others to draw pictures or write. But there are sure to be many who would like to play an episode from the book. Whatever it is, they will want Mr. Toad in it for he is the most fun

[1] Speech at Kent (Ohio) State University.
[2] Kenneth Grahame (Charles Scribner's Sons, 1908).

to play. More likely than not they will choose his escapade in
the gaol, for that has just the kind of action and humor they
most enjoy. Because they know the incident and the characters
well they will take great delight in playing it.

A fourth-grader would certainly want to play several of the
incidents from *Pinocchio* after hearing it read. And a sixth or
seventh would like to dramatize an episode or two from *The*
Prince and the Pauper. Because a wise teacher always reads
books a little more difficult than most of the children would
read themselves she spurs them on to dramatize good material
by making it so clear and so interesting to them that they have
perfect confidence in their ability to use it.

ORIGINAL PLOTS— NOT GOOD

Children sometimes create the plots for their plays, especially
when they are doing an integrated project based on an historical
event such as the Gold Rush, or on an idea like that of space
travel, described in Chapter 8. Most often, however, when they
create from an idea, the result is not a sustained play in several
acts but a single scene developed in one period of high enthusiasm such as those described in the preceding chapters.

A group of intelligent, imaginative children can make up a
complete plot, but at best they will need unusually strong guidance from an imaginative leader. Furthermore, many of the children are left with a feeling of inadequacy far behind the imaginative ones. It is extremely difficult to originate a good plot, as
any playwright will testify; and children, with their limited experience in life, have to rely largely on stories they have read
and moving pictures and television plays they have seen.

What comes out is a play that is always inferior to one based
on a really good story. Though an original plot gives much exercise for the imagination, a beautifully written story can offer
a more significant experience. Horizons are widened, insights

and understandings are deepened; and there is so much opportunity for imagination in turning a story into a play that what
children lose by not creating a plot they more than make up by
having their imaginations and emotions stirred by working on
material of real quality. It is like the big shove that sends the
toboggan flying down the icy hill faster and farther than it could
go on its own power.

INFLUENCE OF TELEVISION

It is inevitable that when children watch television for several
hours every day, their interest in literature is influenced in one
way or another by what they see and hear. Ask one teacher what
it does to children and she will say that it plays havoc with their
tastes, lowering their sense of comedy to slapstick, and making
them sophisticated to the extent that they have no interest in the
rich folklore which boys and girls formerly enjoyed.

On the other hand, some librarians will say that television
seems not to have cut down on children's reading, though in
many cases they know only the distorted versions of classics
which have been rewritten by Walt Disney and others. Many
of them even think that Disney is the author of *Bambi, Alice in
Wonderland, Uncle Remus,* and the rest.

A television program can arouse tremendous interest in a
book, sending children by the thousands to the libraries for novels which are far beyond their ability to read. It acquaints them
with information about far-off places and peoples so that their
world is much wider than the world the children of past generations knew. At the same time, some teachers say, they know less
about experiences near at hand, their home experiences being
fewer because the family spends so much time looking at TV.

General taste in serious drama is being raised by the increasing number of fine plays, and young people's knowledge of
Shakespearean drama needs no longer to come from books only.

Many eighth-grade boys and girls studying Shakespeare in creative dramatics are finding such presentations of great interest and value.

Because there are as yet so many programs which are a waste of any child's time, and some that are actually harmful to young children, many intelligent parents control the hours that their children devote to television and help them to be discriminating in their choice. A family with a number of interests, especially if they involve *doing* things together, seldom has the problem of indiscriminate watching of television programs. Teachers often help to popularize really good programs by talking about them in the classroom and encouraging their pupils to choose the best.

Everyone will agree that the potentialities of television are extraordinary, that there is scarcely any limit to its educational possibilities. It is to be hoped that not only educational channels but every network will steadily improve the quality of the programs they offer to the coming generation. They could, if they chose, contribute both to the enjoyment and to the taste of children by presenting in various forms the best of the classic and modern literature.

CHOICE OF STORY

The choice of the story is of high importance. It must be suited to the age and taste of the children and be challenging to their abilities, though not too difficult for them to dramatize with satisfaction to themselves. It must be worthy of the time to be spent on it; and it must be of the kind to gain in effectiveness by being made into a play.

This means that we must know children and learn what things interest them. We must study the tastes of boys and girls at the age level with which we work but remember that other things besides age help to determine what they like. Environment, temperament, previous experience, and present mood are just as significant; and all should be considered in choosing material.

Children of varied ages and abilities do quite different things with the same material. If "Sing a Song of Sixpence" were to be dramatized by four widely different groups, the material might scarcely be recognizable in the four plays which came out of it. But in spite of the fact that all children beginning creative dramatics should work with simple material, older children with experience grow much more if it challenges their keenest thinking.

LITERARY QUALITY

A story to be used for playmaking should have certain qualities characteristic of good writing:

1. A WORTHY CENTRAL IDEA OR MOTIVE. *Paddy's Christmas,*[3] for instance, concerns the meaning that Christmas should have: not merely holly and mistletoe, not just getting presents, but making others happy.

"Our Lady's Juggler" presents a touching example of how each can serve in his own way.

Many, many good stories, however, do not start with a theme. Their purpose is not to set forth an ethical truth but to show some aspect of life with fresh significance, like the immortal *Tom Sawyer* and "Rip Van Winkle"; or to tell an absorbing story about a worthy hero like Robin Hood of legendary fame; or for the motive of pure entertainment, like *The 500 Hats of Bartholomew Cubbins.*

Nonsense stories sometimes have a purpose beyond the good fun which makes them popular with children. "The Three Sillies," "The Husband Who Was to Mind the House," *Mrs. Goose of Animaltown,* help us to see our own follies. But quite aside from any meaning they may have, they do much to culti-

---

[3] See Story List in the Appendix for all stories mentioned in this chapter.

vate a young child's sense of humor by introducing him to what May Hill Arbuthnot calls "a gay, exuberant world of irresponsible behavior and impossible results." [4]

2. ECONOMY IN THE NUMBER OF INCIDENTS, each of which should build a little higher than the one before and lead directly toward the climax.

Three is the magic number in stories: three sons, three trials, and in many cases just three incidents. Some tales have more, but those for the younger children—such as "The Billy Goats Gruff," "The Three Bears," and a host of others—have three, which always seem rhythmical and right. Some stories for older children have many more. Dickens' _Christmas Carol_ is an espe- *CHRISTMAS* cially good example of many incidents building steadily toward *CAROL* the climax, yet even this classic has three spirits who dominate the *3* main part of the tale.

Because the people of long ago loved a good story they often encouraged a storyteller to spin a long, long tale which really had several plots. In some of the older versions of folk and fairy tales we still have a series of stories told as an elaboration of a single tale. But in the course of centuries, in the countless retellings, many of their complexities have fallen away from them with the result that most of our printed versions are told with economy, leaving but a single impression.

3. A CLIMAX THAT IS STRONG YET DOES NOT APPEAL TOO GREATLY TO ANY ONE EMOTION. The climax is the turning-point of the story, when emotion is at its highest peak. A story can build too much suspense in reaching its climax so that a sensitive child is tormented by nightmares after he reads such a tale or sees it enacted. The emotion may be horror or merely intense anxiety lest the hero may not win.

Such stories are rarely found in good books for children though there are many among folk tales intended for adults.

[4] _Children and Books_ (Scott Foresman and Co., 1947).

When we choose stories we need to consider carefully the age of the children with whom they are to be used. What makes a good story for older children is often too frightening for the younger ones. *Treasure Island, Tom Sawyer,* "The Moor's Legacy," all so satisfying for young people of ten and older, are far too strong for the five-year-old.

One small boy whose mother thought he was old enough for *Treasure Island* was taken to a children's theatre production of that play. Before the first act ended his fingers were in his ears and he asked his mother to cover his eyes—though he stoutly refused to leave the theatre! Other children too young for a play which older children are thoroughly enjoying slip down behind the seats in front of them or cry to be taken home—the strongest kind of argument for a special series of children's theatre plays just for them.

4. A QUICK AND SATISFYING ENDING. Regardless of the length of a story or play, a child's interest drops as soon as he knows how it is coming out. Too, in the plays children create, they are impatient of a long denouement, or solution of a situation. After the climax of a tale, rewards and punishments are administered with dispatch. Perrault's "Cinderella" takes only a few words to tell that Cinderella forgave her sisters, and ends thus:

She was conducted to the young prince, dressed as she was; he thought her more charming than ever, and, a few days after, married her. Cinderella, who was not less good than beautiful, gave her two sisters lodgings in the palace, and that very same day matched them with two great lords of the court.

5. CHARACTERS SHOULD SEEM REAL, WHETHER THEY ARE SUPERNATURAL OR HUMAN. The minor people are often types, but they are only part of the background for the main characters, who should be as individual and three-dimensional as Homer Price or Jo March.

Even in a fairy tale the people must seem real and believable.

For hundreds of years children have felt the reality of Cinderella and Snow White, of Rumpelstiltskin and Jack and Goldilocks.

They must be consistent always. It would be unthinkable to have Cinderella seek revenge on her stepsisters. Rumpelstiltskin would never reform.

When characters are animals they are usually humanized, so that they walk on two feet and have the characteristics of human beings. To crawl around the floor as cats or dogs or goats is such an unrewarding experience that we shall do well to suggest that when such animals appear in a story, they be made imaginary characters.

6. DIALOGUE SHOULD GIVE THE IMPRESSION OF NATURAL CONVERSATION. If conversation were taken direct from life it would be very dull and long-drawn-out. In a well-written story, it is selected and condensed. Speeches are usually brief and direct and seem to belong to the character making them.

Who but Mary Poppins could say of the "medicine" which she administers to Jane and Michael, "For you it's strawberry ice; for you it's lime juice cordial; for *me* it's rum punch!"

And could we have any doubt as to the identity of the following from *Winnie-the-Pooh*, even if no name were attached? "Balloon?" said Eeyore. "You did say balloon? One of those big colored things you blow up? Gaiety, song-and-dance, here we are and there we are?"

These are, of course, extraordinarily clever bits of dialogue. Except in *Alice in Wonderland* and the Mark Twain books, one doesn't expect to find it so well done. But many modern stories do excel in this respect, even when they are very thin as to substance. Indeed, all of the best books for children are so beautifully written that an adult going back to them after many years is astonished to find that they measure up to the best he has read in the adult field.

A. A. Milne, though he considered himself mainly an author

of adult books, says in his *Autobiography* that such merit as attaches to the verses in *When We Were Very Young* was won by taking pains: "more pains, perhaps, than is usual." He says that it is the work of a light-verse writer taking his job seriously even though he is taking it into the nursery. "It seems," he says, "that the nursery, more than any other room in the house, likes to be approached seriously."

POETIC JUSTICE

Ideal, or poetic, justice should characterize the stories we choose for young children. This alone does not make them worthy, as shown in the flood of cheap literature and comic strips, most of which have a more or less just distribution of rewards and punishments.

But poetic justice sets standards for children of what most of us believe is admirable, as well as what we think is despicable. Stories exemplifying poetic justice build sympathy for virtues such as courage and good sportsmanship, for integrity and for kindness, and arouse antipathy for cruelty, jealousy, and pettiness. If we were to tell stories of people who look out only for self-interest or take revenge on their enemies, and leave children with the impression that these were acceptable kinds of behavior, we would confuse those who already had begun to learn that "we should do to others as we would that they should do to us," and make it more difficult to teach them that "it is a prince's part to pardon." For though in most stories there is both good and evil, the important thing is that the sympathy of the reader be kept on the side of the right. There should *never* be obvious moralizing nor pointing out of ethical truths. Children want to see cause and effect and judge for themselves, and the influence of the story is far greater if they are allowed to do so.

There are many who think we give children a wrong picture of life in literature that is characterized by poetic justice. Even these people think we are justified in doing it, however, for they say, "Let children be happy as long as possible, for they will be disillusioned soon enough!"

Admitting that there are terrible injustices on every side, we can be sure, if we have a true sense of values, that there is much more truth in the Bible verse, "Whatsoever a man sows, that shall he also reap," than is known by anyone except the person who does the sowing and reaping! Justice is often slow in coming, and it is not always evidenced in material ways; but in the long run evil is usually punished and goodness rewarded.

It is indeed a question as to whether the material rewards and punishments which are meted out to characters in stories do not serve to build in children the belief that if they do good deeds they, too, will receive *material* rewards. Disillusionment is surely in store for those who expect worldly success as a reward for being good.

Though young children cannot yet understand that goodness is so infinitely worthy to individuals and to nations that, as Hughes Mearns expresses it, "it is even worth failing for," older children should gradually come to realize the very rich reward for integrity which comes in peace of mind and the ability to look people straight in the eye.

STORIES WHICH MAKE THE BEST DRAMATIZATIONS

If a story is more effective read than dramatized, it should not be used for a play. Only when its value to the child is heightened by coming alive in a dramatization should it be used in this way.

At once this eliminates stories which are superior chiefly because of beauty of language. Antoine de Saint-Exupery's exquisitely written story *The Little Prince* is one of these. Other stories have very little action, or the kind of action which cannot be done with any degree of satisfaction: *Horton Hears a Who*, for example, by Dr. Suess; *A Camel for a Throne,* by Eloise Lownsbery; *The Saturdays,* by Elizabeth Enright; and *Charlotte's Web,* by E. B. White—all of which are so much more delightful and worth-while to read than to play that it is a pity to risk spoiling them by attempting to dramatize them.

As to poetry, story-poems and ballads are much more adaptable than are lyrics, though as ideas for pantomimic dance, lyrics often inspire beautifully creative work. Aside from Mother Goose jingles, there are numbers of poems with a bit of a story: "The Elf and the Dormouse," "The Goblinade," "Hiding," "The Butterbean Tent," "The Weather Factory," "The Enchanted Shirt," "Get Up and Bar the Door," "King John and the Abbot of Canterbury," and many others.

Stories with characters much like the children playing them do not often gain by dramatization. In reading such stories children like to identify themselves with the characters; but in playing them they do not sufficiently get away from their own personalities to make the experience worth-while. Seldom are they really absorbed in their playing, and too often they are self-conscious and uncomfortable.

It seems to be much more difficult to find stories of modern life which dramatize well than stories of other periods. Certain *Homer Price* incidents, *Mrs. Mallaby's Birthday, Twig, Andy and the Lion, The Hundred Dresses, The Magic Bed-Knob,* are a few examples of the exceptions. But the great majority of modern stories do not offer dramatic situations which make satisfying plays. Any leader looking for a good story to use will find at least twenty good folk tales or classics to one story of modern life.

THE FIVE- AND SIX-YEAR-OLD

Much of the material used by the child of five years is suited to dramatic play rather than story dramatization. He is still being a jet plane or a fireman or a cowboy with no thought of definite beginning, ending, nor climax, unless he has attended a nursery school and has dramatized stories.

The first plots he uses will be simple and short because his span of attention is brief. His limited experience in life implies that he has not a great deal on which to base imagination; therefore, we cannot use tales of princesses and leprechauns, of fairy dells and far-off lands. Instead, we shall need to find stories related closely enough to the familiar so that he can readily understand them. He especially enjoys a familiar character having imaginary adventures.

Our stories must have action, plenty of it, if they are to hold a little child's attention. For he likes things that go! Trains and tigers, airplanes and trucks. Their sound as well as action intrigues him, and he enjoys a realistic imitation of animal cries and motor sounds when a story is told or read to him.

Rhythm and repetition charm him because of his sensitivity to sound. The recurrent rhythm which comes from the repetition of incidents in "The Three Pigs" and "The Three Bears" has the additional value of making the story easy to grasp. There is a pleasurable sense of familiarity to the very young child when he hears, "Now, the *third* little pig met a man with a load of bricks." Just one new element to grasp. It gives him that same good feeling which we who are older feel when we find we can recognize the French words in an opera!

The characters in stories for the five-year-old must be like the people he already knows, such as the postman, his church school teacher, or his own family. Animal characters are especially delightful to him, and he accepts without a question the fact that most of them talk like human beings. A few magic characters such as elves and brownies are understandable to him, especially if he sees pictures of them, because they look like human beings, only smaller. By the time he is six he comes to know kings, queens, dwarfs, gnomes, and the rest of the story-book characters through pictures, stories, and plays.

The idea of the story must be within his interest range. The little engine who wanted to take his train of cars over the mountain to carry Christmas gifts to the children on the other side wins his genuine sympathy. Of *course* the children over there want their gifts, and it's nice of the little engine to carry them!

To many adults the sense of humor of little people is baffling. They are entirely unmoved by most of the situations which are funny to older children. What appeals to them as comical is merely the slapstick fun of people falling down or having their hats knocked off. They love words with odd sounds and will laugh with glee at characters with names like "Tweedledum" and "Tweedledee." They enjoy some of Lear's nonsense rhymes for that reason, and they like nonsense stories like "Epaminondas" and *Mrs. Goose of Animaltown.*

The outcome of their stories must be completely satisfying, with everything coming out all right: the Billy Goats Gruff getting safely over the bridge, the Big Bad Wolf cooked for dinner, and the Little Duckling content at last with his own little voice.

Mother Goose

BEST

There is no better material for the dramatizations of little children than the gay, rhythmical Mother Goose jingles. They have action which can be played: "Three Little Kittens," "The Old Market Woman," "Miss Muffet." They are full of captivating characters who, though familiar people, often do the most surprising and amusing things! They have names which are highly amusing to five-year-olds: Jack Sprat, Old King Cole, Lucy Locket, Wee Willie Winkie. There is suspense: "Who stole the tarts?" "Who killed Cock Robin?" The rhymes are wonderfully pleasing to the ear!

Other Stories and Rhymes

Regardless of all the newer stories introduced to children of five, "The Three Bears" and "The Three Billy Goats Gruff" continue to hold highest place for beginning dramatizations. They have everything that children enjoy: lovable animals as characters, simplicity in pattern, with rhyme and repetition, plenty of good action, just the right amount of suspense, a climax and satisfying ending, with things coming out all right.

Every five-year-old likes to play "The Elf and the Dormouse," too, especially with music. All the children are likely to be elves dancing about in their new little suits until a sudden shower (*heard in the music*) sends them scurrying to toadstools for shelter. For the moment it is fine to be so well protected from the rain until the elf sees on the other side of the toadstool a fat dormouse, fast asleep! He is frightened. What to do? He thinks and thinks—and an idea comes to him. Seizing the imaginary toadstool, he tugs and tugs (*all this is rhythmical pantomime accentuated by the music*) until he suddenly breaks it off! (*Climax in music.*) Then he runs gaily home. To complete the story, the dormouse, wakened by the rain pouring down on him, exclaims, "Good gracious me! Where is my toadstool?" and scrambles off to another shelter. One group of children had a man meet the elf as he scurried away and ask him what he was carrying.

"A toadstool to keep the rain off. You'd better get one, too!"

"It wouldn't be big enough for me, I'm afraid," answered the man. "But it gives me an idea. I'll go home and make one, and I'll call it an umbrella!"

Whether or not this small bit of dialogue is added, the children have a gay time being elves and dormice; and they begin to get more characterization and real story sequence than they have had before.

"The Rabbit Who Wanted Red Wings," "Little Duckling Tries His Voice," "Ask Mr. Bear," and "Why the Evergreen Trees Keep Their Leaves in Winter" are almost as popular. Less known but excellent for five-and-six-year-olds are "Fancy Dress," a charming spring poem, and "The Adventure of Three Little Rabbits."

One group playing the latter story suggested that all the children except the two playing the goodman and his wife be the rabbits who hopped in the window and got stuck in the treacle. This the teacher was glad to have them do so that all could play at once.

They used a low table for the window sill over which they hopped, and soon they were all beautifully stuck in the treacle. After the wife had built up a rousing fire to cook the rabbits for dinner she went out to call the goodman to catch them for her. By this time, as the story goes, the heat of the fire had so thinned the treacle that the rabbits could get their feet free, and when the two entered the door "all they could see was the powder-puff tail of the last little rabbit disappearing over the window sill."

Now, of course, it required far more time for fifteen rabbits to get out the window than the original three of the story; and the children who played the goodman and wife were not experienced enough to note that they would have to wait a few moments before coming in. As it was, half the rabbits were still waiting their turn to get out the window when the pair entered. Quick as a flash the goodman whipped out an imaginary gun, and "bang, bang, bang!" he picked them off fast.

The dramatization would have ended badly for the rabbits if the goodman had been a better shot! What happened was that the rabbits paid no attention whatever to the gun, and soon they were all safely away from danger!

Teachers with a love for children's literature are often tempted to use stories and poems which are too difficult for their children

to dramatize. Although it is true that even the simplest material
which is given to five-year-olds makes a more delightful play
when dramatized by children several years older, we should at
least avoid the mistake of suggesting that they play a story which
is beyond their ability to do satisfactorily. They may like to hear
some of the Milne stories and poems, for instance; but it would
be a pity to spoil their later enjoyment of this material by trying
to make plays from it before they are old enough to appreciate
Milne's delicious humor.

CHILDREN OF SEVEN AND EIGHT

Granted that no two children are alike, certain story interests
can be counted on to predominate in groups of boys and girls of
any particular age. The seven- or eight-year-old, for instance, has
had a great many more experiences than the child just starting to
school; and it is natural to suppose that his everyday surroundings are less novel to him. Having adjusted himself to them, he
now seeks wider fields and new experiences. He is interested in
people and things which are more remote.

Though boys and girls of this age like realistic stories also,
their enjoyment of fairy tales is at its height. They delight in the
magic of tales about far-away kingdoms—tales of dragons and
fairy godmothers, of swineherds who are really princes, and of
children lost in the woods who come upon a house made all of
sweetmeats! The pleasure in such stories should be fostered and
encouraged, especially in a mechanistic age such as this when
interest in scientific discoveries tends to crowd into the background the fascinating world of make-believe.

Now and again people tell us that children no longer care for
fairy tales. Yet it is a fact which any children's theatre in the
country will verify that the greatest crowds of the whole season
flock to the theatre when it offers the boys and girls a play based
on one of the great old fairy tales such as "Cinderella," "Hansel

[handwritten margin note: EVERYDAY SURROUNDINGS LESS NOVEL]

and Gretel," "Jack and the Beanstalk," or "Snow White and the Seven Dwarfs." Regardless of alarmists, the life of these stories, which has already gone on for centuries, will continue as long as the world lasts.

We shall find stories of magic happenings highly popular as material for dramatizations. The stories may be longer, too, for children can concentrate better and understand situations which puzzled them before. The characters are still very definitely good or bad rather than mixed good and bad, but they are more varied and often less familiar in type. Suspense is held longer, and so the climax builds higher. Humor is a little finer in many of the tales. And there is poetic justice in all the modern stories and in most of the older ones.

Folk tales, whether realistic or fairy stories, are made to order for playmaking. In form they are usually simple and logical, extraneous events having been dropped through many tellings. They have a childlike outlook on life, and the emotions they arouse are simple and obvious. They stress justice, courage, loyalty, sympathy for the weak. They are democratic tales in which true worth counts for more than position. A lad who is poor but brave and clever may win the hand of a princess. Labor is always dignified and a poor man may talk to a king.

As to standards, they show what the race generally considers of high value: honesty, fair play, loyalty; and what we despise, as pettiness, underhandedness, poor sportsmanship, jealousy. Beauty and ugliness of character are presented so definitely and objectively that even the most ignorant or immature person cannot fail to understand. Always they show the certainty of reaping what one sows; and because they repeat this pattern over and over again they set standards of life as well as standards of form.

Not all folk tales can be used, of course, for the seven- and eight-year-old. Because they were originally told for men and women, some have subject matter that is unsuitable, even grue-

[margin notes: FOLK TALES FOR PLAYMAKING; REAPING WHAT ONE SOWS]

some. But such tales as "To Your Good Health," "What the Goodman Does Is Sure to Be Right," "The Bailiff's Wonderful Coat," "Three Meals a Day," "The Brahmin, the Tiger, and the Jackal," and countless others from the folklore of many different peoples, make a rich contribution to the fund of stories on which plays can be based.

Fairy Tales

Modern fairy tales come and go, while a few great stories that have come from the folk of long ago will be loved forever. Someone has written, "A fairy tale, like a cat, has nine lives. It can pass in many queer shapes, and yet not die. You can cut off its head, or drown it in sentiment or sea water, or tie a moral to its tail, but it will still survive and be found sitting by the fire some winter night."

It is because the folk among whom these old tales originated really *believed* in fairies, believed in supernatural happenings, that they are more sincere than are modern fairy tales. There is nothing playful or condescending in them, and though most of them have not the literary style of modern stories, they are more sturdy and more truly childlike. As a rule they concern the fundamental things of life. A person's whole life happiness is at stake in "Cinderella" and "Snow White." What every child wants to see happen is for justice to be done these gentle heroines—for them to be freed from their lowly position as drudges in their own homes and win the freedom and the happiness they deserve. In contrast, what is the desired end in the modern fairy tale *The Wizard of Oz?* That Dorothy may get back to Kansas!

The old tales use the supernatural sparingly—only enough magic to accomplish the necessary ends. Many modern fairy tales, such as *The Wizard of Oz*, pile magic on top of magic until a child becomes satiated with it.

The supernatural characters in the old tales are not fairies in gossamer dresses such as we find in many modern fairy tales and plays. They have wonderful variety: ogres, witches, elves, gnomes, goblins, leprechauns, "wee folk," dryads, mermaids, giants. It is in this aspect—variety of interesting characters— that "The Wizard" has won popularity despite its faults.

Among the traditional fairy tales which children of this age like best to use for plays are "The Sleeping Beauty," "Rumpel-stiltskin," "Taper Tom," "Why the Sea Is Salt," "The Elves and the Shoemaker," and "East of the Sun and West of the Moon," in addition to those before mentioned.

Modern Stories and Poems

Second- or third-graders have a good time in the fall with the lively little poem "The Weather Factory," in which the weather folk—Whipper, Snapper, and all the others—are busy as can be making the weather which will be needed for fall and winter. Plenty of imagination, with much action and good humor, characterize this charming and usable poem. "The Goblinade," too, is a well-liked fall poem, especially good for Hallowe'en week.

A seasonal story which lends itself to dramatization is "Old Man Rabbit's Thanksgiving Dinner." Though the characters are all animals, they are humanized so that they do not have to go around on all fours, always a disadvantage in dramatization! How Old Man Rabbit gave a Thanksgiving dinner without knowing it is a story with simplicity, lively action, and a good idea. It is suitable either for child players or puppets.

Before Christmas time the children like very much to play *Paddy's Christmas,* an appealing tale with a fine idea; or *Why the Chimes Rang,* a story which is flexible as to age appeal, highly effective to play, and deeply impressive for all who participate in it.

The Plain Princess is enjoyed especially by girls, and though strongly moralistic, has charm and humor enough to make it acceptable. *The Moffats,* though far more delightful, is not often used because the kind of action and humor in the stories seems better suited for reading about than playing.

A sure favorite, however, is "The Peddler and His Caps," in a delightful version by Geraldine Siks. Though it has come down from an old source, it has only in the last few years appeared in our children's books. Whether young children play only the very funny monkey episode or more experienced children develop the interesting village scene also, the story is a boon to teachers and children alike.

CHILDREN OF NINE, TEN, ELEVEN

From the years in which children's interest in imaginative literature is high, they come gradually to like realistic stories better. At nine, ten, and eleven the boys clamor for adventure, excitement. They are interested in hero stories, both real and fictitious, and they like tales of pioneers, Indians, and cowboys.

Physical bravery is admired above moral courage at this age, and because there is always a flood of cheap adventure stories which give a false picture of life it is important that we satisfy children's hunger for excitement with really good hero and adventure stories. For though boys and girls are not at all idealistic at this age level, and though they are prone to suspect that adults in general are against them, they are often strongly influenced by heroes whom they admire.

Both boys and girls of nine and ten like also to dramatize the fanciful stories which have been beyond their ability up to this time; and since they provide material for rich experience, we are likely to postpone some of the adventure stories until they are ten or eleven.

Among the modern stories liked very much by fourth grades is a Swiss tale in verse *A Bell for Ursli,* by Selma Chonz, simply and charmingly told, and well suited to dramatization. *Andy and the Lion*, by James Daugherty, is even more popular with the children. The humor is exactly on their level; and the idea of the boy who reads so many lion stories that he dreams he is Androcles furnishes situations that are not only enjoyable but also very playable.

Realism and Magic

Certain modern books that "join on to real life," yet have surprising magical characters are devoured by most of the fourth- and fifth-graders, and enjoyed by many of the sixth-grade children. Of these, *Mary Poppins* and *Mr. Popper's Penguins* are more usable as children's theatre plays than as material for informal dramatizations, though Mary's arrival at Number 17, Cherry Tree Lane, with the unpacking of her astonishing carpet-bag, the episode of "Bad Tuesday," and "Miss Andrews' Lark" from *Mary Poppins Comes Back*, are three popular incidents for playmaking.

Two more recent books that combine the real and the fanciful very cleverly are *The Lion, the Witch, and the Wardrobe*, by C. S. Lewis, and *The Magic Bed-Knob*, by Mary Norton. In the latter, Miss Price, who is "learning to be a witch," buys the children's silence by giving magic properties to Paul's bed-knob! In "The Hurdy-Gurdy Man," by Margery Bianco, all seems to be realistic until the hurdy-gurdy proves to have magic tunes that can make sour-faced villagers dance in spite of themselves and change to friendlier human beings.

It is very doubtful whether the *Arabian Nights* tales—pure magic, with no slightest trace of realism—will ever lose their enchantment for the older children, especially "Ali Baba and the Forty Thieves" and "Aladdin." Both for formal and informal plays they still prove more richly dramatic than almost any other imaginative tale except perhaps "The Emperor's New Clothes," which never fails to stir the imagination of fifth-grade children.

Besides the appeal of its situation and the interest of its characters, its satire makes for irresistible comedy. It remains always one of the "sure-fire" stories for a creative play.

Hero and Adventure Tales

After boys and girls have had considerable experience they are ready to play the *Robin Hood* stories. Here are adventure and excitement, lively action, and a hero whom they all admire! Though he has had many imitators and competitors, it is safe to say that he will outlast all the others.

Historical background for these stories is important, for the children should understand why Robin Hood became an outlaw. Without condoning the custom of taking money from the rich to give to the poor, we should see to it that they know something of the cruel and unjust laws which caused men to rebel and break them.

Some of the best stories for dramatizing tell of Robin Hood's meeting with Little John and of the latter's initiation into the band; "Robin Hood and Midge, the Miller"; "The Widow's Three Sons"; and "The Shooting Match at Nottingham."

The Howard Pyle prose version of the ballads—*The Merry Adventures of Robin Hood*—is completely satisfying, with all the rich flavor of the bold hero and his merry men. Anne Eaton writes of it in *A Critical History of Children's Literature:*[5]

This truly great children's book has been read by children and their elders for over seventy years and there are no signs of its losing its popularity. [The reader] finds himself in the green glades of Sherwood, or watching the life of the day as it passes on the high road sharing the springtime adventures that could only have taken place in a younger, more innocent world.

A quite different adventure tale—one that is unfailingly a favorite with the eleven-year-old—is *Tom Sawyer*. Like all the

[5] Cornelia Meigs, Ann Eaton, Ruth Hill Viguers, and Elizabeth Nesbitt (The Macmillan Co., 1950).

rest of Mark Twain's novels, it seems written to be played. Though the book is full of dramatic episodes, the whitewashing incident holds the top place with children and is therefore most often used. This novel, combining realistic human nature, adventure, imagination, and humor, is the most essentially American of all books for children; and certainly it is the most popular.

The Sorcerer's Apprentice appeals to children on this age level, and it is interesting to them to hear the recorded music and experiment with it before playing it with words. Pantomime with the music of *Tyll Eulenspiegel,* too, is successful with some groups. And the children always like Indian stories with the rhythmical beat of the tom-tom.

"The Nuremberg Stove" is wonderfully fine as a longer story for many fifth- or sixth-grade groups. "The King of the Golden River" is another, even if one uses only the very dramatic first episode. "Old Pipes and the Dryad," and "The Knights of the Silver Shield," too, have been made into creative plays by many a sixth-grade group.

Several Christmas stories are rich in possibilities for dramatization. The recent tale of Menotti's opera *Amahl and the Night Visitors,* in which the three kings stop at the cottage of a poor widow on their way to seek the Christ Child, has simplicity, charm, and real meaning. There are unusual opportunities for interesting action: when Amahl hobbles over to tell his mother that some kings are at the door, knowing well that she will think they are only creatures of his imagination; when the villagers come to entertain the royal guests; when the mother attempts to steal some of the gold so that she may be able to buy food for her own child; and when, after Melchior has told them about this Child who is the hope of the world, Amahl offers the only valuable thing he possesses, his crutch, and the miracle happens.

Ruth Sawyer's "The Voyage of the Wee Red Cap," a delightful Irish parallel to *A Christmas Carol,* her Spanish legend "A Christmas Promise," and Eric Kelly's two Christmas stories, *In Clean Hay* and *A Christmas Nightingale,* are four more excellent possibilities for creative plays in December.

Complete Novels

The sixth grade is an ideal age for integrated projects, and because a number of weeks will be devoted to one of them, the children can often use a whole novel as its center. *Bhimsa, the Dancing Bear,* by Christine Weston, for instance, is a beautifully written story of India that has been used most successfully for creative plays. Not only do the children learn much about India in creating a play from it, but they find plenty of material in it for an adventurous play.

A class studying the Southwest could not do better than to use Holling C. Holling's *The Tree in the Trail* as the meeting-place for all they are learning about that period. If they were especially interested in Kentucky pioneers they would find *Tree of Freedom,* by Rebecca Caudill, a dramatic story to use as a play. Several of Clara Ingram Judson's stories of European immigrants in our country—*The Green Ginger Jar* and *The Lost Violin,* to mention only two—have been found to offer valuable experiences for the children.

CHILDREN OF TWELVE, THIRTEEN, FOURTEEN

The most striking change in story interests which develops as children reach twelve, thirteen, and fourteen years, is that along with their liking for realism, mystery, and excitement, comes a feeling for idealism and romance. Not, at first, the romance of lovemaking. At twelve that makes most of them scoff, and at thirteen or fourteen, become very self-conscious.

The kind of romance which comes from looking at the world through rose-colored glasses, which idealizes life, and lifts both hero and adventure out of the commonplace, is enjoyed at this age. _Treasure Island_ and _Ivanhoe_ are romantic, as is _Robin Hood_, though by this time most of the children have outgrown their great interest in that dashing hero.

Boys and girls seldom let you see their idealism of such things as friendship, patriotism, and religion. They are more moved at this time by ceremonies and rituals than are either younger or older children. And they respond to finer ideas and emotions in their literature than ever before.

The Boy Who Found the King is one of these finer stories with a lift which appeals to many children. "The Rabbi and the Diadem" is another. The latter is short, with a strong ethical lesson, yet with much mystery and suspense. Dickens' _A Christmas Carol_ is a favorite year after year; and "The Christmas Apple," which is the old German's story in _This Way to Christmas_, has strong appeal and great beauty. A parallel to _Why the Chimes Rang_, it tells of a quaint little clock-maker who carves a very beautiful clock as a gift to the Christ Child but is forced to sell it to help some children. On Christmas Eve he takes as his gift only an apple—all he has left for Christmas dinner. As he makes his way to the altar he hears the whispered reproaches of the congregation until, of a sudden, there is a hush. The miracle has happened! The Christ Child has reached down from Mary's arms to take his gift!

Occasionally we may have a very superior group who may be entrusted with either "Our Lady's Juggler" or "The Bishop's Candlesticks." Both are beautiful stories of high spiritual quality, and we need to be very sure that our children can rise to them. Much, naturally, will depend upon the attitude we are able to build toward them. For the young people who are ready for them they can offer a wonderfully fine experience.

Contrasting with these stories of strong ethical quality is the "comic tragedy" of "Hungry Hans," which seventh-graders always find great fun. They also enjoy "The Three Sillies" and the old ballad "Get Up and Bar the Door." Some groups like "The Dumb Wife Cured," the story which Anatole France used in his play *The Man Who Married a Dumb Wife*. "How Thor Got His Hammer Back" and several other stories from Norse mythology are full of adventurous comedy for children of the seventh grade, especially if they have had some background in Norse myths.

Though ballads require much imagination in order to embroider a story that is told without detail, there are some favorites in this field of literature in addition to "Get Up and Bar the Door," which has already been mentioned. The traditional ballads "King John and the Abbot of Canterbury," "Lizzie Lindsay," "King Henry and the Miller of Mansfield," and an occasional Robin Hood ballad go well, as do the modern ballads "The Enchanted Shirt," "King Robert of Sicily," and a few others.

"The Page of Count Reynaurd," a clever story in *Troubadour Tales,* which tells of a contest in the writing of ballads and the way a plagiarist is exposed, is excellent material for dramatizing; and so is "Count Hugo's Sword," in the same book. But neither of them equals "The Moor's Legacy" in *Tales of the Alhambra,* which never fails to fascinate a group of twelve-year-olds.

Shakespeare Stories

If the plays of Shakespeare are introduced to boys and girls in the way they were intended to reach people, that is, by giving children a chance to see or take part in them, there would be far more enthusiasm for Shakespeare in high school than there is at present. In schools where children are prepared by a considerable amount of preliminary work in dramatics, they look forward to Shakespeare as being the most interesting material they can use.

Only the scenes in any story which are best adapted to the playing of the young people are used, though the whole story is told or read to them from such a collection as *The Shakespeare Story Book*, by Mary McLeod. Of the comedies, *A Midsummer Night's Dream, The Comedy of Errors, The Taming of the Shrew, The Merchant of Venice,* and a few scenes from *The Tempest, As You Like It,* and *Twelfth Night* are the best. From the tragedies, the witches' scenes in *Macbeth* are superb material from the standpoint of bodily action, rhythm, and utter freedom of characterization. Sometimes the girls plead for the sleep-walking scene, too, and though it is so far beyond them, they often surprise one by the effectiveness of their playing.

Several scenes from *Julius Caesar* can be done well by thirteen- and fourteen-year-olds. And one episode from *King Lear,* the dower scene, is good. A few eighth grades have attempted scenes from *Hamlet* with success. The process of dramatizing these stories is described in Chapter 6.

In a year's work in this field, three or four of the stories can be used. Some of the tales have a number of good episodes to use with eighth-grade children. The first dramatizations are likely to be the artisan and fairy scenes from *A Midsummer Night's Dream,* two or three incidents from *A Comedy of Errors,* or a series of episodes from *The Taming of the Shrew*: Katherine taunting Bianca, and Baptista separating them; Grumio pretending to misunderstand Petruchio when the latter tells him to knock at Hortensio's gate; the very humorous homecoming scene when Petruchio brings in his bedraggled bride and, by throwing the supper all over the room, shows Katherine what a temper is like when it belongs to someone besides herself. In another episode Katherine begs Grumio for something to eat, and he exasperates her by offering her the mustard without the beef; whereupon Petruchio brings in a platter of meat but sees to it that she does not get a morsel. He finds fault with her new dress and hat and sends them back in spite of the fact that she likes them, and later makes her ridiculous on their way back to Padua. In the wager scene she proves herself beautifully tamed and Petruchio leads her off triumphantly.

Early in their study should come the witches' scenes from *Macbeth,* but the Rialto, casket, and court scenes from *The Merchant of Venice* should be saved until the boys and girls have had considerable experience; for the court scene, especially, is difficult to do creatively, depending as it does on definite cues.

The dower scene from *King Lear* gives children experience in portraying characters who have great dignity yet tremendous emotion. They are far from equal to the part of Lear; yet the situation is more understandable to them than that of many easier stories, and some groups are deeply interested in playing it.

If *Twelfth Night* is used, only the subplot, involving Sir Toby, his lively companions, and Malvolio, are suitable, and even these scenes have to be adapted. No one will feel that children should play drunken parts; so they are merely made rollicking and noisy. The letter scene is very funny to children and so is the duel between Viola and Sir Andrew. But the story has more pitfalls for children than most of the others.

The Tempest and *As You Like It* are mildly successful for boys and girls. But *Julius Caesar* is very excellent for the development of understanding of the way a mob reacts when worked upon by a clever orator. This story can be used as well in the first half of the course as the last.

PROPAGANDA PLAYLETS

One source of material which has not been mentioned, though it is drawn upon for innumerable plays, is propaganda—propaganda for good health, for safety, for athletic games, for plays, for causes like the Red Cross and the Community Chest, and, in fact, for whatever needs promoting.

Some pictures given out at an educational conference show scenes from a pageant on forest conservation played by school children. Some of the boys and girls represented trees destroyed by fire and carelessless. Others—lying on the floor—were eroded soil; and the ones representing uneroded topsoil were standing on top of the ground! Such an absurd use of dramatics, no matter what the cause, is well-nigh unbelievable.

Everywhere, people want playlets or skits for propaganda purposes because they emotionalize material and make the idea more pleasant to take. Facts in school are often sugar-coated by dramatizing them, and warnings against such dangers as fire-hazards or traffic violations are more vivid by seeing them acted out in moving pictures.

All this, in reality, is a recognition of the effectiveness of creative drama. Yet there is danger in making it so common that it is cheapened as an art—made the "cart-horse" of every other subject.

A teacher should use her best judgment whenever she is asked to have her class originate a "skit" for any sort of propaganda. In half the cases some other means of promoting the idea is just as good or better. A real fireman giving a demonstration, a scientific exhibit, a short professional moving picture may be most effective. An original playlet is often fairly good as propaganda but nearly always a very bad exhibition of art or science. Furthermore, if used often, it will deaden the interest in dramatics both of the children who participate and those who are audience. It will also lower their artistic standards. As a consequence, therefore, we should use this kind of material very sparingly.

STANDARDS

Trivial stories, whether from books or from children's magazines and papers, should not be used even though ethically sound because they are not worth the time spent on them. Dramatizing a story is quite a different matter from casually reading it. The process requires time and very real thinking to make the story come alive. When a thin, slight story is used, the play which comes out of it is correspondingly bad; and the children who struggle to clothe it in flesh and blood turn to something more vital than dramatics for their enjoyment. A child's experience in drama should be kept a delightful thing, like experience in music, the dance, and every other art.

Let us read widely, experiment carefully, and study thoroughly the reactions of the children to every story used as content for their dramatizations. In addition, let us see to it always that the stories we use have the *quality* which makes them worth the time and thought which we are to spend on them.

CHAPTER 6

Presenting the Story

JAMES M. BARRIE'S REFRESHING WHIMSY _A Kiss for Cinderella_ has a delightfully absurd scene showing a little London slavey's dream of Cinderella's ball. Everything in the room is shining gold, even to the rocking chair in which the Queen sits to knit. The beautiful court ladies who are competing for the favor of the King's son prance around the room in the manner of high-stepping steeds, "to the heavenly music of royal hurdy-gurdies." (The little waif once saw a horse-show!)

Cards with "2nd" and "3rd" printed on them are pinned by the Prince to the persons of the court beauties as they pass, the "1st" being reserved for the lady of his choice—Cinderella, of course! And the refreshments of "sandwiches, hard-boiled eggs, cake, and an orange or a banana" are served in paper bags.

All the gorgeous people and events of the dream ball appear as if filtered through the experiences of the ragged little slavey. The lords and ladies of the court look like people she knows, the Prince himself strangely resembling her friend the policeman.

Less startling than the dream of Barrie's little heroine, but strongly colored by their own experiences, are children's interpretations of stories. As they read a book, boys and girls see its people and happenings in terms of their own lives; therefore, no two children (and, indeed, no two people of any age) get the same thing from the printed page. Because their experience is

116

usually very limited, children do not see so much in a story as they will when they are older. What to an adult may seem rich material for dramatization may not mean very much to children unless the grownup helps them to realize its possibilities by reading or telling the story to them. If they get the tale *plus the deep appreciation of the storyteller,* they will see more in it than they ever would have dreamed was there.

Stories to be dramatized need to be read or told with unusual care. Ordinarily, a person can miss parts of incidents, character descriptions, and images, and still get the story reasonably well. But if a child is to help dramatize it, he needs to know everything that happens, see all the images, become acquainted with the characters as real people, and appreciate the story's significance.

When children read for themselves the material they are going to dramatize, they seldom get enough out of it to make a good play. For younger children the mechanics of reading limits their appreciation, and even with older boys and girls the help of a good teacher or leader will set them much further on their way than if they have only their own interpretation.

TO READ OR TELL?

Few people would quarrel with the statement that a story well told is more interesting than one that is read. The storyteller's direct contact with the audience means that the story goes straight to the children, without a book to intervene; and boys and girls always listen eagerly when it is told.

The preparation for telling a story requires much more time and care, however, than for reading it from a book. If not done carefully, it is greatly inferior to reading. For when the story is to be dramatized, the children need to have all the help that the book gives. A synopsis will not do at all even though it contains the complete plot. The dialogue is needed, both for direct use and as a model for further conversation. So is the description of characters and places. And a synopsis does no more than *suggest* the element of the story which children like best—the emotional appeal.

[margin note: SYNOPSIS]

[margin note: EMOTIONAL APPEAL]

All these things in a well-told story stir a child's imagination away beyond what a reading can do. Lacking the time for preparation or the skill to tell it effectively, however, the teacher or leader should read the story, remembering that only very superior reading will make up for what is lost by not telling it.

PREPARATION FOR TELLING

The storytellers whom everyone loves to hear have back of them a rich experience in the telling of stories and in life itself. There is a mellowness in their telling which cannot be had in a month or a year, no matter how hard one works at it.

Children listen with interest, however, even when stories are not skillfully told. This is encouraging to beginners, who are sure of child listeners even while they are learning to tell stories. It takes many years to build up the kind of life experience which the best storytellers possess, and in the meantime one may take heart from the response of children whenever a story is told with sincerity.

The actual preparation of a story for telling begins with careful reading and rereading of the material. For one must *know the story well!* It should be so assimilated that when it is told it seems to be the storyteller's personal experience.

[margin note: KNOW STORY WELL]

Very few storytellers memorize their material. It is safer not to do so, for memorized stories are almost sure to sound formal. Furthermore, a lapse of memory leaves one helpless; whereas if one has thoroughly grasped what *happens* in the story, it is possible to go on even when details escape one.

[margin note: DON'T MEMORIZE]

Certain aspects of the story, however, may be memorized to advantage. If the beginning and end are well written, it is a

[margin note: DIALOGUE MAY BE MEMORIZED]

good idea to fix them in mind. Kipling's beginnings of the *Just
So Stories*, for instance, are so charming that no one should miss
them.

In the high and far off times, O Best Beloved—

The neat and conclusive ending of "The Three Billy Goats
Gruff," too, is much better than one could devise:

> And so,
> Snip, snap, snout,
> My tale's told out!

Dialogue is often memorized, especially when the story is a
well-known classic or when the conversation is especially clever
or fine, as this from Eloise Lownsbery's *The Boy Knight of
Reims*[1]:

"Whenever the master is angry," advised Colin, "keep still and
say nothing. Sit down quietly and go to work and think to yourself:
'You have no real power over me. I am not afraid of you.'"

"No," Jean answered, "I'm not afraid of him. He can't break me.
I can stick here if I have to. But, do you know, all the same, I think
we should do something for the honor of our craft."

Picturesque or humorous words, phrases, or sentences are
usually retained by a storyteller. It would be a pity to change
such phrases as this from *Uncle Remus*: "Good mawnin'. How
does yo' symptoms seem to sagashuate?"

Or the conversation between Pooh and Christopher Robin
when the latter aimed his gun carefully at the balloon which was
holding Pooh up in the air and hit the bear instead.

"Ow!" said Pooh.
"Did I miss?" Christopher Robin asked.
"You didn't exactly *miss*," said Pooh, "but you missed the *balloon*."

[1] (Houghton Mifflin Co., 1927).

HOW TO LEARN THE STORY

Casual readings of a story will never fix it in a person's mind. It must be learned by thinking intensely as one reads the story again and again. The imagination must work on it until each detail is clear in one's mind.

READ AGAIN + AGAIN

INCIDENT BY INCIDENT

Ruth Sawyer, a skilled and delightful storyteller as well as writer of children's stories, believes in learning them incident by incident or picture by picture, whichever way one's imagination works better. They should never be learned word by word.[2]

In the reading, associate the words with the pictures or incidents until they seem inseparable. Then try telling the story aloud. It will be necessary at first to go back to the book often. But gradually the story will come. And in getting it this way, one learns much more than words. The whole pattern of the story, the pictures, the people, the climax are so naturally impressed on the mind that they cannot be forgotten.

TELLING THE STORY

An artist makes a story so much his own that it sounds like an improvisation. That is the ideal to be sought by every storyteller, and it is only to be achieved by knowing the story so well that it is a part of one. There is joy in listening to a story told in an effortless way by one who seems to be the actual *source* of the story.

A warm, friendly manner; a directness which includes all the children; and a zest which seems to say, "I know a good story which I think you'd like to hear!" arouses the interest of a group of children every time. An introduction linking the story with their experience has the effect of making it more real to them. To set 'the mood and unify a group of children for the telling of "The Unhappy Echo," for instance, a camp counselor would naturally

[2] *The Way of the Storyteller* (Viking Press, Inc., 1942).

lead the conversation around to the echoes which come across
the lake to the camp. "Do you ever wonder about them?" "Does
it seem to you as if a real person were answering?"

One teacher of playwriting often says to her students, "Sit in
the audience when you write a play." One might also say to the
storyteller, "Sit in the audience when you tell a story." That is,
think always of the child's point of view. Remember that when
telling a story with dramatization in mind, one must make it   CRYSTAL
crystal clear: the setting, the exposition, the plot, the characters.   CLEAR
The children must see and understand it thoroughly if they are
to base a play on it.

When there is anything in the story which might be confusing, anything which deviates from the dramatic line of the plot,
it is better to simplify and rearrange the language and, perhaps,
even the situations in order that the impression made may be
single and clear. Because first impressions are persistent, it is
well to take great care that they are right.

One who sees the pictures of the story vividly can make others
see them, too. They are made clear to children by the eyes of the
storyteller as well as by the words of the story. Gestures are unnecessary to show them, though there is no reason why one's
hands should not be used if it is a natural expression for the
storyteller.

Since the tale is being presented for dramatization, all of the   ACTION
action needs to be very vivid. Good action words are used, and   NEEDS
the happenings are visualized. Having the events of the story   TO BE
very clearly pictured in their minds, children will be ready and   VIVID
eager to supply the physical action.

Characterization being of first importance in a play, the one
who presents the story to boys and girls has the responsibility of
making characters seem real and understandable. They should
not be one-sided like paper-dolls but should be presented "in
the round." This sometimes means using one's imagination to

make real people out of characters who are sketchily drawn in the story. The children get their ideas from the storyteller's description; from what the character says and the way he says it; from what he does; and from the reaction of the other characters to him.

Direct discourse should be used almost entirely in presenting the story. Even when conversation is indirect in the printed form, the teller will do well to make it direct. This always heightens a child's interest, and at the same time it gives the players something to take hold of in the dramatization. "She asked Elf if he had really been in a story" is not nearly so alive as, "Why, Elf!" she whispered. "Were you—*really*—in a story?"

INVOLVE CHILDREN NAMES

What makes children ask for a story over and over again is the emotional appeal. They say they like it to be "exciting." They want to be moved to laughter or fear, to wonder or admiration. The older children, especially, enjoy suspense. So, in telling the tale, the good storyteller keeps them looking forward with keen interest to what is about to happen and sees to it that the climax is both strong and satisfying. Almost invariably, such a presentation arouses the enthusiasm of the children to play the story and helps them to make it come alive.

Timing

The skill of the storyteller is perhaps nowhere more evident than in timing. It is something one has to learn by experience, though after one has been made aware of its significance he begins to observe it both in his own telling and in that of others.

Each story calls for a timing of its own. There is the lively rhythm suggesting the constant running of "The Gingerbread Man"; the slow stateliness of "The Sleeping Beauty"; the gay, light-stepping Milne stories; the strong, firm movement of "Robin Hood."

In building toward a climax the timing is even more crucial.

Some climaxes can be made most impressive by a gradual slow-ing-down; more are heightened by speeding up the rate of tell-ing. A pause just before the highest point is strongly effective, but it is not a mere mechanical device. It must be fraught with meaning and arouse the most intense interest in what is to follow.

NO RULES FOR TIMING

No rules can be laid down for the timing of stories. When one truly appreciates a piece of literature, he may time it correctly without even being aware that he is doing so. Good taste and sensitivity will guide even the inexperienced in general timing. It is the specific timing for greater effectiveness that requires real artistry.

The Telling of Humorous Stories

For many people the telling of a humorous story is much more difficult than any other kind. They are the people who lack a strong sense of humor. They cannot, of course, hope to make others laugh at what is not funny to them.

The first requisite, then, is to have a sense of humor oneself. If an incident or a story seems deliciously funny to a person, he can make it humorous to others. He has to learn how to get the most out of it, but he *will* learn, for he cannot be satisfied to enjoy a funny story all by himself.

MUST HAVE A SENSE OF HUMOR

He may find that he is so anxious to tell the climax of the story that he does not take time enough to lead up to it or that he gives so many details that people tire of waiting for the point. But gradually he learns just how much to tell and just how to time his stories. And once he has established a reputation for telling humorous stories well, children and adults alike will laugh easily and often when he tells them.

Many stories are funniest when told with exaggerated serious-ness. But there is a certain light in the storyteller's eyes which belies the gravity of his face and voice and lets the children know that it is really pure fun. It is especially important that younger

SERIOUSNESS

children shall see this light; for if they are not sure whether the story is intended to be funny, they are afraid to laugh and, as a result, they do not fully enjoy it.

Sincerity in Presenting the Story

Whether or not a person can tell a humorous story to give children the maximum amount of fun, it is of greatest concern that it be told sincerely. A storyteller should never talk down to children, never make light of the material he is using, whether it be funny or serious. Respect for boys and girls is one of the requisites of the storyteller, just as it is a requisite of a teacher.

One storyteller creates something beautiful out of the story, another makes only a commonplace thing. Experience counts for much, of course, in the acquirement of skill in telling a story; but what is in the heart counts most. And when the story has been told and the dramatization begins, the quality of the play which the children make will depend to no small extent on how the tale was presented by the teller.

[handwritten margin note: MUST HAVE RESPECT FOR CHILDREN]

CHAPTER 7

Creative Plays Based on Stories

MOST CHILDREN DELIGHT IN MAKING UP COMPLETE PLAYS. TO
the older boys and girls improvised incidents and characterizations are only preliminary to creative plays based on stories.
Many have attempted to dramatize old fairy tales by themselves;
and they welcome the fascinating and orderly process of playmaking under the leadership of an adult.

That the experience of dramatizing may be more than merely
putting a story into dialogue form, intelligent guidance is indispensable. A grownup who understands children and knows
the requirements of good drama[1] can give boys and girls rich
and enjoyable experiences by helping them to see exciting possibilities in the story, and to be selective in making use of them.

THE LEADER PREPARES

Whoever depends upon inspiration in guiding children in
creative drama is on very uncertain ground. For unless a teacher
has much to give she will get only the most mediocre results.
The safe procedure is to follow the plan of a certain brilliant
after-dinner speaker who, on being praised for his very clever
response to the toastmaster, said, "My speech was not extemporaneous. I was sure that Nelson would introduce me in one of

[1] See Chapter 9.

125

three ways, and I simply prepared speeches in reply to all three of them."

As good leaders, we prepare for "all three" of the possible directions the play is likely to go. Knowing that we may have to discard all of our plans, we realize that only by exploring all of the possibilities we can think of shall we be ready to guide the children in such a way that the experience will have real worth.

If the material is simple like "The Old Market Woman" who went to market "her eggs for to sell," we need only to read between the lines of the poem to see its possibilities for playing. What about it will appeal to the children? How shall we be able to make it believable that the old woman doubts her own identity? We think out what is likely to happen in the class. Will the children want to begin the play when she is putting on all those skirts and telling her dog that he will have to stay at home while she takes the eggs to market? Or will they think it should start with the market scene? Why does she go to sleep on such a public place as the king's highway? Is the peddler who "cuts her petticoats up to her knees" a scoundrel or merely a practical joker? What people come along and see her asleep with her skirts cut off up to her knees? What are their various reactions? Which ones are amused? Which pity her? Who would be most shocked at her lack of decorum? If anyone knew her wouldn't he waken her?

Any preparation would necessitate ideas on these and other aspects of the story. And if we are very familiar with it, we shall know what questions to ask to call forth other ideas from the children. Certainly, we will say the poem in such a way that they can see the old woman is an exceedingly simple soul!

RESEARCH   Some stories will require real research. Medieval tales, for example, require a knowledge of the customs of the times; and if the scene is laid in a castle with drawbridge, moat, and ramparts, we need to know about the way the grand folk lived: the duties of the mistress, the diversions of both adults and children, the way the page boys were educated for knighthood, and many other aspects of life in those times. If we can tell the children about these things and suggest books to read, we can be of great help in making the whole era live for them.

Stories of foreign countries mean research as to geography, customs, the names which will be appropriate for extra characters, values of such coins as pesos, farthings, guilders, rubles; kinds of dwellings, foods, and clothing. And we need to find pictures of things which are not easy to describe.

SETTING THE MOOD

A part of our planning is what we shall say to introduce the story—just the right thing to make the children eager to hear it. We think through various approaches and choose the one which we believe will be most appealing to the children because it is closest to their own experience. At the same time it should be an approach that will lead directly to the heart of the story and center attention where it belongs.

Suppose we planned to tell the little story poem called "Fancy Dress" [2] in which a fairy makes a ball-dress from apple blossoms. SEASON We naturally would choose the story for spring; and what would better set the mood for it than to bring a branch of the fragrant blossoms? Showing them to the children, we might say, "Aren't they lovely? Wouldn't the blossoms make a beautiful dress for a fairy? They remind me of a poem in which a fairy was invited to a fancy-dress party and she did make herself a dress from apple blossoms. Would you like to hear it?" This centers all thoughts on what happens in the story and at the same time gives them an immediate and pleasant experience.

We very often consider the season when choosing a story since the children are already in a receptive mood for it. A winter day

[2] See Story List in the Appendix for all stories mentioned in this chapter.

when the snow is just right to build snow men is an ideal time to introduce them to the poem "The Snow Man," which is perfect for a creative play. December is the month for Christmas stories, and little if any introduction is necessary to motivate them.

EXPERIENCE An actual experience may in some cases best set the mood for a story dramatization. A picnic or a walking trip at camp may take the group past a lonely side-road. "Where would it lead us?" Then and there, if the poem "Roads" is in the leader's mind, she might say Rachel Field's fascinating poem; and later it could be played.

MATERIAL THING A material thing like an old coin, an interesting headdress, a picture, a small chest with a key, could be the point of departure for a creative play, as might also a souvenir from some country the group is studying in school. With a good factual background from their social studies which children like to use in a dramatization, only a slight introduction may be necessary.

CURRENT HAPPENING A current happening may be the link which connects present interest with the story. Queen Elizabeth's coronation recalled the perfection of her conduct as a princess in contrast to that of "The Princess Who Could Not Cry," and the conquest of Mt. Everest motivated an older group to play out the story which had excited them through radio accounts.

MUSIC Music can create a perfect mood for story-playing, as illustrated by the children who were inspired to work out "The Nutcracker of Nuremberg" described in this chapter. Whether or not music is written for a story, it can create a feeling for many kinds of dramatizations: "The Hurdy-Gurdy Man," "The Sorcerer's Apprentice," "The Blue Bird," "The Conjure Wives," and hosts of others.

A warning should be given about introductions that are long or that lead children's minds away from instead of into a story. In introducing "Mrs. Mallaby's Birthday," one inexperienced

teacher asked her group about their own birthday parties, leading into the playing of a modern party that became so involved
that she never did reach little old Mrs. Mallaby! And more than
a few leaders have found to their dismay what happens when
they introduce an animal tale by asking, "How many of you
have pets at home?" What a flood of conversation this brings
about! One such experience in trying to recapture minds that
have flown away in every direction teaches a young leader to
plan an introduction that *unifies* her group.

MAKING THE STORY CLEAR

If we have set the mood successfully for the presentation of
our story, we should have more than usual concentration from
our children as we tell it. Occasionally we suggest something
special to look for, as to note how much "The Goblinade" tells
us about this particular little goblin. Or if we have introduced
"The Emperor's New Clothes" by asking fifth-graders if they
have ever been in a situation where they were afraid to tell the
truth, the point of the story will make a deeper impression upon
them.

As to the art of presenting the story, Chapter 6 has considered
this in detail. It is enough to emphasize here that one telling of *Know it*
a new story is not enough in preparation for a dramatization. *well*
The children need to know it *well*. Every part of it should be
clear—the plot, the characters, the meaning.

PLANNING THE PLAY

If we have asked the class to notice some particular aspect of
character or meaning, we, of course, begin our discussion with
this. Otherwise, we sometimes ask, "Do you like the story?" Or,
"What do you think of it?" Or, "Would it make a good play,
do you think?"

Instead, we may leave the question of dramatization until

later, and discuss the characters or some other aspect of the story. "What did you think of the father? (In "The Nuremberg Stove"). "Did you have any sympathy for him?" "Could he have avoided selling the stove which was so precious to his family?" Such questions as these may start a discussion which will expand to include the whole story. If children are truly interested and feel at ease with us, they will not depend entirely upon questions to bring out ideas in the story. They will take the initiative, and with a minimum of guidance will formulate their ideas on what the story means.

"TRYING ON" characters. While discussing the characters of the story, we usually "try on" some of them. To do so at this time not only breaks up what may be a rather long discussion period, but gives the children a chance to get the feeling of the characters before actually playing them in the dramatization. Each character played should be engaged in some sort of action, whether from the story or not. All may be the goblin in "The Goblinade," creeping stealthily along to frighten some little creature; or Mary Poppins unpacking her astonishing carpet bag; or the courtiers in the Tyll Ulenspiegel story who are appalled because they can see nothing on the wall where their portrait is supposed to be.

From here we shall plan the form our play is to take. For young children there is less planning and much greater simplicity than for fourth grades and older who have had some experience in playmaking. It is important that everything should be completely natural, with no thought of stage or curtain or audience. They are not "pretending" to be Goldilocks or the three billy goats or any of the other storybook people. They are *being* these characters.

For this reason their dramatizations are played all over the room rather than divided into scenes and played as if on a stage. An aisle is usually the road, the desks may be a forest, and any open space may be a house. If there is a time sequence, the scenes are simply played in succession. Young children are not bothered by the lapse of a few months or years!

When there are several episodes in the story, as in "The Three Bears," they learn to keep one at a time in the center of action, with not more than a minimum of pantomime going on among the groups who will be playing later. In most cases, when the bears go off into the woods they do not continue their action but wait until Goldilocks goes to sleep in the house before they come alive again. It is quite possible for several groups to be playing in their own little localities during the whole time. But if many children are involved, it creates much confusion and usually a good deal of noise. Furthermore, each group becomes so interested in its own pantomime that it seldom notices when its turn arrives to be the center of attention. For these reasons, most leaders—and children, too—decide that it is better to focus on one scene without distraction from the others.

As children grow older and more experienced in playmaking, they have more concern for form. So we commence our planning with the opening of the play. At what point in the story shall we begin? With some knowledge of what a good play should be, we can indirectly guide the children so that the opening is logical and effective. Regardless of whether we shall ever play it for anyone outside of the class, we want it to be a good play— understandable and dramatic. Several of the children will have ideas as to how it should open. Even if the first suggestion is good, it is well to encourage others to give their ideas and then let the group decide which they like best.

Many times someone will suggest a scene in which all the exposition is given at once, perhaps by a soliloquy. We shall hope that others will have better ideas so that as we restate all of the suggestions, the children will see for themselves which is best. If all the ideas are poor, a leading question will often stir their thoughts so that they will suggest something better. And if they are the ones to think of the better idea, it means more to them than if we stated it directly.

OPEN WITH ACTION

For instance, in planning a play based on the old tale "The Stone in the Road" someone always suggests that it open where the Duke is placing the stone in the middle of the highway. Another thinks that the Duke should be talking to himself about the laziness of his subjects and the way they depend upon him. Fortunately, someone usually comes forward with the idea of a scene in which various people come with quarrels for the Duke to settle or appeals for help in doing work they ought to do themselves.

If no one makes this suggestion, we may need to ask, "Which is more interesting: to hear about the laziness of the people or see it in action?" This is really telling them a principle of playwriting, but the question is better than a flat statement would be. All that the children need is to *see* what is really an obvious fact.

Theoretically, it might be well to try a scene according to each suggestion. But the time element makes it a questionable procedure unless the majority of the class vote to play it a certain way. In that case the only democratic procedure is to do so. Usually, however, when children are given the chance to vote on the best of several suggestions, they will choose wisely. Furthermore, no child need feel rebuffed if his suggestion is only one of a number to be rejected.

The Scenes

1st SCENE PLANNED IN DETAIL

Having decided upon the opening, the children next plan the scenes which will lead to the climax of their play. The first scene is planned in detail, complete with beginning and ending, setting and properties. If the story is at all complex, they find that they will have to omit some incidents, and explain, if necessary, what is supposed to occur between scenes. The classic example of condensation is in "Cinderella," which, in some versions, tells of three balls, in others, two. But we find, when we dramatize the story, it makes a better play to have but one ball.

Unless we expect to perform our play for an audience, it is not at all necessary to dramatize every incident anyhow. When we do have an audience, we can, if we wish, have a narrator as a connecting link, and play only those scenes which are necessary steps in leading to the climax.

The question of how far it is permissible to deviate from the story in a dramatization cannot be answered with finality. With very young children, the story is often simply a device to push off the imagination. Traditional material, like Mother Goose, has no known author. These stories and rhymes changed constantly in the years when they were being handed down by word-of-mouth before their form was fixed by being printed. We are relieved, therefore, of the obligation to keep them exactly as they are, and can feel free to let our children have a glorious time shaping them as they wish. But good taste should keep us from radically changing old tales which have become classics, as one storyteller did when, in telling "The Three Bears," she ended, not with the usual exciting flight of Goldilocks out the open window, but by having Papa Bear rudely order her away, telling her never, never to come back!

We have an obligation to known authors not to change the idea nor the outcome of their stories, and though the technique of plays differs from that of stories, there is a limit to the amount of liberty we should take with the literature we guide children in dramatizing. The people of the story should not be tampered with, certainly, though characters and details may have to be omitted or added. It is not only allowable but desirable to read between the lines and add incidents which are in harmony with

CAN'T CHANGE KNOWN AUTHORIES STORIES

the story. But we have no right to distort an author's story by allowing the children to make radical changes.

CHOOSING THE CAST

The most democratic procedure is to choose the casts from those who volunteer for the parts. If we make it a privilege to play, not urging anyone who does not feel inclined to take part, we keep the spirit of fun in our playing. We are careful, however, to choose a few children with ability to carry the scene so that it will go well and give the group a feeling of success. If several of such children take part each time, the less imaginative players are carried along with them, often surprising even themselves by their contribution to the scene.

The problem of some children's volunteering, like Nick Bottom, in *A Midsummer Night's Dream,* for every part, or for a part in each playing, while other more reserved or timid children sit back and watch, is one of which we have to be careful. It is too easy to allow half the class to do all the playing, either because they enjoy it so very much or because of the wish to be the center of attention. Yet what pleases a good teacher most is to bring out the timid, inhibited child who is afraid to volunteer. We watch constantly for the raised hands of children who do not often take part. We are even alert for eyes that say a child would like to play but dares not. Sometimes we respond just as if it really had been a signal, and give him the part.

"Who hasn't had a chance to play today?" We usually ask this in the middle of a class period. Then we may give each child in this group the opportunity to choose the part he would like to play. This generally brings everyone into the playing, though the timid ones are likely to choose to be servants or guards if there are such parts so that they can be certain of being adequate. Girls often play men's roles, and boys enjoy an occasional woman's part if it has great spirit or good comedy.

Whatever they do, if it is ever so slight a characterization, we encourage them. And a bit of praise will help them to volunteer next time, perhaps, for a role which gives them a little more opportunity. Praise and encouragement coming from the teacher will do much, but if it comes from their contemporaries, it may work wonders. Many a child has blossomed amazingly by general approval, changing gradually from a feeling of inferiority to real leadership in the group.

PLAYING IN SMALL UNITS

Each scene of a play may involve several small incidents. The festive first scene in "The Sleeping Beauty" includes the preparation for the feast, the arrival of the guests, their gifts for the princess, the appearance of the wicked fairy and her curse, and the conclusion with the good fairy's softening of the princess' fate. Even the most experienced cast does not attempt to play it all at once. Each little part is played several times with different casts before putting it together, so that by the time the complete scene is played, some of the details have been worked out and the characters have been established.

If a long scene is played in its entirety the first time, the cast is likely to lose its way. A single person could think a scene through, but when a number of people must play together with extemporaneous dialogue, they find it a complicated and difficult proceeding. Much better progress is made and the result is far more satisfactory if each cast plays only a short scene.

After all the players have been chosen for a scene, the teacher often says, "Places!" as a signal for the cast to go to the stage (or to whatever place they are to play). "In character!" reminds them to assume their roles, and, after a pause, "Begin!" starts the action. At the close, if a signal is needed, the leader often says, "Curtain!" or "Cut" or "End." Such directions are optional, of course, but they do make for clean-cut scenes.

PERIOD OF EVALUATION

When the players return to their seats there is always a period of evaluation. In some classes the cast even lines up to receive comments. At this time the children who have been watching first commend the players for good work. Someone may say, "The Queen was very happy. She kept looking at the baby and smoothing the covers in its cradle." Another is impressed by the grace of the fairies. "I think the soft music helped to make them feel like fairies."

When all the "good comments" (as the children often call them) have been given, there is always constructive criticism. "How can we make it better?" brings forth plenty of what would be adverse criticism if the children were not required to suggest what would make the scene better. This is something to insist on, for it helps both to develop the play and to form a habit of making criticism constructive. So they may suggest that there be more conversation, that the fairies admire the baby, that the king have more part in the scene, that the servants show greater respect.

Just before the next cast plays the scene we sum up the suggestions made for its improvement, or at least three of the best ones. Because children are imitative, it is difficult for succeeding casts to avoid using the pattern made by the first children. We need to make a great point of "doing it your own way" and praise a cast for thinking out different ways of playing a scene.

COMMENTS ARE IMPERSONAL

Comments are made impersonal by using the names of the characters rather than the children. If an unpopular child brings forth criticism more harsh than he deserves, it is our place to lead the way in praising him for what he does well or even tries to do. Children are fair in almost every case, however, and few instances of hurt feelings occur if we have established a friendly feeling in the class.

Without guidance, though, boys and girls tend to criticize things that are inconsequential such as a slip of the tongue, failure to dispose of an imaginary property, walking through the wall instead of the door in a make-believe setting, turning one's back on the audience, etc. Though we accept such criticisms, we make it clear that these things are of much less consequence than some other aspects of playing.

Often the children fail to see what would improve the scene. This is the time for us as leaders to make our contribution. Just as we should see to it that good work from every child is commended, we need also to supplement the suggestions if they are not vital. For if we are too easily satisfied, there will be little growth. Usually, a question is all that is necessary to bring out the point from the children themselves, even to the suggestion of what might be the subject of conversation in a scene which had been stilted and unnatural, or a point of ethics which had been questionable. Without real evaluation, playmaking remains always on a low level. This is a time for learning, for having ideas crystallized, for gaining fresh insights and finer attitudes. Children rarely know whether they have achieved anything significant or not, so it is important that every evidence of growth is commented upon and every child feels a new impetus to achieve.

CONCENTRATING ON ESSENTIALS

The really vital aspects of story dramatizations are these:

1. STORY. Was the part of the story which was to come out in this scene perfectly clear? If we had not known it before, would we understand it? If it was not complete, which characters could give the needed exposition and how? Was the central idea of the story made clear?

2. CHARACTERIZATION. Were the characters true to life, natural? Did they seem to be the real characters of the story? Would people think and act and speak as they did? Were they consistent? Did the players stay in character from beginning to end or did they ever get out of character?

3. DIALOGUE. Did it make the story progress? Did it seem to belong to the characters? Did it keep to the point or wander off into unnecessary chatter? Was it consistent with the speech used by the people in the story?

4. ACTION AND GROUPING. If we had not had words, how much of the story could we have understood through the action? Could it have told more than it did? Did as many things happen as should have happened? Did the characters do the things which would be natural to them? Were there awkward places? How could the players have avoided them? Was the grouping pleasing? Did it mean something?

5. CLIMAX. Where was the high point in the scene? Was it made important enough? How could we build up to it more effectively? Did it emphasize the central thought in the story?

6. TEAMWORK. Did the characters play together? Could we see by their reactions to one another what their relationship was? Did they listen to each other and show what they were thinking and feeling? If they were a family, did they *seem* to be one?

7. TIMING. Did the scene *move?* If slow, what was the matter? If over too soon, was it because it was played too fast or lacked needed details? What can we do about it?

8. VOICE AND DICTION. Could everyone be heard? If not, was it because some spoke too softly, turned away from us, or were indistinct? What suggestions might be made?

The way in which we apply these points will naturally differ greatly according to the age of the children and the material used. We shall not refer to them directly in working with young children nor apply all of them at any one time with older children. We shall need to help both young and older ones to clarify further their ideas of the characters when they seem blurred or distorted; to plan how to tell the story better by the playing; to think of further action to make our play more full of meaning. Specific ideas for more conversation will be needed, and little drills to help correct the inevitable "jists" and "gits" and other careless pronunciation. We must remember never to embarrass individual children by correcting their grammar in public, however, for its only effect will be to arouse the fear to say anything at all.

Sometimes we allow a member of the group to choose a cast and conduct the evaluation period. This is good experience for the child acting as chairman if he is capable of doing it but less valuable for the group because of lack of guidance, and it probably never should be done for a whole period at a time.

TIME DEVOTED TO EACH STORY

Because the work on a single dramatization could go on and on without achieving perfection, it is always a question as to whether to devote a long time to one good story or a short time to each of several. By working intensively on one project, the children learn to be thorough, to get all possible values from it, to become well acquainted with every character, to acquire some skill in interpretation. On the other hand, their experience is broadened by coming to know more characters and more situations, and their enjoyment of variety is satisfied by fresh stories of different types.

MORE EXPERIENCE THE BETTER

It would seem, then, that we shall do well to play several short stories of different kinds and with varied characters before devoting a longer period to one substantial, well-liked story. Roughly, we should work on one story until the children have gained from it all that they are capable of getting at their present stage of development. But if interest wanes before that time, the dramatization should be brought quickly to a close, or else we should inject new ideas which will revive their interest.

Once a week is not ideal for creative dramatics. But if this is all that is possible, we shall do well to use a good deal of pantomime; many situations, original and otherwise; very short stories;

and scenes from longer stories which the children all know. A good deal of their work can be complete in one period, for it is not easy to carry a dramatization over from one week to the next.

Two periods a week of half an hour for younger children and three-quarters of an hour for the older ones is much more fruitful than double the time once a week. A classroom teacher does not often have set periods but uses playmaking when the time seems right for it. Some small projects may be completed within one period, but most of them will carry over. Several class hours will be devoted to each story, as a rule, but the longer dramatizations may require one or two months.

5ᵗʰ — The Nutcracker of Nuremberg

The two fifth-grade groups at Miller School [3] had been fascinated by the recordings of *The Nutcracker Suite,* and thought that the story which inspired Tschaikovsky to write it would make a wonderful Christmas play. They realized that it was too elaborate to dramatize in its entirety but they were eager to work out several of the scenes and play them for the school. So in the next dramatic class their teacher experimented with parts of it, the children spontaneously playing the battle of the mice, and trying some of the dances.

The second time they worked with it one of the girls brought some old curtains and costume jewelry and gave her idea of the Arabian dance. Several others worked out an effective pattern to "The Dance of the Flowers." Each time the children came they had a background of music for whatever scenes they played.

At another meeting their teacher partly read, partly told the beginning of the legend: the eager anticipation of the two German children, Fritz and Marie Silberhaus, as they waited outside the curtains of the drawing-room to be called in to see the Christmas tree and the merry party of neighbor-children waiting

[3] Evanston, Illinois.

to greet them; the tinkly music-box and the whispering and gig-
gling of the children; then the burst of light and music and
laughter as the drawing-room curtains opened; and the gaiety as
they danced around the tree and then opened their gifts.

The next step was to plan and play the opening scene. (They
had heard the whole story when they first listened to the music,
and they had roughly planned which scenes they would work
out.) Their first playing followed the story closely, but the
children used a good deal of imagination as they opened the gifts
under the tree. One was a suit of armor for a knight, and soon
they were playing the knighting of a squire. A toy sword brought
about a series of duels for the hand of a fair maiden, and the
playing ended with the opening of a nest of boxes which one of
the girls imagined she found under the tree.

The following session was taken down in shorthand:

"You remember that last time someone opened a big box, then a
smaller and a smaller one inside," began the teacher,[4] "and we
thought that it would be good to have the Nutcracker opened that
way so that the attention of everybody would be centered on him
at once. The Nutcracker was really found leaning against the
tree, but I think it would be all right to take this liberty and use
our own idea. And now we are going to see the Nutcracker in our
imagination. What does he look like?"

One child said, "I see the coat with little gold buttons, and a pair
of gold trousers." Another said, "Fuzzy beard, and a real funny
hat like a witch's hat—red and purple. He has shiny, sharp teeth."

"He is a little man," added a third child, "dressed in a coat, with
big teeth almost as big as his face; with bulgy eyes and a little pipe
—with purple on the inside of his cape."

The teacher made no comment on these "imaginings" based on
their impressions after having previously heard him described, but
began the story where they had left off the previous day.

Marie, in opening the box containing the Nutcracker, immediately took a fancy to him and exclaimed, "Papa, who is he?" Papa

Ann Heekin.

came over and explained that he came from the old and respected race of Nutcrackers in Nuremberg. Then he showed how, if one opened his mouth and pushed a nut in and pressed the jaws together, the nut would open.

The boys were not so excited as the girls about the Nutcracker. Marie, being tender-hearted, asked if she might take care of it, and Godfather Drosselmayer said yes. The girls then took the Nutcracker off and Marie chose a very little nut to crack so that she wouldn't break its jaws.

Fritz, with the other boys who had been playing with toy soldiers, now grew interested and came over to ask Marie to let him crack a nut with it. When Marie gave it to him, he chose a big black walnut which proved too hard for the Nutcracker's teeth so that they broke and three teeth fell out.

Realizing that he had done something that might get him into trouble, Fritz shifted the blame onto the Nutcracker—said he wasn't much good at his job, and that he would make him go on cracking nuts until he lost all his teeth! The girls accused him of being mean with his toy soldiers. The boys said he was a bad Nutcracker and should be punished.

Here the teacher stopped the story to ask, "Did you ever have something you like very much broken by someone?"

A number of hands shot up, and one boy said, "I had a model plane, and my sister got mad at me and threw it down and stamped on it."

"I had a new electric train," said another boy, "and my little brother broke one of the coaches so bad that it cost me $14.50 to get it fixed."

"You can appreciate how Marie felt then," said the teacher. By this time she was crying so hard that her father came down to where they were. "What is going on here?" he asked. Marie tried to explain but Fritz interrupted. "No arguments on Christmas Eve!" said Judge Silberhaus. "Marie, you take the witness stand." Fritz interrupted again as Marie tried to explain, until his father said, "Is your name Marie?" All the boys and girls giggled and Fritz was quiet until his father said, "Now, Master Fritz, what have you to say?"

"Well, I did break his jaw," said Fritz, "but he didn't know his business."

"My dear Fritz," said Judge Silberhaus, "I entrust the Nutcracker to your sister's care. I see he is unwell and I give him solely to Marie until he is well again. And you, Fritz, who are so fair with your military discipline, when did you ever hear of a wounded soldier returning to his duty? The wounded always go to the hospital."

"Yes, yes," sympathetically agreed the boys and girls. "Judge Silberhaus is right!"

This ended the scene they were to work on during this period. It was given them as a review, since it is necessary to be thoroughly familiar with a story before making it into a play.

"We'll begin today's scene just as Marie is opening the box which contains the Nutcracker," said the teacher.

"Couldn't there be some presents for the other kids, too?" asked one of the boys, who was going to feel left out if he didn't get at least one!

"Surely," replied the teacher, "and perhaps refreshments, too."

"I should think they'd get their presents at home, not at a party," objected one of the girls.

"Oh, they might get one here and the rest at home," said another child.

"Remember, you must know what these gifts are—*see* them. Open them and handle them," reminded the teacher. "And it is important that you know what everyone is *thinking*—the adults as well as the children. What would Mrs. Silberhaus be thinking about?"

"About her family and her guests," was the answer. "And the refreshments."

"What is she doing?"

"Talking with Godfather and the Judge."

After locating the tree and deciding where the girls would take the Nutcracker to play with it, children were chosen for the first cast and they began as the boys and girls were exclaiming about their gifts. During the whole scene there was soft *Nutcracker* music that might have come from a little music-box.

MARIE: Look at this big box! *I* know what it is! I bet it's one of those great big boxes that goes down and down to a little one!

A GIRL: (*as Marie continues opening the imaginary boxes*) Another one!

MARIE: Wait till you see the present I'm getting!

GIRL: Maybe that's it. What is it? Open it!

MARIE: (*taking it out*) What a funny little man! I know—it's a Nutcracker! It came from Nuremberg!

GIRL: Gee, isn't he sweet! And such sharp teeth! and so many!

ANOTHER GIRL: Let's get some nuts and take him down here. Ask Mrs. Silberhaus if we can have some nuts. (*One of the GIRLS says "O.K." and runs up to the MOTHER while the conversation goes on*)

MARIE: Maybe he's a little warm. I should take off his coat. Look at that funny hat! (*The GIRL returns with the nuts*) I'll use just a little nut.

FRITZ: (*as he and the other BOYS come down*) Let me see it. Can I try it once?

MARIE: Just a minute. Isn't he cute? He comes from an old and ancient line of Nutcrackers from Nuremberg.

(*FRITZ takes it, picks out a large nut, and cracks it*)

MARIE: Oh, you broke his jaw! (*Cries*)

FRITZ: That's not my fault. He should be able to crush nuts. I just put one in his mouth. He should know his trade.

GIRL: Gee, that's too bad. Three teeth came out!

MARIE: You're mean! You always shoot your soldiers.

FRITZ: I don't. I only punish them when they're bad. That silly old Nutcracker!

MARIE: He's not silly!

GIRL: I think he can be fixed.

JUDGE SILBERHAUS: (*coming down*) What is going on here? What is wrong, Marie?

MARIE: He came along and took a big nut and put it in the Nutcracker's mouth and opened the jaw real wide and it broke.

FRITZ: I did not! I did not!

JUDGE: Wait a second, Master Fritz. No arguments on Christmas Eve! Marie, you take the witness stand.

(*FRITZ interrupts as MARIE starts to answer a question*)

JUDGE: Is your name Marie? (*The BOYS giggle*) Now Fritz, what have you to say?

FRITZ: Well, I just put a nut in his mouth.

GIRL: Here is the nut. Just look how big it is!

For some reason the playing stopped here the first time, before the Judge put the Nutcracker in Marie's care and gave Fritz a little lecture on being fair to a wounded soldier. They doubtless would add this later.

In the evaluation the teacher asked, "What part seemed to be the most real?"

"Marie's crying," said one of the girls, "when she found the jaw broken."

Another child said, "The Judge was good."

"Yes, he was," said the teacher. "He thought and spoke in character."

"Some of them used modern slang," added another. "Gee" and "cute" and "O.K."

"Fritz was a little too rough."

"I should think they ought to get ideas of how to fix the Nutcracker, like taking him to the woodshop."

"Why don't we begin the scene when Marie and Fritz are outside the curtains and peek in?" asked one boy. This suggestion was not commented upon, but the boy had suggested what would likely be the way they really would open their play since it was such an effective beginning.

It did not seem to occur to any of the children to ask how Marie knew that the Nutcracker "came from an ancient line of Nutcrackers from Nuremberg" since she had not asked her father about him.

Two other casts played the scene without developing it to any considerable extent. But the interest was high, and when noon was only three minutes off and the teacher was about to send them home for lunch they begged to do it "Just once more."

Analysis of the Lesson

This was a good first playing of the Nutcracker episode. As with any beginning dramatization, it lacked the interesting details which the children would add later, but it did tell the story with reasonable accuracy, and showed a little characterization. It was evident that they were very familiar with the episode.

True, they left Mrs. Silberhaus and Godfather Drosselmayer with nothing at all to do in the scene. And too little was made of the part where Fritz broke the Nutcracker. One would expect Marie to be loath to hand over the precious puppet to her rough brother without a strong admonition to "be careful," and protestations when he chose a big nut to crack. This scene could be built up greatly.

The suggestions made by others in the group would have helped to develop the scene if the second cast had noted them. Perhaps it would have made them more impressive if the teacher had briefly summed them up before the second cast played. As usually happens, the first cast set a pattern that the next cast imitated. It always helps if the teacher puts a premium on new ideas and stresses several objectives for each cast.

Though the story for the most part is fantasy, being Marie's dream, this first scene is realistic and calls for less imagination than do the later ones. Nevertheless, the children were greatly interested, and there were enthusiastic volunteers for each playing.

What Happened Later

By the time the children had worked several weeks more on the story, it had developed into a charming play which they presented not only for the school but also for a parent-teacher audience.

Before the opening scene where Marie and Fritz were waiting impatiently for the party and watching the snow (through the imaginary window looking toward the audience) the play was introduced by four little white snow fairies in large snowflake bonnets, dancing in from three auditorium doors to the soft opening music of *The Nutcracker Suite*. Arriving at the front of the auditorium, they chanted a little introduction to the play. Then Fritz and Marie appeared before the curtains for the opening, and looked out at the snowflakes who danced away as the children left the window.

The party scene was played with much more detail and more participation on the part of the adult characters, with imaginary presents given to each. One of Godfather's gifts was an imaginary belt which required the united efforts of all the boys to fasten around Godfather's ample girth. As the deed was accomplished, Godfather straightened up with a smile and a triumphant, "It *fits!*" which brought great laughter from the audience.

The Dance of the Flowers, the scene of the Sugar Plum Fairy, with the Chinese, Arabian, and Russian dances, and the Battle of the Mice, with the final vanquishment of the Mouse King and the Nutcracker's emergence as the prince, made an exciting and beautiful play that entertained kindergarten children and parents alike. As the prince bowed low before the sleeping Marie, and the Snow Fairies hovered around her, Fritz came running down the steps calling "Marie!" and the dream was ended.

The children had made, under supervision, the unusual Christmas tree and the other properties, and had designed and made the flower headdresses. The story, partly realistic but with much fantasy, seemed exactly right for them, and the need for much dancing greatly pleased the girls. Neither the dances nor the dialogue were "set" so that the whole play was characterized by charming spontaneity.

13 and 14

DRAMATIZATION OF SHAKESPEARE STORIES

One project on which it is thoroughly worth-while to spend a good deal of time is the dramatization of a Shakespearean tale. It is never advisable to use these rich but difficult stories until children are thirteen or fourteen years old. But given a year or more of preliminary work, children on this age level may have an unforgettable experience from working with them.

But why dramatize stories which are already in play form? Why make crude plays out of great ones? If one is going to use them, why not memorize Shakespeare's own dialogue?

The answer to these inevitable questions is obvious if one bears in mind that our objective in playmaking is not product but meaningful experience. These stories are well liked by boys *DIALOGUE MUCH TOO DIFFICULT* and girls, but the dialogue is much too difficult. If dramatizing has the effect of cheapening the plays for the children, of making them look forward with less interest to future analytical study of Shakespeare, then it is a mistake to use them now even if they *are* good material. But experiments over a period of years have proved that a dramatic introduction to Shakespeare, *well done,* causes children to approach their high school study of his plays with heightened interest. They neither think him "highbrow" nor boring, and high school English teachers have often expressed appreciation for the leavening influence in English classes of children who have been introduced to Shakespeare by the creative dramatic method.

BACKGROUND MATERIAL

RESEARCH Rich background material should be provided for children's dramatizations of stories from Shakespeare if they are to get the most from this experience. Information and pictures concerning Elizabethan England, its life, customs, and dress; something about Stratford and the little that is known about Shakespeare's boyhood; pictures of the Globe Theatre and a description of the way the plays were presented—all such preparation will help them to understand the dramas and heighten their interest in doing them. If books such as *Medieval Days and Ways, Every-day Things in England,* and *An Introduction to Shakespeare*[5] are available, some of the children will like to read them and tell interesting facts which can be used.

Mary McLeod's *Shakespeare Story Book* will furnish good versions of the tales for dramatization. It has the advantage over Lamb's *Tales* in that the stories are told in a style more interesting to children—at least for the purpose of dramatization. In order that the group may have some choice, we shall give them brief synopses of several stories, say, *A Midsummer Night's Dream, A Comedy of Errors,* and *The Taming of the Shrew.* If we make them all sound interesting, the group may be divided almost equally. We decide to play first the one on which most of the group agrees, promising to use the next in popularity for our second project.

Besides the fact that the whole story of the play would be a bigger undertaking in dramatization than most classes could manage, the central idea is sometimes entirely unsuitable, as in the *Dream,* a tale of unrequited love. So, when we present the story, reading some parts, telling others, we spend less time on the love story and present the artisan and fairy scenes with greater care and more detail.

Then we talk it over and decide on the scenes we want to dramatize. Knowing which ones will give them the most valuable experience, we have purposely made them very clear and interesting. But we discuss the whole story and choose the first incident we want to play.

We find that we really do not know very much about the characters by reading these stories; and, since little dialogue is

[5] See Bibliography for all books mentioned.

given, the children haven't much idea how they talk. Because we are concerned to keep the dramatization true to the real Shakespeare, we read the scene from the text of the play to the children who are to dramatize it. We want them to have more substance for characterization and more flavor for their dialogue, and this is the only way to get it.

Yet here will be their play ready made! Won't they take over the dialogue? What opportunity will they have for creative expression? To be sure, they now have their story in play form. They have dialogue which, if they choose, they can learn word for word. But, though it may seem strange in view of what has been said before, they have much scope for creativity in characterization, dialogue, and action.

What happens is this: the group usually keeps the general pattern given in the text. Within this pattern, however, there is plenty of room for original action and spontaneous dialogue. Stage directions are very few. The language is difficult in its phrasing and we have to do more or less translating as we read. With the exception of a very few children, the boys and girls will use their own dialogue rather than Shakespeare's. In fact, the group is not pleased with any child who does memorize any considerable part of the speeches. Many phrases which are meaningful and appealing to them will be taken over, and the children will make an effort to fit their own language to Shakespeare's. This is to be desired, for one of the objectives of this study is the beginning of appreciation for these great plays. There is more opportunity for study of people in Shakespeare than in any other material the children have used, and they thoroughly enjoy working on characters who are so real and so interesting.

Pantomime

Because these stories are notably richer in action and characterization than those which the children have studied before, we shall use a good deal of pantomime in the beginning stages of our dramatization.

Pantomime gives a kinesthetic sense of characterization by concentrating all one's attention on bodily expression. Not having to think of what to say, the player can concentrate on action and thus get a better sense of how his character feels. It will be fun to pantomime one or another of the artisans in some typical action and have the group guess whether it is slow-witted Snug; Bottom, the show-off; or one of the others. Each character may pantomime an action belonging to his trade, done in his characteristic fashion. When playing the scene in which Puck puts the ass's head on Bottom, it is amusing to pantomime the reaction of each one of them to the transformed weaver! Puck, running about playing pranks on each of them, is another good situation for pantomime. Becoming familiar with the way each character feels and moves before using speech will make for careful interpretation of the parts.

Short Scenes

Very short scenes or parts of scenes will be used first for pantomime and later with words. This is not easy material, and the players gain deeper appreciation of the characters and more assurance in playing them if they attempt only a bit at a time. Neither appreciation nor skill can be hurried, and we are wise not to count on dramatizing many Shakespearean scenes.

SHORT SCENES FOR PANTOMIME [margin note, handwritten]

Adults whose experience with Shakespeare has not been of the kind to remember with pleasure are astonished at the zest with which adolescents play Petruchio, Katherine, and Grumio in *The Taming of the Shrew,* or the two Dromios in *A Comedy of Errors.* Without the evidence of their own eyes, they would not believe the great freedom of thirteen-year-old children in playing the witches' scenes in *Macbeth.* Boys and girls are often self-conscious at first from the necessity of "letting go" so thoroughly.

But given a teacher who knows how to set the mood for these
weird scenes and lead the children little by little into a feeling
through their whole bodies for these strange, supernatural creatures, and soon it is hard to hold them back! Everybody wants
to be a witch, and we have a difficult time getting people to be
Macbeth and Banquo. Sometimes, when the class is not too
large, everyone plays a witch until it is time for the human beings to come on, at which time two of the boys may disappear
into the wings and walk out a moment later as the Scotch gen-
erals!

A dimly lighted stage and rumblings of thunder on a piano
are additions to the uncanny effect which all the children love.
The shedding of shoes helps to give them a feeling of ease in
assuming the character of these strange creatures who seem to
emerge from the elements. They like to make their voices sound
as if they belonged to beings who are not human. They know
they would not have the harsh, cackling voices typical of such
a witch as the one in "Hansel and Gretel" because they are unearthly creatures who come out of the fog and the wind. They
try strange low tones, wailing high voices, eerie laughs.

They often achieve remarkable rhythm in these scenes from
Macbeth. Using the

> Double, double, toil and trouble,
> Fire burn and cauldron bubble,

as a recurring phrase, they are influenced in making the whole
scene rhythmical: their swooping movements, their pauses, their
promises and warnings to Macbeth.

It should be said by way of warning that we do not get such
playing as this without knowing how! It requires skill and experience on the part of a teacher and a good deal of previous
work in playmaking by the children. A group should not attempt
Shakespeare until it has had a considerable amount of experience

with easier material. But when teacher and pupils are able to work out creatively scenes from the plays mentioned here, the various incidents from *The Merchant of Venice, Julius Caesar, Twelfth Night, King Lear,* and the others which have been suggested in Chapter 5, they will find that of all the stories which might be chosen for thirteen-year-olds, these are the richest and most challenging.

CHAPTER 8

Integration

DRAMA IS AN ART, NOT A TOOL FOR MAKING LEARNING EASY.
Facts put in dialogue form are a far cry from drama, which
breathes with life and meaning. Nothing else, however, has
such power to make living the great events in history; or, through
role-playing, to clarify problems in human relations. It can motivate expression in art, in creative writing, in music, and in
dance.

To illustrate the difference between putting facts in dialogue
form and drama, we might compare two ways of using an event
in the life of America's first statesman, Roger Williams.

The first way would be used to test the student's knowledge
of an historical period, the dialogue form being used to make the
lesson more interesting. A conversation might include Roger
Williams and the men of the General Assembly of Providence
regarding Williams' beliefs concerning civil and religious rights.
Such dialogue, called forth by the question of admitting Quakers to Providence, *could* be dramatic, but if the purpose were
simply to test accuracy in historical facts, the experience would
never be the unforgettable one which young people would have
if the event in Roger Williams' life came alive for them in
drama.

The purpose of the second way of studying Roger Williams
would be to make impressive the *meaning* of what happened at

that time. By developing a dramatization showing the attitudes of the people as well as the events recorded on the printed page, the children may live through an exciting session of the General Assembly in action, and hear Roger Williams express some of his views on the right of the people to follow their own consciences. They will learn much about the evils of intolerance as they see how revolutionary were some of Williams' beliefs which we now accept as a matter of course: the belief that the state has no right to dictate what its citizens must think or say; that this country was founded so that people might worship as they chose; that no colony should turn away any sect or any race because they worshiped differently from the majority. It is rather thrilling for them to learn that for a time Roger Williams' voice was the only one in the great wilderness that was to be the United States of America which spoke out for freedom of religion, and that it is largely because of him that we have no one national church.

One of the many dramatic incidents in Williams' life concerns his defense of the rights of Quakers to settle in Providence, especially one Mary Dyer who had been banished from the Massachusetts Bay Colony after having been beaten and thrown into prison and all but put to death for her outspoken views.

Histories do not agree in all particulars about Mary Dyer, some saying that she actually was put to death in Boston, others that she came to Providence, which was a haven for those who sought religious freedom. According to one story, she and her son, on arriving in Providence, were summoned to a meeting of the General Assembly when Roger Williams was away from the settlement for a few days. Certain of the Assemblymen were determined that these "troublemakers" must be sent away, and knowing well that Williams would defend their right to stay, proposed to take advantage of his absence and get the business safely over with before his return.

How one of the leaders turned the feeling against Mary Dyer by producing a letter from the Massachusetts Bay Colony threatening that if Providence gave refuge to the Quakers they would close all trade channels with this colony; and how, as Mary Dyer was about to leave, Roger Williams appeared to defend her and completely changed the attitude of the people by his earnest persuasion, makes an exciting plot. The episode may be partially fictitious, but it could have happened. And it offers a magnificent opportunity to make some of Roger Williams' views impressive.

What boys and girls get from dramatizing such scenes from history is not merely learning facts—which most of them would promptly forget—but experiencing a period in history which has real significance for today. For even yet we have not caught up with some of Williams' enlightened beliefs; and it is a good thing for our young people to see the fight that stereotyped thinkers have always put up against views they considered revolutionary—views which often in contemporary times have become generally accepted.

History is full of dramatic events; and if we as teachers would help our pupils to play out the episodes which have most meaning for today, perhaps the common saying that "the one thing we learn from history is that we do not learn anything from history" would no longer be true.

Consider, for instance, the case of the American Indian, who in our histories has appeared most often as a terrible enemy, massacring and scalping the helpless colonists. Little is ever said of the reason for their enmity, nor of the dramatic contrast in their attitude when they were treated fairly. Only let children experience the manner in which most of the colonies appropriated the Indians' land or paid them mere baubles for it, and their sense of justice will make them condemn such treatment. On the other hand, let them play out William Penn's insistence in

Pennsylvania that land bought from the Indians must be paid for at a fair price. The example he set of treating Indians as friends, not enemies, resulted in the Quakers being able to go wherever they chose, unarmed and unafraid.

We want our younger generation to love their country, but we should not keep them ignorant of wrongs that have been done and are being done if we are concerned that they learn *from* history as well as learning facts. And since the treatment of the Indian even in the present day is a blot on our country's history, there is value in making vivid by dramatic treatment the contrast between the breaking of sacred treaties with the Indian which still goes on today with the one that Penn made in Pennsylvania—the treaty which the great French philosopher Voltaire said was the only treaty "never sworn to and never broken."

The playing out of other historical occurrences, if wisely guided, can give boys and girls a better understanding of their own times. This does not mean that we are using drama as a tool for teaching other subjects. It does mean that we are integrating subjects with a play at the center and in so doing we are helping to make unforgettable certain truths which have significance at the present time.

INTERRELATIONSHIP OF SUBJECTS

Subjects are no longer taught in isolation in the best of modern schools. More and more their interrelationships are recognized and they are grouped accordingly. One evidence of this change is the grouping of geography, history, and civics into "social studies," and reading, writing, speaking, and listening into "language arts."

For some years the pendulum swung so far toward correlation and integration in elementary schools that it was thought that everything in the school program should be closely related to everything else. In more recent years education has grown away from this extreme view, though John Dewey's idea that subjects should not be kept in "water-tight compartments" has had great influence in the recognition of natural relationships.

While the arts often provide freshness and variety in the school program, with no direct connection with any other subject which the children happen to be studying, a correlation of art, music, literature, writing, and drama—all or several of them at a given time—provides rich experiences for boys and girls.

Rachel Field's little poem "Roads," [1] read in a study of literature, is an incentive for art in the painting of the children's conceptions of the places past which the road winds: the "harbor towns and quays"; the "scarey" pointed house of the witch; the shop where the tailor sits cross-legged, sewing; Miss Pim, the milliner, "with her hats for every head" (and what little girl does not enjoy picturing quaint Miss Pim and her gay shop?). Then there is that "great dark cave" with its shining treasure, and the mountain "blue-humped against the sky." What wonderful motivation for art!

The pictures the children paint may be the incentive for playing the poem. Or the dramatic play may come first; and after they have acted out the things that happen at the witch's house, at Miss Pim's, and at all the other places, they will have many more ideas for their art.

Some teachers of preschool and kindergarten children say that dramatic play is the best motivation they know for art expression. After the fun of playing "Sing a Song of Sixpence" or "Little Miss Muffet" or "The Three Bears," the children's art work is immeasurably better, they say, than without such experiences. It also creates the feeling for many kinds of rhythmic movement or dance.

A group of fourth-grade children[2] studying undersea life

[1] See Story List in the Appendix for all stories mentioned in this chapter.
[2] Chapel Hill, N.C. Dorothy Koch, teacher. Adeline McCall, supervisor of music.

painted a large mural of soft green to represent the ocean. To
this background they attached cutouts in gaily colored paper of
crabs and sea-horses, oysters, octopuses, various kinds of fish—
everything they had been reading about in their science lessons.

Using the characteristic movements of first one and then another of these—each in a different rhythm tapped out on a drum
—every child made his own dance pattern as he moved about
in the group before the mural. On the occasion of a demonstration everyone began with the random movements of an octopus,
changing with the drum beat to a sea-horse, a crab, a water-
spider, or whatever else was suggested.

Though these rhythmic movements might as logically have
been taught as a basic part of dance or drama, they came in this
instance in the children's study of music, and demonstrated once
more the close relationship of the creative arts. It was a pleasurable activity for the children and taught them bodily response
to various rhythmical beats.

A DRAMATIC PROJECT BASED ON NATURAL SCIENCE

Another project based on natural science was inspired by a
study of insects. Two superior fourth-grade groups[3] prepared it
for an assembly program and the venture proved so successful
that they were invited to present it on a number of special occasions.

They decided to call their play "The Adventure of Alfred the
Ant" and make it a fun play instead of the heavy factual dramatization they could have developed. In this one production they
used not only science but also art, creative music and writing,
craftsmanship, puppetry, choral speaking, and probably other
skills.

The play began on the apron of the stage, before closed curtains. Two or three children were reading science books, and

[3] Fort Wayne, Indiana.

another was stretched on the floor peering through a microscope. Into the scene came a little elf who invited them to go on an adventure in science; and of course they eagerly accepted his invitation.

Then the curtains opened wide enough to display a marionette stage, with a window shade which served as a curtain. When this was raised, Alfred, a surprisingly large ant, was discovered on a log in the midst of an outdoor scene painted by one of the children. Into his humdrum life came butterflies, caterpillars, crickets, and other insects, telling him of the fascinating world beyond his narrow horizon, tempting him to sally forth to see it.

The following scene showed Alfred far from home, on the edge of a pond, watching the fish and turtles and frogs as each took his turn at entertaining the others. Much fun resulted in the efforts of a big bullfrog, who was master of ceremonies, to keep order when a great chorus of approval swelled up after each performance.

The climax came in the next scene, in which a wicked spider tried to entice Alfred into his web. At the crucial moment, when the spider was stealing out to get the poor ant, the day was saved by a group of ladybugs who called shame on the spider.

"I was only inviting him in for supper," whined the culprit.

"*Whose* supper?" demanded the ladybugs. And, protected by his fearless rescuers, Alfred escaped from the scene of danger and started on his homeward way.

The final episode was a lovely night scene in which fireflies (tiny Christmas tree lights which flickered on and off) guided Alfred safely home. There were night sounds made by children —of crickets and owls—and a song "How Lovely Is the Night," sung by an unseen chorus. At the end, a relieved, oh, a very relieved voice exclaimed "Alfred!" so happily that there was no slightest doubt about his welcome home!

INTEGRATION IN CHRISTMAS PLAYS

Christmas plays invariably call for the closest harmony of music and drama, with art expression in the colors and blending of the robes, as well as in the lights—if any special lighting is possible. In Nativity plays, in dramatizations of Eric Kelly's *In Clean Hay*, Ruth Sawyer's "Wee Red Cap" or "Christmas Apple," as well as in Menotti's *Amahl and the Night Visitors* and many other Christmas stories, the play is the meeting-place for all of the other arts.

Amahl is, of course, an opera; but the story is used by children for whom the presentation of the opera is impossible. Certain of the records of the opera can be used—for scenes of pantomime, for the boy's piping, and for the dance which is an integral part of the action. This dance of the villagers, being an honor shown to the "Night Visitors," does not stop the story. It is drama of the kind described by Roy Mitchell in *Creative Theatre*.[4]

For Mitchell conceives dance to be a form of theatre. He emphasizes the fact that "the theatre's essential art is motion," and he compares it with the art of the painter and the sculptor, the writer, and the musician. All of these can *suggest* motion but they cannot make it an actuality. "Motion," he says, "is the peculiar and exclusive property of the theatre which can by the use of the human body—the most plastic and expressive of forms—embody its miracle in actual motion."

He goes on to say that there are four increasingly complex forms of theatre: (a) the patterned dance, which is the most abstract form; (b) the imitative or interpretative dance; (c) the pantomime; and finally (d) miming with words. Whether or not one agrees that dance and theatre are exactly the same art, it is obvious that they are at least so closely akin that it is merely a question of semantics.

[4] (The John Day Co., Inc., 1929).

Certainly pantomime with music is a natural form of drama and much used in playmaking. From the little child's playing of circus acts, and his miming of "The Little Pink Rose" and "The Snow Man," to "The Wonderful Weaver," *Amahl, The Sorcerer's Apprentice,* and *A Midsummer Night's Dream* of older boys and girls, music can establish a mood beyond that which comes in any other way.

Children catch the spirit of Ireland, of Scandinavia, Mexico, Scotland, or any other country through characteristic music; and whether or not they actually use it in a play they develop, it is worth-while for us to search for recorded music which will help them to get the feeling of the people in the story.

A PLAY OF SWITZERLAND

A creative play is often developed in the upper grades as the culmination of the study of a country, a period, a movement, a great person, or one of many other units of study. Such a play is based usually on a fine story from literature—a story that has not only good dramatic possibilities but close enough relationship to their study so that what they have learned will greatly enrich the dramatization.

One sixth-grade group studying Switzerland searched for a good story about William Tell to use as the basis of a play. They decided on a recent version of the Tell legend called *The Apple and the Arrow.*[5] It seemed exactly right for their use because not only was it very dramatic but it was timely, coinciding with the hunger of so many small countries all over the world for freedom and independence. Tell is a hero who has great appeal for children—strong, courageous, freedom-loving, independent—and, withal, more than a little reckless. He never fails to stir their imagination.

During the developing of the play the class had gone on to

[5] Mary and Conrad Buff (Houghton Mifflin Co., 1951).

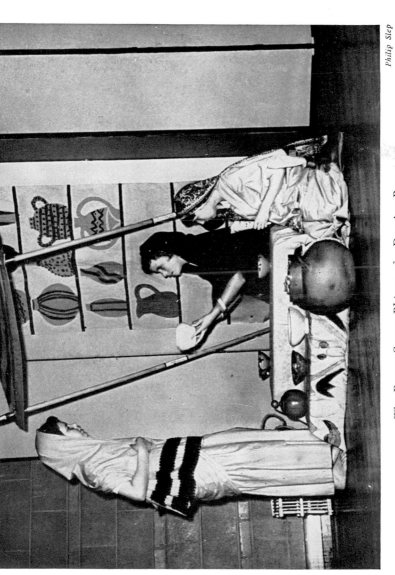

The Bazaar Scene, *Bhimsa, the Dancing Bear*
An Integrated Project
NOYES SCHOOL, Evanston, Illinois
(*Phyllis Mandler, Teacher*)

Lee Balter

The Wager Scene

Eighth-grade dramatization of the story of

The Taming of the Shrew

(see facing page also)

HAVEN SCHOOL, Evanston, Illinois

(*Elinor Rice, Teacher*)

The servants, listening at the door, fall into the room when Petruchio opens it!

"For service to a great ideal"

Formal dramatization of
The Boy Knight of Reims

THE CHILDREN'S THEATRE OF EVANSTON
(*Rita Criste, Director*)

The Goldsmith's Shop

other subjects in their social studies. But in arts and crafts they had designed and made the characteristic bows used at that period, and all the other necessary properties, as well as the designs for costume decoration. They had learned Swiss songs and dances, studied pictures of the architecture, learned about the food which would be served, become familiar with the customs of a mountain country. All these things they made good use of in the action and dialogue of their play.

One performance was given for the school, and they invited their parents to an evening performance, for in a project as ambitious as this the children should have the satisfaction of playing for a real audience. No lines had been learned but so thoroughly had the children lived the story that there was no fear of gaps in the dialogue. Each child knew that he was responsible for certain points which would make the play move, but even if he had missed a cue there were plenty of others who would have carried it along.

Probably every child grew in his sense of responsibility while co-operating with his fellows in this important project. He had improved in his ability to think on his feet and express his ideas without fear. As a constructive use of creative imagination it was a challenging and satisfying experience.

Because the people in the story were strong and virile, with deep feelings concerning human dignity and freedom of conscience, it offered an unusual chance for controlled emotional release—the kind of thing every child needs and wants, but for which he has very few legitimate opportunities. Because it dealt with fundamentally fine values in life, there could be no question as to where sympathy would be. Altogether, many kinds of learning were involved, not the least of which were qualities of personality and character. And though the project had necessitated much research by the teachers, they felt that it had been an exciting and valuable experience.

AN INDIAN PROJECT

Most boys and girls around nine, ten, and eleven years old delight in Indian rhythms and dances. Often they make their own tom-toms and rattles and create an astonishing variety of Indian rhythms.

The story used in one play of this kind [6] had to do with a young Indian boy who, while hunting, came upon a white lad whose foot had been badly hurt by thorns. After relieving his suffering, the Indian took the white boy to the near-by camp where his father, chief of the tribe, made the injured boy welcome. A feast was given in his honor that night, and the young braves entertained him with tales, told in pantomime, of the exploits of their heroes. Each story was accompanied by tom-toms and rattles played by the rest of the tribe, seated in a circle on the ground. No two of the pantomimes had the same pattern, but all the braves followed exactly the beat of their own distinctive rhythms.

The most intense eagerness characterized the whole process of working out this play, especially on the part of the boys, from the day they began originating Indian rhythms to the time when they produced it for the rest of the school. Creative writing came out of it in the prayer for rain in one incident of the story. Many children wrote prayers, from which they chose this one for the Indian boy to say:

> O great Spirit,
> Let the clouds above the tall pine trees open,
> And let the refreshing drops of rain
> Make a silver shield against the drying sun,
> Moistening the thirsty earth,
> Healing the crops of their dry leaves,

[6] Rita Criste, dramatic teacher in the Evanston (Illinois) elementary schools for this and the following play.

                And unfolding the hidden seeds
                That store our crops.

The art work reflected their interest, too. The pictures of the Indian braves had an unusual feeling of action. The decorations for the stage and for the Indian headdresses were highly effective; and every program cover had an interesting design.

A CHINESE PLAY

They called it "How Knowledge Outwitted Conceit," those sixth-grade boys and girls who developed this Chinese play at one of the schools. They chose China as the setting because they had found that country a fascinating study in social science. And their dramatics teacher had discovered a story from Chinese history which so fired their imagination that they voted to base their plot upon it.

It was the story of the vain emperor who caused the Great Wall to be built—that emperor whom Madame Chiang has said the Chinese children are taught to regard as "infamous." It told of his inordinate jealousy of those who had ruled before him—a jealousy which became so strong that he proclaimed that all the learned books telling of the wisdom and the deeds of his ancestors should be burned and all knowledge should begin with his dynasty.

Aghast at this shameful decree, the scholars of his kingdom made a secret pact that they would memorize the finest of these books and rewrite them if the time came when they dared to do so. Accordingly, they stored them in their minds; and when, a few years later, the vain emperor was gathered to his ancestors, they set to work to reproduce them while the whole country rejoiced.

For the vivid drama which grew out of this bit of history, the children wove a factual background like a tapestry, with threads from many sources. With their teachers they read various books on China. They studied the history of the period and visited the oriental exhibits at the museum to see the costumes. In their art periods they painted several large panels of Chinese heroes, made the books which the scholars reproduced, stenciled Chinese designs on their costumes. With their dramatics teacher they slowly developed the play itself, each child contributing what he could. At all times their work was characterized by the eager interest and zest which always accompanies a creative project.

The culmination of their work, a performance at the end of the semester, was a climax, though not the really valuable part of what they had done. Because the children had lived so long and so intensively with the production, this ancient Chinese civilization had come alive for them. They felt authoritative in what they were doing. It was their own, and each child could have played any part in the play.

What the individual children got out of this creative experience they could never forget; for they had lived, as it were, in those remote times and in that far-off land; and their horizons could never again be so narrow as they were before. They understood, so far as they were capable of understanding, a culture completely different from their own. And the China of today became more intelligible to them because of their experience in a period of its past.

All dramatic situations involve emotions, and when from day to day the children took their turns at playing creatively the cruel emperor, the patient scholars, and the crowd of citizens who begged for mercy, they had a legitimate outlet for many kinds of feelings. If they themselves had secret fears, here was a chance to play them out and so release the tensions they caused. When a child who was distinctly antisocial played the evil ruler, his own hostilities were brought out in to the open and often

minimized by the very act of putting them into his characterization of the emperor. And in a story such as this, in which sym-
pathies are rightly placed, no slightest danger could come from
experimenting with emotions of many kinds.

As a socializing experience it could hardly have been more effective. The children were engaged in a project which seemed to
them infinitely worth-while and thoroughly satisfying. The incentive was strong, therefore, to work together harmoniously and
to subordinate their individual desires for the good of the whole.
Innumerable ideas were suggested by participants; and after evaluation by the group they were either accepted or rejected. And
by the most democratic procedure possible they built up a play
in which all were proud to have a part.

When the day came for the final performance, the children
did not recite lines memorized from a script. Yet no character
could possibly forget what to say, for the play was his own crea-
tion, and every speech and every reaction came from inside. He
might use different phrasing occasionally, but he was thinking
and feeling constantly, never merely recalling words and directions.

When the curtains opened on the climactic scene of the little
drama, the audience of parents and friends was surprised to find
itself swept into a dramatic situation which was amazingly real.
A red glow from off stage lighted the faces of the frightened crowd gathered to watch the burning of the books. Amid
harsh orders and mournful cries, the oldest of the scholars threw
himself at the emperor's feet, begging him to save the most precious of the books. Angrily, the emperor refused and ordered
that the man himself be cast into the flames. The climax was one
to satisfy the most inveterate seeker after thrills; for, as the curtains closed, the man was dragged out toward the red glow, and
a wail swelled up from the crowd which really made one shiver!

After reaching such a height, the last scene (supposed to be several years later) would have been anticlimactic except that the festivities celebrating the rewriting of the books ended in a procession gay with music and colorful lanterns and headed by a great green dragon propelled by the legs of many little boys. And so the play ended with a merry laugh!

The Dark Side of the Moon

Two sixth-grade groups in the same school,[7] having been given the opportunity to develop an integrated project with a creative play at the center, spent some time in discussing what kind of material they most wanted to use. Since it had long been the custom for the sixth grades to work out a project of this kind, many such plays had been developed. Previous classes had dramatized stories of Japan (*The Samurai Sword*), Russia (an original plot), India (*Bhimsa, The Dancing Bear*), Germany ("The Nuremberg Stove"), France (*The Boy Knight of Reims* and *Joan of Arc*), and each one had broadened knowledge and developed attitudes based on strongly motivated research.

This class, guided by their teachers, groped about for some time among ideas of space and space travel, together with ideas of constellations and the myths with which they were connected. The science and science-fiction which they had read and seen demonstrated on television influenced them to invent a story of the future—a story which was pure fantasy even though it involved a good deal of scientific knowledge.

The play began with a group of about twelve children who had evidently become so interested in studying the constellations that they had formed a club which met once a week to watch the stars. On this particular night they were locating first one and then another of the planets, while they wondered about the vast spaces and how soon man would be traveling to the moon.

[7] Miller School, Evanston, Illinois. Armin Beck and Amelia Vorhees, teachers. Ann Heekin, dramatic teacher.

"Hi, there, Jupiter," shouted one of the boys. "Can you hear me?"

"Mars looks so close, it seems as if the people there—if there are any—*could* hear us," said one girl. "Hello up there, people of Mars!"

Soon the rest of the children, caught up with the fun of it, were shouting—to the moon, to Saturn, and to all the other planets they knew.

"Listen!" said one of the girls suddenly in a low voice. "Did you hear what I heard? It sounded as if someone answered us!"

Others had heard the strange sound, too, and for a moment all were silent. Then one of the boys scoffed, "You're hearing things!" and he gave a big shout. Again there seemed to be a reply and even he was quiet.

"Look," whispered a girl. "Someone is coming!"

Then, not from the sky, but down a pathway before them (which to the audience who watched was the middle aisle!) came a small figure in flowing garments.

"Who are you?" someone asked uncertainly.

"I am Echo," was the reply. And in the conversation which followed she told the children that long ago, as earth folk ceased to believe in the old myths and superstitions, the people in them left the earth to go and dwell on the dark side of the moon. She alone had refused to go, and now she was dying. Her only hope was to get to the moon.

"That should be possible before long," said one of the boys encouragingly. "I read that perhaps in two years there might be some interplanetary travel."

"Two years will be too late for me," replied Echo sadly.

"I wish we could build a space ship and take you there," said one of the boys. "But I'm afraid there is no chance of that!"

"You might," said Echo doubtfully. "Strange things can happen in my magic cave." Then she led the children to a cave where things not humanly possible, she said, had sometimes occurred. She showed them grotesque rocks "that used to be witches," and told them that though she had not found any strong enough magic to take her to the moon, she believed that they might be able to build a space ship there.

And from here on, the element of the fantastic, the unreal, entered more and more strongly into the play. The children, with Echo's magic, contrived a space ship (only the back part of which was visible on the stage!) and six of them, with Echo as guide, climbed aboard and blasted off amid light and sound effects which were highly convincing to the audience!

As the curtains closed on this scene, instead of houselights coming on, the ceiling of the auditorium became the heavens, with a blue, star-studded sky (projected from three so-called "planetariums" brought by the children). With soft music as background, it was an effective way of sustaining the atmosphere of the play until the curtains opened on the moon scene.

The second part of the play involved many children. In fact, the cast was so large that even two home-rooms were not enough to man it, and a number of children played two parts.

The scene was, of course, the moon just as the earth children arrived—with offstage noises that drew out to meet them all the mythical figures who lived on the dark side of the moon. Introduced by Echo, now strong and well, the children met the genial man in the moon, who welcomed them with festivities in which five myths were enacted: a Chinese, an African, a Greek, a Norse, and an American Indian. It was a gay and festive scene, with music and dancing, and finally with the goodbyes of the children who needs must leave in time to get home before their parents began to worry about them!

Again the contingent at the home-made control board set off the light and sound effects. Echo said her last thank you to the children; and the curtains closed with the impression of a ship hurtling through space in order to reach the earth before dark!

"The best experience the sixth grade had all year" was the way one of the classroom teachers expressed it. Nothing else had so interested, so unified the group; and they worked with the most intense enthusiasm from the beginning of the project until the end.

The greatest fascination for some of the boys was the scientific research and experimentation. They made the most careful and detailed charts, and worked long hours on the control board for light and sound effects. When one of the girls was asked who built the space ship, she replied, "Just the ones who knew the most about electronics!"

For two months the greater part of their school work was built around the play. Their study of astronomy led into Greek mythology—then into the myths of other peoples. They learned to spell the new words which had enlarged their vocabularies, wrote book reports on space and space travel, listened to documentaries on space on radio and television, discussed good and poor science-fiction which they read, and rejected the kind of sound effects being used on a popular television program as "not having imagination!"

In arithmetic they made scale models of the stage and properties; in arts and crafts some beautiful mobiles, which were hung in the auditorium, as well as designs for the simple costumes. In language they pictured themselves as people in myths, and did some creative writing in character.

For social studies they read articles and heard talks about the moral and spiritual values related to space travel. "If or when we meet peoples of other planets, what should our responsibility be?" "What do we have that we should be proud to offer them?" "How receptive would we be to their ideas?"

It was an experience these children will not soon forget. It was in line with their reading, their interest in the unknown, exciting future. As leaders we could wish that we might more often find projects so challenging, so fascinating to the children we teach. For when children are truly interested the hardest work is play to them.

CHAPTER 9

Play Structure

AN INSPIRED TEACHER OF ANY ART ENCOURAGES HER CHILDREN to "do it your own way." She believes, though, in giving them tools to work with in the form of a few definite principles to help them make satisfying pictures, create interesting puppets, write verse that is not mere imitation.

To be a real guide in playmaking, we need to know what it is that gives a play quality so that we can be of more help to children in the plays they create. Like able leaders in other arts, we teach the principles indirectly and concretely. We praise children who think out sound ideas for weaving events into play form, and comment on them in such a way that all the children will gain some new insight.

A group of children dramatizing "The Peddler and His Caps" [1] may plan to begin the play at the peddler's home when he is making caps to sell.

"How can we make it clear who he is and what he is doing?" we ask.

"By having the peddler talk to himself," Larry says.

"Can you think of any other way that he could make these things known?"

"By pantomiming," offers Linda. "But then I don't know how he could show he is a peddler."

[1] See Story List in the Appendix for all stories mentioned in this chapter.

173

"I know a way," volunteers David. "He could have a wife and maybe some children, and we could tell by what they said and did what kinds of caps he was making and what he was going to do with them!"

"A good idea," we say. "It always seems more natural, don't you think, to talk to someone else instead of to one's self? People don't think aloud, as a rule." And by thus commenting on a child's suggestion, we make the children realize that there is a better way of giving exposition than by the unnatural soliloquy.

It might be objected that since the children's ideas are what we care about, it makes no difference whether a story dramatization is developed according to dramatic principles or not. So long as the children are happy and satisfied, what difference does it make whether the product is good? They generally are not doing it for an audience.

The answer to such a question would be another question: does it make any difference about the quality of a child's work in the graphic arts or in music so long as he is happy? We know of course that it does make a difference; that if he puts his best effort into the modeling of a figure or the mastery of a song, he grows not only in skill and in taste but more important still, he grows as a person.

By all means the children should be happy about their play if the experience is to be a valuable one; and they will be happier if they feel that they have accomplished something out of the ordinary. Satisfaction comes from stretching their imaginations to create a play of which they can be proud; and there will be respect for the whole activity if they have confidence in a leader's knowledge.

The assurance on the part of a teacher which comes from acquaintance with the basic principles of dramatic construction will do much to make the experience of guiding children rewarding. No good playwright follows these principles at all times, nor should a teacher of creative drama insist that her children do so; but even though perfection is not the end sought, it is of immense help to any leader to know the rules of the game.

SUBJECT MATTER

In an adult play, the subject may be a problem, as in Galsworthy's *Loyalties;* or the study of a single character, like *Candida,* by Shaw. But in a children's play the *story* is the most important thing. At the center is usually a hero; but the story of his adventures is what interests young people most. There may be a central idea or theme, such as the search for happiness in *The Blue Bird,* or the fear of speaking honestly as in "The Emperor's New Clothes"; but most children do not understand abstract ideas, and are more impressed by qualities of character in the people of the story.

Since Chapter 5 discusses the kinds of stories suitable for creative plays, all that needs to be said here is that whatever material is used should invariably be of good quality.

THE PLOT

The elements of a play are *plot, characters, dialogue.* The plot is the plan of action. It includes a number of episodes and the arrangement of them for the progress of the play from beginning to end. It should have a problem, complications, and a solution. Usually, though not necessarily, there is a conflict between good and evil forces.

In "Snow White and the Seven Dwarfs" the conflict arises from the Queen's jealousy of the lovely and gentle Snow White. In *Peter Pan,* it is Peter against Captain Hook. In "Aladdin" it is the wicked Magician trying to get Aladdin's power and wealth. In "Jack and the Beanstalk" Jack struggles with the Giant to get what is rightfully his.

The evil force in many children's plays is personified by someone seeking the destruction of the hero or heroine. In "Midas and the Golden Touch," however, the evil struggles with the good *inside a man*. It is not so easy for children to understand this kind of conflict, but it would be well if there were more stories for older children where the hero's struggle was not with an evil person, but rather with difficult circumstances, forces of nature, weakness or evil within himself. In searching for good stories to dramatize, we might well consider this point. Pioneer tales, for example, are likely to concern a hero's struggle against the forces of nature. Heroes and heroines in many novels must struggle against poverty or physical handicaps.

Some stories are very little concerned with conflict between good and evil. Like *Tom Sawyer,* they simply show some aspect of life with fresh significance; or they are just enchanting tales like "Ali Baba," *Alice in Wonderland,* and *Mr. Popper's Penguins.*

There should always be *unity* in the plot—not necessarily of time, place, and mood—but the unity which results when everything bears on the central idea. In *The Silver Thread,*[2] for example, there are no happenings which are not related in some way to the gift from the Woman Beyond the Hills—the gift which will always show Cubert where safety lies if he faces danger bravely and never turns his back.

The plot should be clear and meaningful to the children for whom it is intended. Granted that the subject matter is within their comprehension, the episodes are logically arranged, each developing from the preceding one, and all are directly related to the main idea, children are seldom puzzled or confused. In dramatizing a story that is at all complex, we should always help the children to be objective in this matter and make their plot

[2] Constance Mackay (Henry Holt & Co., Inc., 1910).

very clear whether they are to present it for another group or not.

The Opening

If a play is the dramatization of a story or novel, *the point at which it opens* requires much thought. When it begins too early in the story, the children's span of attention may come to an end before the play is completed; when it opens too near the climax, they may not be able to make it clear what led up to it. In the dramatization of an eventful novel like *The Prince and the Pauper,* the opening scene could very interestingly show the family life of little Tom Canty in Pudding Lane, and when children dramatize the story they very often do start here; but there are so many richly dramatic scenes leading up to the climax that if they are going to play it for anyone else, they are more likely to begin with Tom's fateful visit to the palace.

The story should start out at once in a well-made play, preferably in the midst of things happening. Action is better than talk, as all good playwrights know, for an audience "locks its ears until its eyes are satisfied." As one little girl in a formal audience expressed it, "I was so busy looking that I forgot to listen."

By sitting in a children's theatre audience, we find out that it is useless, therefore, to begin a children's play with anything really important for an audience to *hear.* Peter Pan[3] is a classic example of the way an author can set the mood of a play entirely with the action of the opening scene. As the curtain rises, the cuckoo clock strikes six, awakening Nana, the Darling's dog-nurse. Springing to her feet, Nana crosses the nursery, turns down the children's beds as a good nurse should, and then goes into the bathroom to prepare Michael's bath. And from these

[3] J. M. Barrie (Charles Scribner's Sons, 1928).

surprising and humorous bits of action, a child audience knows that it is in for a jolly play where anything can happen.

Such an opening is fresh and different, arousing immediate interest and eager desire to see the rest of the play. Unusual, too, is the action of the monkeys at the first of *Rama and the Tigers*,[4] and the outlandish sounds with which *Mr. Popper's Penguins*[5] begins.

No one is interested in the opening of a play or a dramatization in which people are disagreeable or actually quarreling. A lively beginning, with dialogue or pantomime that makes us wonder is a sure way of securing the rapport of all who are watching. The dramatization of such a ballad as "Get Up and Bar the Door" should never start out with the couple quarreling. In fact, we can introduce it so that it is very gay with the preparation for a festival the following day. This makes not only for a good opening, but provides a delightful contrast when the quarrel does begin.

Once started, *the story of the play should never be interrupted.* Attention is always lost by songs or dancing, introduced to stretch it out or use more players. This is not to say that songs and dancing may not be an integral part of a play, as the ball in *Cinderella*[6] and the boy's singing in *The Christmas Nightingale.*[7]

In one dramatization of *The Emperor's New Clothes,* given for an audience, the procession in which the Emperor walks was interrupted by some magic tricks done by one of the crowd on the street. Well managed as they were, and fascinating to the children, they stopped the story, and the Emperor, whose big scene it should have been, completely lost the attention of the audience.

[4] Charlotte Chorpenning (Coach House Press, Chicago, 1938).
[5] Rosemary Musil, Elmhurst, Illinois (Ms.).
[6] Charlotte Chorpenning (Children's Theatre Press, 1940).
[7] Eric Kelly (Children's Theatre Press, 1940).

Exposition - EXPLANATION OF SITUATION + CHARACTERS

The *exposition,* or explanation of the situation and the characters, is given in various ways. Sometimes a Prologue or Narrator is used, as in a pantomime of "Ali Baba and the Forty
Thieves," in which an oriental storyteller appears at various
times to explain the pantomime. This is a very formal kind of
exposition, charming for quaint or dignified plays, but less suitable for many others.

The names of the characters—Cassim, Witch Hex, Gretel
Brinker, Rumpelstiltskin—often tell us something about nation-
ality or character. If the play is given with setting and costumes,
the scene of the play and the appearance of the characters give
some of the information we need to know. Mainly, though, exposition is given by the *dialogue and action.* What a surprising
family the Darlings must be to have a dog-nurse for their children, we think in the first scene of *Peter Pan!* And even the
youngest child who sees *Cinderella* needs only a speech or two
from the stepmother and her daughters to know about Cinderella's unhappy lot.

What one character says about another and the way he speaks
and acts toward him offer as much exposition as what the character himself says and does. But with even a little experience in
reading and seeing plays, one knows that it is poor playwriting
to have one character tell another what that person would naturally have known before. Because certain things need to be
made clear, it is a common practice to introduce a stranger or
some person who has been away for a time so that he can be
told what is needed to make the situation clear. This is better
than soliloquy but not so good as bringing in the information a
bit at a time in the course of natural conversation—by far the
best technique in regard to exposition.

Episodes

An episode or incident is one of a series of events comprising the plot. Some of these episodes are main events, the others minor incidents. They need to be kept in proper relation one to another. In "The Sleeping Beauty," for instance, the main events are:

1. The Curse of the Thirteenth Fairy.
2. The Pricking of the Princess' Finger, Causing Her to Fall into the Long Sleep.
3. The Awakening.

The minor events or incidents are:

a. The Happy Christening Party.
b. The Softening of the Curse by the Twelfth Fairy.
c. The Exploration of the Palace by the Princess on Her Fifteenth Birthday.
d. The Fate of the People of the Palace.
e. Their Awakening.
f. The Wedding.

Variety in episodes keeps interest high. Two or three scenes of the same length, in the same mood, or with similar action always mean loss of interest. In contrast, "Snow White and the Seven Dwarfs," with its refreshing variety of scenes—the formal palace scenes of beauty and intrigue, the forest with its near tragedy relieved by the song of the bird, the lively scene in the dwarfs' cottage, and the place where the witch mixes her strange brews—though a problem in the staging if the play is developed into a formal production—does keep interest high.

Economy of episodes is necessary when long and involved stories are dramatized. Such stories are rarely used for young children since their span of attention is short. Older children like both to see and to act in plays of an hour or more in length if the play is absorbing. But even for this length of time, it is necessary to economize on scenes if a play is based on a complete novel such as one of the Mark Twain books. Combining or condensing incidents, or omitting minor plots or characters is always necessary; and doing so often improves the play by tightening the plot.

What is shown in a play makes a much greater impact on children than what is told about. Think of the graveyard scene in *Tom Sawyer*, Uncle Wigg's tea party in the air in *Mary Poppins*, the sale of Aladdin's lamp to the Magician by the Princess! How cheated a child would feel if any one of these wonderful scenes was told about instead of played! The omission of certain episodes (called "obligatory" scenes) might completely spoil a performance for an audience. Such a scene as the trying on of the slipper in *Cinderella*, or the Emperor's procession in *The Emperor's New Clothes*, are so unquestionably necessary that no one would dream of having them described instead of played. In creating a play, the children's interest is the best kind of guide to us as leaders in the choice of episodes to be shown, and we shall do well to avoid guiding our children in such a way that they will rely on mere talk.

Suspense—a compelling desire to know what will happen next —is built by holding back the knowledge of something which is about to occur. It can be aroused only when the audience is in sympathy with one or more characters so that it cares what happens to them. When the audience knows beforehand what this is, suspense results from the desire to see how the characters will react when they are faced with the situation.

The older the children, the more they like *complications*. The rogues in the Chorpenning play *The Emperor's New Clothes* want to expose Han, the wicked minister of the Emperor's robes. They find a secret cupboard in which he has hidden goods stolen from the weavers. As he approaches they try frantically to close the doors but they always slide open again. Just in time they stay closed, and the suspense diminishes. But throughout the act there is one complication after another: the Empress startling the rogues by coming in through a secret door, the risk when the General, Han, and the Emperor enter, one at a time, to look at the stuff on the loom, the delay in Zar's scheme to expose Han, the uncertainty of success when the idea does come. It is all very exciting, but the comedy is so strong that the strain is not great.

The *crisis* is the point at which the situation is the most serious for the hero or heroine. It looks dark indeed for Janie and Tommy, the two children in *Mr. Dooley, Jr.*[8] when all their plans for rescuing a poor little dog from a harsh owner seem to have gone awry. Tommy has been unable to sell his bicycle in order to get the money to pay for the dog, the children have well-nigh wrecked the living room by trying to redecorate it, and by the time they are supposed to pay for the dog they not only do not have the money but they are in disgrace.

The Climax

The *climax* or turning-point comes when the dog's owner is discovered to have falsified to the pet-shop owner and is only too glad to turn the dog over to the children in order to avoid being arrested. The *climax* is the time when emotion is at its highest peak; and it should come, in a children's play, practically at the end. There is just time in *Mr. Dooley, Jr.* for the expression of joy of all concerned over the outcome or solution, known generally as the *denouement* of the play.

We as leaders in creative drama need to study a plot carefully in order to plan how to guide children to create a strong climax. It takes skill to build to it effectively, and only rarely do children make the most of it. But a good teacher helps them to become aware of the problem and gradually they learn how to manage it.

[8] Rose Franken and Jane Lewin. (Samuel French, Inc.).

In general, a plot should be believable and interesting throughout. The development should seem natural, inevitable. It should have strong emotional appeal. If it is carefully worked out there will be no loose ends to leave one wondering. Details will be convincing. If a person is sent for he will not appear immediately —unless he has been looking through the keyhole! A *cover scene* will be provided which will have a real function in the plot besides consuming the time it will take for the person to be summoned. Nor will meals be eaten in split seconds, though time will have to be telescoped to a certain extent in the short space of an hour or two allowed for a play.

CHARACTERS

"Plot is what the characters do; characterization shows why they do it." [9]

In life we do not often know what motivates people to act as they do. Even though we are acquainted with a person for years, we may have the chance to know only certain aspects of his character. But in a story or play we should be given causes for the behavior of the people so that we understand why they do and say what they do. If the author fails to give us this insight, their behavior is meaningless.

When children dramatize a story, the characters are created for them except for minor people whom they may add to the cast. By studying the characters in a story written by a good author, their understanding of people is broadened. They "try on" these characters and, according to their degree of maturity, keep them consistent to the author's idea.

The characters of a play should be recognizable as human beings who act as we think people *would* act in a given situation. They must seem real and convincing even if they are as fanciful

[9] H. D. Albright, William P. Halstead, Lee Mitchell, *Principles of Theatre Art* (Houghton Mifflin Co., 1955).

as Rumpelstiltskin or Puck. As a rule, they have more vitality in a play than they have in life. Certainly they should be interesting to watch, not dull or colorless unless a point is made of their being drab. Even then they are often made humorous by contrast.

A good playwright *individualizes* his characters so that each has his own unique personality. In great plays such as Shakespeare's the characters are so real that we consider them as truly living people rather than as creations of an imagination. But even a good playwright uses some type characters as background for the important ones.

A *type character*, so called because he is typical, is easy to recognize because he is so common. In a children's story or play the ridiculously pompous prime minister, the cackly old witch, the sharp-tongued stepmother are a few of the types that have appeared so often as to become *stereotypes*, too conventionalized to be really interesting to anyone with enough experience to be discriminating.

While an important character may have many individual traits, the minor character in a play often has just one that is pronounced. He may be a show-off, a timid person, a bully, so that even in a crowd he may seem real. This is a very useful thing to remember when guiding children to create crowd scenes.

The author reveals character in a number of ways. The name, appearance, and manner of speaking and moving all show individuality, as well as what a character says and what is said to and about him. Think of the many ways we have of knowing Rip Van Winkle! There is his Dutch name, and an odd one at that. His appearance and way of talking and moving instantly characterize this good-natured ne'er-do-well. Then we hear from his shrewish wife all about his shortcomings, and though we realize that he may deserve her tirades, we sympathize with him as a henpecked husband. And by the time that we have seen how

well the children and the other villagers like him, we have a
picture of Rip so well-rounded that he becomes entirely real to
us.

Consistency is exceedingly important in creating a character.
Rip never fails to act according to the picture we are given of
his personality. If an author creates a character who seems convincingly honest and straightforward, he cannot reasonably
have him stoop to an unworthy action. The lovely Snow White
does not seek revenge on the wicked Queen who has tried to
take her life. The Queen brings her punishment on herself.

There should be *balance* in characters, with some strong and
dominating, others timid or weak; some serious, others light and
humorous. Variety in personalities makes for interesting and
widely different points of view. Conflicts usually develop from
strong contrasts in character, some conflicts being so serious that
one character must change or be destroyed.

Everyone, especially a child, enjoys seeing the deserving un-
derdog rise to heights. In many of the oldest folk tales that have
come down to us, the small but clever jackal outwits the fox or
elephant or whale. In our own literature Bre'r Rabbit comes out
ahead of the larger animals. And we all know how often it is the
youngest son, scorned by his older brothers, who wins the hand
of the princess! So, in many plays, the small, the weak, the
lowly, triumph over the pompous, self-important characters. Children have a very strong sense of justice, and whether they are
seeing or creating a play, they want the people to get what they
deserve.

In children's plays the people are necessarily less subtle than
in adult drama, for children's life experience is too limited to
prepare them to understand subtlety. Nor do the characters often
change. Those who are good stay good, and the bad seldom reform. It takes a powerful experience to make Midas see that
there are more desirable things in the world than gold; and no

child could fail to understand the motivation for his change of attitude. Nevertheless, the discussion of character with older children brings them gradually to appreciate the finer points of personality, and can be one of the most valuable aspects of story dramatization.

DIALOGUE

Every play for boys and girls should be told in action, with a minimum of dialogue. "Show it, don't tell it," Charlotte Chorpenning used to say; and it is a fact that the most successful plays for child audiences *show* what happens, and depend much less on dialogue than do plays for adults.

This does not mean that children prefer pantomimes to spoken plays. Quite the contrary. But they like the speeches to be short and to the point. And it is true that in life people speak most often in short, simple sentences. The long speeches written into many children's plays are not only impossible to say naturally, but are actually not listened to by the younger children, who become lost in the maze of words. This however, is not likely to be a fault of children's own dramatizations. Conversation that wanders far from the point is much more usual, for it is not easy to be selective when dialogue is spontaneous.

Conversation should seem to *belong* to the person using it. The Irish minstrel has the lilt of poetry in his speech. There is beauty in the way Light expresses herself in *The Blue Bird*. Bill Bones is a pirate in *Treasure Island*, but he has a characteristic way of speaking that differs from Pew and Silver and all the rest of the pirates. Tom Sawyer and Aunt Polly, Muff Potter and Injun Joe all live in a small Missouri town around 1840, but even in the same period and locality each has a way of speaking all his own.

The remote times and places of many plays often pose a problem in language. While a child may be entirely capable of understanding the story, the speech of the characters gets in his way. This is true of the Bible, of Shakespeare, of dialect stories, and of such formal dialogue as is found in *The Prince and the Pauper;* and it is sometimes wise to simplify it to a certain extent when presenting the story. When it is a question of dramatization, the children will take hold of as much of the original language as they are able, for the sound of it is fascinating to them. For the most part, however, they will use the language they know best.

If the conversation in plays were drawn directly from life, it would sound dull and repetitious. Every playwright must select and condense in his use of dialogue if it is to hold the attention of an audience. For it must be remembered that a play is art rather than life. It must only *seem* like life. We should not hold too high a standard, however, in improvised speech. We can only praise players for dialogue that *is* to the point.

CONCLUSION

Let it be emphasized that if conditions are as they should be, few if any of the little children's dramatizations will be given for an audience, even for an informal one. Many of the values of playmaking are lost if the stress is placed on performance for an audience. Their own group and their teacher comprise enough audience for kindergarten, first, and second grades.

As children grow older, the communication aspect will be stronger, and there is no harm in playing occasionally for other groups of their own age or younger, especially if performance for an audience has not been the dominant purpose of the project. When any of such groups have done an excellent piece of work, it is a satisfaction to share the results with other children. Seventh and eighth grades, especially, like to do creative assembly programs, for which they need not use scenery and costumes. But even if such dramatizations are never presented for audiences, it still is important that we who are teachers or leaders know the requirements of good plays. Sooner or later we shall need to observe most of them, especially if we teach older classes. Certainly, a working knowledge of dramatic principles will make us far more intelligent guides of playmaking with children; and if we are called on occasionally to direct formal children's theatre plays, where adults, or adults and children together, make up the casts, we shall find that our knowledge of what constitutes a good play will help us to be much better directors.

CHAPTER 10

Playmaking in Religious Education

THE THIRD-GRADE GROUP IN CHURCH SCHOOL HAD BEEN STUDY-
ing the life of David.[1] They had heard the story of the shepherd
boy—the sweet singer who calmed the turbulent spirit of King
Saul and won the friendship of Saul's son Jonathan, the lad
who conquered Goliath the Philistine, and finally became the
successful commander of Saul's armies.

Though the story is much more suitable for fifth- or sixth-
grade children to play, the fact that it was a part of the regular
course for the third grade suggested that one of the simpler episodes be chosen for dramatization. Among the possibilities for
these young children were (a) an incident showing David's care
of his sheep and his encounter with a lion; (b) his triumph over
Goliath; (c) the cave incident in which David refused the
chance to take revenge on Saul. The last of the three was chosen
by the teacher because it was simple and understandable, and
especially because it has real meaning for today's children.

"What do we mean when we say, 'I'll get even with him!'?"
asked the teacher.

[1] See Story List in Appendix for all stories mentioned in this chapter.

189

"I'll do the same thing to him," someone answered. "Or maybe I'll do something worse!"

"Suppose you were playing a game with another boy or girl, and that child didn't play fair. Are you getting even if you cheat *him?*"

The children agreed that you *would* be getting even, but if you did get even that way, you would be no better than he was; you would be a cheat, too.

"This 'getting even' has something to do with the David story we are to have this morning. You know how Saul tried to kill David. Why did he?" One or two children gave the reasons, and the teacher continued. "David knew that Saul was a sick man— not really responsible for his actions. He wasn't sick in his body but in his mind. He had been fond of David, but now he had turned against him; and so David had to leave the palace and live out in the hills where Saul could not find him. Other men who were friends of David went with him and they all hid in a deep cave which they found.

"Now someone told King Saul that David was hiding in the hills, so he started out with many men to search for him. They looked for several days, but David and his followers kept out of his way, spending most of their time in this cave.

"One evening David's men saw the king and his followers coming toward them and they were afraid that he had found out their hiding-place. So they went far back in the dark corners of the cave and hid. They heard voices coming nearer and nearer, and finally they heard King Saul speak just outside the entrance.

" 'Stay on guard out here,' he said to his men. 'I will rest awhile in this cave.' Then David's men knew that Saul had no idea they were there, and they kept very, very quiet in the back of the cave.

"Saul came in, tired out, threw down his spear and shield and stretched out on the ground, glad to have a place to rest.

"For a while David's men kept very still, until they saw that Saul was asleep. Then one of the men said in a whisper, 'Now you can kill the king. It will be easy.' David didn't move at first, so they urged him, saying, 'If you do not kill him now, he will surely kill you.'

"Then David drew his sword and walked quietly over to Saul. It would have been very easy to kill him. His men, watching, expected him to do it. David stood there for a minute and thought. Finally he said to himself, 'Saul is our king. I must not do it.' He leaned over the sleeping man, and with his sword cut off a piece of Saul's cloak. Then he went back to his men.

" 'Why didn't you kill him?' they asked. David said, 'May the Lord forbid that I should do harm to the man who was anointed king!'

"The men were not pleased with this, and they said, 'Let *us* put an end to Saul!' But David would not let them do it.

"Before long Saul woke up, took his spear and shield, and went out of the cave. He had no idea what had happened.

"Then David ran out after Saul. 'King Saul!' he cried. Saul turned around in amazement, and his guards moved as if to seize David.

" 'I have done you no wrong,' said David. 'Just now you were in that cave. My men wanted to kill you. I could have done so but I did not. See,' he said, holding up the piece from Saul's robe, 'I have cut off part of your robe. God knows I have done you no wrong.'

"Then Saul knew that he had wronged David. Now he was sorry. Tears ran down his face and he said, 'David, you are a better man than I am. You have returned good for evil. May God reward you for what you have done! Now I know that you

will surely be the king some day. Go in peace . . . Come,
men.' And in shame, King Saul led his men back home."

After a moment the teacher asked, "Would this be a good
story to play?" The children thought that it would; and since it
had been made so clear to them both now and the first time they
had been told David's story, there seemed no need to discuss any
part of it except to make sure that the children knew about
caves.

"Where could we have a cave?" she asked. The first child
suggested the cloakroom, a long, narrow passage off the classroom
where it would have been impossible to have any action. The
teacher did not discourage this idea but asked for other suggestions. Fortunately, someone thought the half circle in which
the class was sitting would make a good cave if they used the
wall back of the teacher's chair for the other side. Though this
would not have been her choice it was entirely acceptable, and
the class chose it for their playing.

Then, without further discussion the leader said, "I'll be
David the first time. Who would like to be my men?" More
than half the class volunteered, and the others remained in their
chairs as the walls of the cave, one or two suggesting that they
were bats, and using their arms in characteristic motion, while
most of them were rocks covered with cobwebs.

The teacher's idea for this first bit of playing was merely to
"try on" the characters in order to give the children the feel of
them. She took the part of David herself since she was teaching
the class temporarily and knew that if she happened to choose a
child lacking in leadership and imagination the playing would
get off to a most unsuccessful start.

"Come, men," she began. "It is drawing toward evening and
we must look for a place to camp for the night. Caleb," address-
ing one of the boys, "go over to the top of that hill and see if

there are any signs of Saul's men. The rest of us will gather sticks for a fire."

The "men" spread out and began to pick up wood and talk among themselves, when Caleb came running back to say that he could see Saul's men coming this way.

"Then we must find a better place than this to camp," said David. "And we cannot build a fire. Look for a good hiding-place."

The men hurried around looking, and almost immediately one of them said, "Here is a cave where we could hide!"

"Go into it, men," ordered David. "But take care, for it may have passages leading downwards. Don't fall into them. Be careful! Joel, wait here with me. We'll watch to see whether they know where we are. Quietly now. . . . There they are, see? Down to the right. They seem to be turning up this hill . . . They are coming directly this way. Hide, Joel!"

This was the point at which the teacher intended to stop the first playing. But just then one of the boys who had not played asked, "May I be Saul?"

"Go ahead and take your men," said the teacher, though she was very doubtful as to whether he could carry it through. But he led his men along, and they discovered the cave and played the scene according to the story. When he came to the final speeches of Saul, he was most hesitant; but spurred on by David's speeches to him, he managed to get out the substance of what Saul said.

It was such a successful first playing that the teacher decided that the children could very well play it alone. However, when the one child capable of holding the scene together volunteered to be the watchman instead of David, it fell very flat and she realized anew how a strong leader can carry all the other players along.

On a Sunday a little later the class was asked to play it for a younger group and put on some costumes ready at hand, and the teacher reluctantly allowed them to do it after three half-hour periods developing it. This time the capable boy played David and did it effectively. But the costumes brought about a predicament which had not been anticipated: Since Saul wore a real robe, David felt that he should cut off a piece of it instead of making it an imaginary action. What to do? His stick sword would not cut anything! He knelt down and carefully tore off a corner of the garment so that when the right moment arrived, he really had a piece of cloth to hold up to Saul!

How much the meaning in the story impressed itself upon the children through the playing was, of course, impossible to determine. It is always a mistake to moralize about a story or to question the children about the "lesson" in it. Some of the children will answer glibly just what they think you want them to say, but it will really mean nothing to them unless the story itself touches them.

That the teacher related it to their own kind of experience made it more significant to them. She was tempted to carry the "getting even" idea further but refrained because she knew that it would avail little for her to talk about it. However, there is no doubt that the experience of playing the story made a much deeper impression on them than if they had merely heard it told.

PROBLEMS OF TIME AND TRAINING

Story dramatization as a way of teaching in church schools is still rare, and will remain so until (a) these schools are extended to more than an hour in length, and (b) the teachers are trained to guide creative drama. The best opportunities at present are in summer vacation schools, in institutes and assemblies of the church, family camps, and in other situations where a concerted time period can be saved.

In time, perhaps, a longer church-school period will be the usual thing since one hour a week for religious training is being recognized as entirely inadequate for any enrichment of the curriculum. When the time comes for the consideration of activities that will be more live and appealing to the children than much of the present procedure, religious education directors will turn to drama as did the churches of medieval times, realizing that here is a medium for teaching with greater potentialities for touching the heart and influencing lives than most of the methods now in use.

PRESENT WAYS OF TEACHING

Church schools at present employ too much the "pouring-in" type of teaching which the public schools have long since discarded in theory, if not entirely in practice. What the child reads, sees, and hears is, of course, very important. But what he *does* is more likely to get over into his life and influence his way of behaving. Jeanette Perkins Brown, in that excellent little book *The Storyteller in Religious Education*,[2] writes concerning the weaknesses of story-telling as the only method of teaching, "Emotions are aroused for which no outlet in action is provided." And she goes on to tell how the listener, completely identifying himself with the hero, not only toils and suffers with him vicariously, but also vicariously enjoys the unearned emotional satisfaction of the hero's earned reward. "Thus," she concludes, "he feels no need for real effort on his part to achieve such satisfaction."

Some church schools do, indeed, spend a good deal of time with hand work—drawing pictures of Bible heroes or scenes, making scrolls, Palestinian houses, dioramas, wall hangings, stained-glass windows. All these have some value, but unless they are means to an end—the end being a play, perhaps—it

[2] (Pilgrim Press, 1951).

may be questioned whether such work is the most valuable thing boys and girls could be doing in the one precious period the church school has them each week.

Is there any other activity which has greater potentialities for influencing children to want to live by the teachings of Jesus? If participating in drama, and living out the stories of The Good Shepherd, The Good Samaritan, the story of Zacchaeus and the rest, means that the influence of these stories can change them for the better even to a slight degree, it would seem worth attempting at any cost.

That dramatizing Bible stories is fascinating to children is evident by the way a class throws off its apathy as soon as such a project is under way. One young woman, recently out of college where she had studied creative drama, wrote:

> For three weeks now I have been working in a summer church school where I have had an opportunity to teach the Old Testament by means of creative dramatics. The results were gratifying, for though none of the children had ever had any of the work they seemed to grasp the idea of it very naturally. How they love what they call the "new way!" Heretofore the general attitude on the part of most of the children has been one of resentment because they had to come to school but after the first day I saw no signs of that. The change was amazing. They were even willing to stay in after school and at recess to work up their scene for the last day.
>
> If creative dramatics had *only* made them like their summer church school, that in itself was enough to warrant the use of the method, but I know that they have retained more factual material than they ever have before.

Because as yet little trained leadership is available among church-school teachers, courses in the creative method need to be put into religious education training, into refresher courses, and into leadership training courses. This will be absolutely necessary if it is to be done effectively. With all its potentialities, creative drama can only be successful if it is guided by good teachers. The first step is the realization of the *need* for it. When this realization is sufficiently strong, everything else will follow. At the present time there are a number of evidences of it among national religious education heads, and steps are being taken in several of the denominations to train leaders for this work.

THE PURPOSE OF PLAYMAKING
IN RELIGIOUS EDUCATION

Though the purposes of playmaking in religious education are the same as they are for this subject in general education[3] the emphasis is somewhat different. In the church school *spiritual values* are especially important, and due to the very limited church-school period, there is never time to use playmaking merely as a happy interlude. The implanting of values and attitudes must be more direct in Sunday School, even though moralizing itself is useless.

The *material* must not only be ethically sound, as it should always be, but it should have real significance for living. It need not be made up of Bible stories exclusively, though they are most often the material since one of the purposes of the church school is to teach the Bible. As it is, a large proportion of both children and adults are almost illiterate as far as the Bible stories are concerned.

The late great Dr. Richard Moulton of the University of Chicago used to say to his students, "No one can consider himself educated unless he knows the two great sources of our culture: the Greco-Roman on the one hand and the Hebrew on the other." Regardless of religious value, the Bible should be known as literature by every educated person.

[3] See Chapter 1.

THE NEW TESTAMENT

Mainly, in Christian church schools, the child is taught that the life of Jesus is the most creative and stimulating that has been lived. How can it be made real, meaningful, and natural to boys and girls? If it seems mystical to them, and full of supernatural actions, if Jesus is so elevated that he appears not to be a real person at all, then he will have little influence on the modern child. Our problem is to choose stories that show the warm, human qualities of Jesus, qualities identifiable with the finest in our own lives. This is not easy because the stories are 1900 years old; yet the qualities are universal and we can find many of them in the lives of people we know.

Immediately the question arises, "Shall we have Jesus as a character in our dramatizations?" There are people who think no one should personify Jesus. These people, then, would dramatize no story in which Jesus appears. At once this eliminates a good deal of the New Testament as material for creative drama.

Many others believe that such an attitude on the part of teachers gives children the feeling that Jesus is the same as God himself. Such teachers fail to realize that Jesus came to earth as a human being—a man who mingled with men. They throw away a great opportunity to help boys and girls when they so elevate him that they represent his presence only by a light—as has been done occasionally in pageants. If, instead, a teacher prepares children for the experience of having Jesus as the central figure in a creative play, making it a high privilege to play this part, the whole group grows in reverence and in the feeling that Jesus was a real person.

Take the story of Zacchaeus, the little tax collector who had to climb a tree to see Jesus. It is a wonderfully good story to dramatize for several reasons. In the first place it gives children a fine opportunity to get vicarious life experience by being a part of the crowd that gathered in Jericho to see Jesus and his disciples pass by on their way to Jerusalem. There is real suspense in the expectancy with which they wait to see this controversial figure about whom they have heard so much. It is built to a high pitch when a boy comes running to tell of the healing of the blind Bartimaeus just outside the city gates (an incident suggested by a group playing the story), and the frantic anxiety of Zacchaeus as the people refuse to let him through to any place where he can see. There is the dramatic moment when Jesus stops and speaks to Zacchaeus in the tree, a strong reaction on the part of the people who resent the fact that Jesus has chosen a hated tax collector to be his host; and finally, after they have followed Jesus and Zacchaeus home, the unexpected climax as Zacchaeus declares his purpose and Jesus makes very clear his reason for choosing this man.

Few short stories in the Bible gain so much by dramatization. From the beginning, when the crowd begins to gather, it is a live and exciting situation. News that Jesus is nearing Jericho on his way to Jerusalem for the Passover brings out people from every walk of life. There are the mothers who hope that the Master will bless the little children they have brought early to the roadside; the curious folk who want to see the teacher about whom everyone is talking, some Pharisees and scribes, perhaps, and young lawyers, who would like to find reason for an accusation against him; the inevitable beggars, the lame, and the sick; maybe an innkeeper who hopes to entertain this wonder-working guest; housewives who would be honored if they might be the chosen ones; and one or two Roman officers to see that the crowd is orderly.

Reactions not only to Jesus and his disciples, but to one another and to Zacchaeus are motivated if each player has a strong feeling of his character as a real person—has even thought of a life history for him or her. If he feels that he *is* this character, he will know how he must feel toward Jesus, what his reaction will be when Jesus chooses Zacchaeus, and finally, what he thinks when he hears the tax collector declare, "Behold, Lord, the half of my goods I give to the poor; and if I have defrauded any one of anything, I restore it fourfold," and Jesus' reply, "This day is God's love come to this house. For the Son of Man came to seek and to save the lost."

When a group of teachers played this story with some children watching, a young woman who (in the playing of the preliminary crowd scene) was the boy who ran in to tell about Bartimaeus had such a light in her face that she was unanimously chosen to be honored by the part of Jesus in the scene which followed. She played it with deep feeling but, hesitant about saying anything that was not in the Bible, she responded only in pantomime to the mothers who besought Jesus to bless their children.

In the evaluation period which followed, the children who had been watching said, "Why didn't Jesus talk to them? It didn't seem right for him not to answer." This appears to be typical of the way children naturally feel about Jesus. A sixth-grade class that dramatized the incident, while regarding it as a privilege to be chosen for the part, had no feeling that it would be irreverent to speak as they thought Jesus would speak in this situation.

The attitude toward playmaking depends entirely on the teacher. Unless she can build a fine respect for the whole procedure in *any* kind of dramatization, she should not attempt it at all, for there must not be a cheapening of any character or story used in this way. On the contrary, dramatization should make fine stories unforgettable, and great ideas deeply impressive.

*Dramatic Play of Little Children
in Church School*

Most of the ideas back of the dramatic play into which kindergarten children are guided come from the New Testament. They play few if any of the actual Bible stories unless it happens that they are in a group with older children. But the idea of God as a loving father can be planted in a number of ways through dramatic play.

"What is love? Does anybody have any ideas about where love comes from?" This is a point of departure for some teachers of little children. "And then," one teacher[4] says, "from tiny episodes that show love . . . mother covering the baby at night or comforting us when we are sick or hurt . . . daddy mending our toys . . . a mother bird feeding her babies (that's lots of fun, too, and sometimes the babies are very chirpy!) . . . a mother cat carefully putting her kittens in a box or on a blanket in a snug corner . . . all such things are signs of love. Then what if a kitten is naughty and runs off? Is the mother cat angry? Yes, for a minute, and then she goes right on loving it and caring for it, doesn't she?

"After we have explored love as we can see it and know it," this teacher says, "we explore ways that God shows his love to us. So I have worked a little with the growth of flowers in the spring—the sunshine—the rain—the flight of birds according to the seasons—in other words, the basic and fine and everlasting things that stand for security and love."

Children enjoy being snowflakes dancing down upon the little seeds asleep under the ground; then being the spring showers and the sun and the warm breezes enticing the flowers to come up. And especially do they enjoy being the flowers

[4] Constance Bard Wyman, Oklahoma City.

waking from their long sleep and growing up to be a part of the beautiful garden.

In order to acquaint young children with boys and girls of other lands, one can sometimes bring some material thing from the Bible countries—a water-jug, a veil, a coin, a scroll, a basket —and create very simple situations about them. If the teacher is imaginative and has a good background in the life of peoples of such countries, she might make up very simple stories to play. Or she might find them in church-school lesson books in connection with missions.

Pictures of places and customs of Bible times may suggest that they play such things as sheep and lambs coming into the sheepfold at night and being counted, examined, and comforted by the Shepherd. Sometimes one of the lambs gets his foot caught in a crevice, and when the Shepherd (the teacher) calls them, all come except this one. The Shepherd misses him and calls him by name over and over again. Finally he hears a faint bleating and goes to find him. As they return, the Shepherd carrying the little lamb, all the other sheep are so glad that they gambol with joy.

A little later they can get meaning from the parable of the Good Samaritan, but since this is one of the very best of stories for dramatization, it would seem a pity to use it before children are able to appreciate its real significance. Because some of the Bible stories are so fine that almost every age can get something out of them, it is a temptation to use them over and over again, so that as children grow to the age when they can really understand them, the stories have lost the freshness of their appeal. The children may feel like the girl about to enter the eighth grade in the public school who said, "I *hope* we won't study American history this year! I've heard it hashed and rehashed so many times that I'm sick of it!" It is true that children enjoy hearing loved stories again and again, but not, usually, at various age levels.

New Testament Stories for Older Children

Besides The Good Samaritan and Zacchaeus, which have been mentioned, some of the other stories usable for play-making are: parables such as The Forgiving Father (suggesting the interpretation of the Prodigal Son), The Talents, The Lost Coin, The Rich Young Ruler, The Wise and Foolish Virgins, and others, remembering, however, that the ones in which the meaning is direct rather than symbolical (as The Good Samaritan and the Prodigal Son) are better than the ones in which the meaning has to be explained.

The Nativity story of course is used for all ages and combinations of ages. Sometimes the story of the angels and the shepherds is played separately, the teacher reading to the children the vivid account of this scene in the novel Ben-Hur, as well as the economically told story in St. Luke.

Imagination must be used to amplify any incident of Jesus' boyhood, but such stories may sometimes be found in the children's lesson books. They are based on life at that time and are rarely good material for drama, though with intelligent guidance it is possible to use such episodes as the one in which Jesus went with his parents to the Feast of the Passover. The anxiety of Mary and Joseph when he is missed, their inquiries of various people, their arrival back in Jerusalem, and the discovery of Jesus in the temple listening to the scholars, could be built into an ambitious dramatization.

Some later stories of Jesus can also furnish very good material. The incident of the lame man at the pool of Bethesda and the one in which four men tore up a roof to let their sick friend down to be healed, as discussed in Jeanette Brown's book, offer not only impressive lessons of faith but material for good drama for the fourth grade and up.

The Bartimaeus incident (merely described in the Zacchaeus dramatization) could stand alone as a dramatization and so could the story of the man with the withered arm. Several of the well-told stories in Elizabeth Yates' *Children of the Bible*[5] have good possibilities for creative plays, notably the one about the boy with the loaves and fishes.

THE OLD TESTAMENT

Some excellent material for dramatic use may be found in the Old Testament, in spite of the fact that there is so much which is utterly unsuitable for present-day children either in subject matter or in moral standards. In choosing Old Testament stories to dramatize, one should make sure that they have real significance for our children. For instance, though the story of Abraham's preparation to sacrifice Isaac had justification at the time that they lived, it would be not only difficult but useless to emphasize by dramatization Abraham's belief that God, whom our young people have been taught to regard as kind and loving, wanted him to sacrifice his little son. It is a dramatic story, but that alone is not enough to warrant its use in this way.

On the other hand, the part of Abraham's story where his people and Lot's quarrel over the land is entirely understandable. In Ethel Smither's excellent version of this story in *Early Old Testament Stories*,[6] the quarrel begins among the women drawing water at the well. The men take it up, each side saying that the women of the other side are interfering with theirs. When Abraham is told about this and the strife among the herdsmen, he goes to Lot's tent and says, "Let there be no strife

[5] (Aladdin Books, 1950).
[6] (Abingdon Press, 1954).

between you and me." And he gives Lot his choice of the land, which shall thereafter belong to his people. That Lot chooses the fertile valley of the Jordan instead of the rocky wilderness brings no resentment from Abraham, who is content that the strife is ended and Lot is satisfied. A story like this, exemplifying not only the saying, "A soft answer turneth away wrath," but also showing a man who is above all pettiness, puts vividly before a young person a fine pattern of behavior—one that is entirely comprehensible to children of the fourth grade and older.

In the whole Bible, though, there is no other story so good for a creative play as the story of Joseph. Whether dramatized in parts or as a complete play, it has all the elements for rich and fascinating drama. It is full of varied action, of interesting characters, of suspense, and of meaning that children of the fifth grade and older can turn to such good account that it is a pity to use it for younger children who get so much less from it. *Early Old Testament Stories* has excellent versions of both the Joseph and Moses stories.

Other Bible story books often have good versions of some of the Moses stories also. One is the account, so often used, of the baby Moses found by Pharaoh's daughter, which in some versions is told from the viewpoint of the sister who watches over him. "The Little Girl Who Could Be Trusted" builds up her part in the story in such a way as to give it more meaning than does the straight account of what happened. And since one has to use imagination in any case, there is no reason why Miriam should not be the heroine of this episode in Moses' life.

Another little girl who is the center of a playable tale is the captive maid in the household of Naaman, commander of the king's armies. The child, having heard that there is a prophet in Samaria (Elisha) who can heal the sick, tells her mistress that if Naaman will only go to him she is sure he can be healed of the dread leprosy with which he is afflicted. This story is less simple to work out than the Moses episode, but it could be done effectively.

But second only to the Joseph story in potentialities for playing is that of David. From the time he is brought to Saul to play for him, there are episodes which children are interested in dramatizing. A record of suitable harp music is sometimes used to represent David's playing as well as to set the mood for the palace scene. Though the slaying of Goliath may be less to the liking of the teacher, it will be popular with the boys, and will perhaps have meaning if David's faith that God will help him is stressed.

The cave incident worked out simply by the third grade could be developed further by the fourth-, fifth-, or sixth-graders; and a wonderfully good scene which should certainly be played by the older children is that in which David sends for Jonathan's lame son after Jonathan is dead and David has become king. With a little imagination it can be developed into a very dramatic scene. Mephibosheth does not know why David has sent for him, and realizing the vengeance which may fall on him, the only surviving kinsman of Saul, he is very fearful. Even the palace servants may speculate as to what David may do to him, so that considerable suspense is built up by the time' Mephibosheth is announced.

David, however, soon dispels the fear of Jonathan's son, telling him that all of Saul's lands are to be returned to him, and from this day he is to live in the palace and eat at the king's own table. David's generous attitude toward Mephibosheth is one of the fine aspects we like to stress in a life that had serious faults but some very fine qualities.

Psalm 24 is thought to have been occasioned by David's bringing the Ark of the Covenant to Jerusalem. Elizabeth

Colson[7] has written an exciting story for children describing the splendid procession in which it was carried up to the tent near David's palace. According to her account, the exaltation of the people who brought it and those who greeted it could easily have caused them to burst forth into the thrilling psalm,

> Lift up your heads, O ye gates!
> And be ye lifted up, ye everlasting doors,
> And the King of glory will come in!

The 150th Psalm especially lends itself to reading with the accompaniment of dance, harp, pipe, and clashing cymbals, as it reaches its triumphant climax,

> Let everything that breathes praise the Lord!

WORSHIP SERVICES

There are many unexplored possibilities for worship services which will give young people a truer worship experience than they now get. Rituals which once had significance often become routine, so that they leave one entirely unmoved. Occasionally, at least, young people need to have a dramatic service of worship—one that will shake them out of their complacency and make them really *feel* the experience.

These are most valuable when they are creative—when they are originated by the young people themselves with the guidance of an adult. Grace McGavran[8] has written a little book called *We Gather Together* which tells about worship services all over the world—some of which are the same as those we know, many of which are different. After hearing about them, the children could very well work out as creative projects some of those which made the strongest appeal to them. If they were

[7] *A Second Primary Book in Religion* (Abingdon Press).
[8] (Friendship Press, 1951).

effective they could later be used as real worship services which included other classes.

The meaning of *praise*, of *thanksgiving*, of *offering*, of *penitence*, beginning with the children's ideas about them, and developing with the guidance of a skilled leader, into dramatic interpretations, has decided potentialities for worship services. So have such projects as are described in Hulda Niebuhr's fine book *Ventures in Dramatics*.[9]

MATERIAL OTHER THAN BIBLE STORIES

There are occasional ethical stories of great charm and significance which can be used in the various phases of religious education. Sophia Fahs' *From Long Ago and Many Lands* contains several; others are Raymond McDonald Alden's "Why the Chimes Rang," "The Boy Who Found the King," "The Palace Made by Music"; Ruth Sawyer's "The Christmas Apple"; the old legend of "Our Lady's Juggler"; Victor Hugo's "The Bishop's Candlesticks," from *Les Miserables*; *In Clean Hay*, by Eric Kelly; and *Amahl and the Night Visitors*, by Gian Menotti.

An exceptionally usable little story from *The Storyteller in Religious Education* is "Nathan's Friend," which has so strong a significance for today that it should be used often for dramatization. It concerns a boy, Nathan, who lives in north Judea and has heard so many abusive things said about the Samaritans that he thinks they must be monsters. He wishes he could have just one look at them; and since there are only a few hills between his home and Samaria, he ventures to climb over them one day. What he sees is a boy like himself chasing his runaway donkey and, without realizing he is a Samaritan, he joins in the chase, eats lunch with the boy, and only by accident do the two boys discover that each belongs to the country hated by the

[9] (Charles Scribner's Sons, 1935).

other. It is not a new idea, of course, but the tale has charm and a feeling of reality. A preliminary scene can show the citizens of Judea ascribing everything that goes wrong to the Samaritans. Two other stories in this little volume have dramatic possibilities, namely, "Thank Offerings" and "The Legend of the Black Madonna."

Not only stories from literature, but incidents from the lives of people they know or have read about are being used in some church-school classes as live material for dramatizations. Meanings of Bible verses and character traits of people in their lessons are brought alive by likening them to people and happenings today. Sometimes the modern counterparts of the old stories are discussed, sometimes dramatized. In this way Bible people are made to seem real rather than a remote and elevated race.

THE LEADER'S BACKGROUND

The ideal person to guide children in religious drama is the regular church-school teacher, not the specialist. Because the regular teacher knows the children and can judge when the time is right for creative drama, he or she is best suited to lead them in this aspect of their religious education. Many of the stories they study, while understandable, are too difficult for them to play, and others are not essentially dramatic. More often than not there will be just some dramatic bit in the middle of a lesson for which the mood is exactly right. A teacher who is sensitive to this can lead into a dramatization without any introduction, and though the children may be caught unaware the first time, they will enter into it without any surprise the second time she does it.

For example, they might be studying the story about the men who let down their palsied friend through the roof to be cured. As they are reading the story from the Bible, she might say,

"Suppose we are the people in that room, listening to Jesus, when all of a sudden we hear a noise above us. Look, men! What is happening?" If the children do not think immediately of how to respond, she may need to say a little more. But if the children have done anything at all in creative drama, she can soon have them re-creating the scene and reacting to the healing of the sick man.

The feeling for doing this and the training which is necessary are the two factors that most often stand in the way (granted that the situation allows time for it). The third factor is the need for a rich background in the historical and cultural aspects of the Bible stories. Here the conscientious church-school teacher is more often well equipped; and this is a very important part of dramatization.

When one merely *tells* a story one can make it effective without knowing more than the story sets forth. But when it is to be dramatized, the leader immediately needs to know much more. In The Good Samaritan, for instance, it is not only important to know about the feeling between Jews and Samaritans but also about the rocky and dangerous road between Jerusalem and Jericho, the distance that the Jew had to travel, the way that people *usually* traveled to avoid danger, as well as various other customs which enter into the playing of the story. If a leader is not informed about such things the dramatization will be barren indeed.

The teacher who would guide children in such story-plays needs to do a good deal of research. For the more children know about life in the time and place of the story, the more real their play will be to them. Pictures help greatly, as well as information about the way people lived, how they were governed, what they felt about various things.

Such books as the beautifully illustrated *Bible Days* by

Meindert DeJong,[10] and *A Picture Book of Palestine* by Ethel L. Smither[11] will prove of great help to both teacher and pupils for the geography, customs, and dress of Bible lands. Florence Mary Fitch's *One God,*[12] with wonderful photographs and descriptions of the ways God is worshiped by Catholic, Protestant, and Jew, and the companion volume *Their Search for God,*[12] showing the ways of worship in the Orient, are a fine contribution for the use of Bible stories. Many other valuable books are available in good libraries: encyclopedias and commentaries on Bible life, concordances, and books on how the early Hebrews lived and learned.

NUMBER OF PROJECTS

Lest it be thought from the number of ideas, stories, and references which have been given that playmaking is suggested as something which is to be used continually, it should be said that no such impression is intended. There are many ways for a child to learn; through drama he can learn much. But it should be used sparingly with any one class. A large project such as the dramatization of the Joseph or the David story by an older group, or two or three smaller creative drama projects for the younger classes are quite enough for a year.

Costumes and properties are not necessary in these creative plays. In fact, they are more likely to be a detriment, absorbing far too much time and attention. They always indicate, too, that the play is to be presented for some other group, and sometimes this defeats its purpose.

Occasionally, the boys and girls who have developed a creative play to the point where it is especially well done (*and*

[10] (The Fideler Co., Grand Rapids, Michigan, 1948).
[11] (Abingdon Press, 1947).
[12] (Lothrop, Lee & Shephard Co., 1944, 1947).

this never happens in one or two periods) want to play it for a younger class. It may be a good plan to do so, for it will mean something to the children in the audience. But even then, very few properties and perhaps a suggestion of headdresses are enough to lift the play out of ordinary "every day." The chief danger of allowing children to give it as a "performance" is that it is very likely to build in their minds the idea that this is the sole reason for creating plays.

Playmaking should always be a delightful experience. It should never be engaged in unless the children wish it, nor should it ever be considered a routine activity. Boys and girls who do not care to participate should not be urged to do so. If the majority wish to dramatize a story, let any who do not choose to play be given some painting or other handwork. Very often they will come in the second time if they see others enjoying it.

Somehow leaders in religious education must find better ways to make church schools reach into the hearts of boys and girls. Somehow its teachings must get over into their lives. If these leaders come to believe that drama is one of the ways to bring this to pass, they can without question overcome all the obstacles and make it a valued part of the church-school program.

CHAPTER 11

Creative Dramatics in Recreation

A VILLAGE THAT LEARNED TO DANCE WHEN A HURDY-GURDY man played a magic tune changed of a sudden from a town of solemn-faced people who liked no one who was different from themselves to a friendly community that celebrated its surprising transformation with a jolly town picnic.[1]

When people can laugh together—as these townsfolk did in Margery Bianco's story when they found themselves dancing in spite of themselves—they can get along with one another. For a sense of humor, especially if it enables them to laugh at themselves, helps to make people better parents and teachers.

Children who grow up in a town that is friendly, that recognizes and provides for the need of wholesome recreation for boys and girls—in which parents enter into some of the youth activities themselves—such children are very unlikely to become juvenile delinquents. Rather, they grow up with affection and loyalty for their home town.

Play is voluntary, it is refreshing. It re-creates us. Whether at home, on a playground, in camp, or in a theatre, it means doing things we enjoy.

---

[1] "The Hurdy-Gurdy Man." See Story List in the Appendix for all stories mentioned in this chapter.

213

"What do children enjoy?" asks Grace Stanistreet, in the magazine *Recreation*.[2] "They enjoy projecting themselves beyond themselves and in so doing they grow. They paint, they act, they sing, they dance. They need to do these things. Without opportunity and encouragement they stop doing them. Many adults know the hurt of not being able to satisfy needs similar to these."

CREATIVE DRAMATICS ON PLAYGROUNDS

Creative dramatics is one of the most rewarding activities on playgrounds. It requires no equipment, its extemporaneous nature fits beautifully the out-of-doors, it is easy to carry on in the changing population characteristic of recreation centers. If young people are rehearsing a memorized play and someone in the cast suddenly goes on a vacation with his family, not only the rehearsals but the morale of the group suffers. But if a child has played the little daughter of King Midas today in a creative drama group and is missing tomorrow it makes no difference, for other children should have their turn anyhow.

All playmaking is recreational, but the sheer enjoyment of the activity needs to be higher on playgrounds than in schools. Study and research go into classroom plays, requiring no small amount of effort. Playground dramatizations should not entail real work except as the children's absorption leads them to work intensively. Always the activity itself should be the most important thing rather than the product in the form of a play.

General participation, with parts for everybody, is one of the assets of informal playmaking. If the group is large and varied in age, it is advisable to divide it into two or more groups. When little children play with older ones, they invariably get the small parts. Furthermore, stories that are right for the six-year-

---

[2] "The Case for Creative Arts in Recreation," *Recreation*, March, 1955.

old are too young for the child of ten. If there is but one leader, the older groups sometimes watch the younger and play afterwards, or come at a different hour altogether.

Dramatic Play of the Younger Children

The excursions on which the younger children are taken very often inspire dramatic play for days afterwards. A trip to the beach on one day motivates imaginary trips in which they pack lunch baskets, ride in the bus carrying pails and shovels, make wonderful houses in the sand, wade, swim—in fact, re-enact all the features of the trip they have most enjoyed. Or they may be invited to see a play, in which case they act out their favorite scenes the next day.

Annis Duff, in a delightful article in the Horn Book[3] called "Life in a Looking-Glass," tells of her little daughter's introduction to a real live play. She had seen several puppet shows but one morning her kindergarten class was invited into the auditorium to see a high school group play scenes from A Midsummer Night's Dream. The stage, which she had known only as a place where people stood to conduct music, became a moonlit forest glade where fairies were visible to the naked eye, and a palace room where lords and ladies, gloriously appareled, celebrated a wedding by seeing a play. "With magic in her eyes," she writes, "our daughter reported not only these wonders but another fabulous fact. 'And guess what! There were real, life-size people in the play!' Her theatre had begun to grow up and she with it."

Later in the article she says, . . . "there is a compelling excitement in the coming alive of all sorts of wonders on a stage. And for youngsters whose minds are hospitable to magic, it is a never-to-be-forgotten thrill."

So it is when little children from a playground see their first

[3] February, 1954.

play. And now that children's theatres are so widespread over the country, many thousands of children are having this experience. With imagination quickened and feelings stirred, children should always have the chance to play out what they have seen and enjoyed.

On those few memorable occasions when the children are lucky enough to be taken to the circus, there is no end to their continued enjoyment of it. The wonderful band, the horses galloping around the rings, the tight-rope walkers, the acrobats, the trained dogs, the elephants, the clowns—yes, and the barkers outside the tents, the cotton-candy makers, the pink lemonade stand, and all the other things that make the experience memorable! It is too wonderful to be over in one short afternoon. With the band records of the Barnum and Bailey circus readily obtainable, the feeling of the show is created all over again and the children's sense impressions are sharpened as they play all the fabulous characters they so enjoyed. It is sad that this picturesque aspect of American life is disappearing, and that children of the future will never have the thrill of firsthand experience with a great circus.

Miss Anne Smith, director of the Community Clubs of Evanston, says that the children's total response in creative dramatics—the response of the whole body, the mind, and the emotions—makes them alive, interested, eager. The children who come to these clubs make stick puppets and masks to use for some of their dramatic play and story dramatizations. Only the lack of enough trained leaders—volunteers who can guide the children regularly in these activities—keeps playmaking from being a still bigger part of their recreational program.

Nursery rhymes are alive and sparkling in their never-ending appeal for little children, and they are always useful on the playground. One can do all kinds of things with them: sing them, use them in choral speaking, play them.

The Leader Tells the Story

After a group of children have been playing an active game on a warm day, they welcome a quiet story hour. If the leader has an idea of guiding the children in dramatization, she will choose stories that make good plays. Not only will they be of acceptable quality, but they will be simple and full of action, with a dramatic climax and interesting characters.

Suppose she chose the charming little story "Ask Mr. Bear." A good time to use it would be on a day when some child's mother had a birthday; but as one cannot count on such a coincidence, the leader can set the mood without any real birthday. In fact, since birthdays are invariably interesting to children, she might not even introduce the story by talking about birthday gifts. After she had told about Danny's asking the various animals if they could give him something for his mother's birthday and found out the perfect gift from Mr. Bear, she might, even without assigning parts, take on the character of Danny herself and approach one and then another of the children, saying, "Good morning, Mrs. Hen—or Mrs. Goose or Mrs. Goat—can you give me something for my mother's birthday?" playing out the story with them very informally without even scattering to have different homes the first time. Later, it could be expanded to include a first scene and characteristic actions and conversations of both animals and human beings.

"The Tale of Peter Rabbit" is another good outdoor play which children love. So are "The Old Market Woman," "Taper Tom," and "The Shepherd Boy and the Wolf." Any one of these would be a good choice for young children on a playground.

A leader needs to be resourceful in both materials and ways of presenting them. She may find that the mood is entirely wrong for the story she had expected to use. When she sees the group she may realize that it is too young or too old, too naïve or too sophisticated, too quiet or too robust. Something in the town or perhaps even on the playground may have occurred to excite the children, and it is very likely that no story is right. If the fire engines have just whizzed by (and she has any children left!) it may be that nothing except playing fire will hold their interest at the moment.

Certainly she should always have in her mind a store of ideas for dramatic play such as are suggested in Chapters 2 and 3. She can use also many of the situations for deepening sense impressions. Activity pantomimes are usually quite successful, as well as variations of charades. She needs always to capitalize on the feeling of her group at the time she presents her material.

Play Festivals for Older Children

As long as possible it is well to use dramatizations rather than memorized plays. Unless an older group is working on a formal play for production, with exactly the right number of characters, some of the children will be left out entirely or have to sit around waiting to rehearse their very small parts. There are few good short plays for children, especially non-royalty plays. If the older boys and girls think the term "creative dramatics" sounds childish it can be called "improvisation" or just "dramatics." Stories and situations must always be carefully chosen so that they will never seem remotely like "baby stuff." They may be as simple as the old favorite "The Stone in the Road," but the subject-matter must not be childish. Such outdoor tales as "The Wise People of Gotham," "The Hurdy-Gurdy Man," *Tom Sawyer, Robin Hood,* have fine possibilities for children of nine, ten, and eleven. And Chapter 4 offers many suggestions for good situations to play.

Some recreation departments end their season in dramatics with play festivals to which each playground contributes a creative play, usually with the simplest of costumes and properties. Someone in the community who knows the field, if such a person can be found, judges the quality of the dramatizations and then meets the leaders afterwards to evaluate their work. This recent practice is far better than the public awarding of prizes. Even if there is merely a recognition of first, second, and third place, it causes much of the interest in the project to be in the competition rather than in the experience of creating the play. The festival idea which is just bringing together the best products of all the centers, is far better than competition, which should be used only for activities which have less intrinsic interest. The quality of this work improves from year to year by each leader's seeing the others' productions. And the value is heightened greatly if a qualified person analyzes the dramatizations afterwards for the leaders.

CAMP PROGRAMS

"Potentially the most valuable of the arts in a camp program is drama, for not only may it integrate and focus all the other arts, but its basic stuff is the give and take of social living." [4]

Camps are an ideal setting for playmaking. Children are here because they have chosen to come. There is a spirit of friendliness and fun, of relaxation and confidence. Each child is encouraged to make his contribution to the life of the camp. He is less afraid of being inadequate than he is in school because the recreational value of dramatics is stressed above the educational, and standards are no higher than he can comfortably reach.

Betty Lyle (in a pamphlet *Camping, What Is It?*) [5] writes that

[4] George New, *Camping Magazine*, October, 1952.
[5] (American Camping Association, 1947).

camping provides a very personal, fun-filled group-living experience in, or near, the out-of-doors. Camping is not hemmed in by a formalized, traditional curriculum. Its activities need not be rigidly scheduled. Whatever else it is—therapy, social adjustment, educational growth—it must be fun for the campers. The conditions of camping provide ideal opportunities for playmaking.

Camping makes use of three related disciplines, those of recreation (with emphasis on activities which provide wholesome fun and satisfaction), those of social group work (here an emphasis on personal development and social growth), and creative education (with an emphasis on the expression and higher integration of self). The dramatic counselor will need not only to have skill in creating plays but some understanding of these different disciplines. A good book on the practice of group work is *Social Group Work Practice: The Creative Use of the Social Process*, by Gertrude Wilson and Gladys Ryland.[6] There is a detailed chapter on storytelling and dramatics.

Role of the Dramatic Counselor

The leader in dramatics should be a trained person, understanding not only his own field of drama with children but also the goals of group work in camping. He or she must remember that the play is a means, not an end, but that it should never be carelessly done. Because the leader helps the campers to make use of their own latent resources, to give form and substance to their feelings and ideas, the plays developed in camp can be beautifully rewarding and satisfying to the participants.

In many camps the dramatic counselor is the only person who does anything at all with dramatics. In others, he is a skilled resource person who works partly through the cabin counselors. When this is the case, the camp may have a pre-

---

[6] (Houghton Mifflin Co., 1949).

camp training program for four or five days before the campers
arrive. During the camping season these counselors guide the
children in their cabin in minor dramatic experiences, the
dramatic counselor observing the activities, discussing them
with the cabin counselors, and conducting all the major activities.

Whether the dramatic leader works directly or indirectly
with the campers, he must be prepared with much material
and many ideas. He must see that the best books of stories and
plays are in the camp library, and if the cabin counselors are
to do any of the work, he should supply the library with texts
on the subject of creative dramatics. He should tentatively have
chosen much more material than will be used, knowing that
the immediate interests of the campers will need to be taken
into consideration.

Imagination and resourcefulness are important qualifications
of a dramatic counselor, for he will need to respond to the
happenings in camp in whatever activities he initiates. He
needs to be alert in sensing and using the ideas of the campers
also, for the more he encourages them, the more creative thinking they will do. With his maturity and training, he may be
able to think of better things than they initiate, but if he is a
real counselor he will put their development above his sense
of showmanship. This is not to say that he should keep hands
off. Without stimulation, creative work, as Hughes Mearns
puts it, will remain on an infantile level. It is the dramatic
counselor's skillful questions, along with an occasional suggestion or illustration, that spur the campers to do things that are
distinctive.

When he is warm, friendly, flexible, permissive; when he
considers the individual child in setting standards, not trying
to force the slow child to a faster pace than he can comfortably

maintain, but expecting all to do the best of which they are capable, he will be a strong influence in developing the personalities of the children.

Material rewards for achievement in dramatics are not good. They cause tension and anxiety and disappointment to those who do not win. Actual accomplishment, contributing to the inner feelings of goodness, worth, satisfaction, are far better rewards. This attitude should be developed so far as possible by the counselors.

It is revealing to read some comments of the campers concerning dramatics from a tape-recorded discussion:

PAULA (age 10): I learned about making puppets, about folk dancing. I learned from the story about this part of the country. I would like to find out more about it. I'll go to the library in the city. I learned how to work puppets. Putting on the play helped us to get along with each other.

EVA (age 9): Esther was a good person to help. She knew the most about puppets. Making up a play was more fun than a written play. Esther took her time when she worked with us. She didn't tell us too much. We could think about things ourselves. She let us put in our own ideas.

A group of adolescent boys and girls discussing a play they had done:

JOE (age 15): We wrote down the scenes we needed and what happened. We didn't write down the lines. I think it's better to say your own words. The author knows the characteristics of all these people and how they would say it, but when you act it's more the way you would say it—how you would speak and talk it. It's the way you imagine it, and that makes it more real.

LOUISE (age 14): We learned most from just having fun. I mean that we learned more about the Huguenots (this play was about a colony of French Huguenots who had settled near the camp) than if we had just read it from a book or if the teacher had just told us what happened. I will always remember it. I know a lot more about it and I feel good. It helped that the counselors weren't way above us—they were friendly. They helped us work on it, but they didn't do the whole thing for us. We did it.

JOE: That's the way it should be. Counselors shouldn't do things for kids. They should just suggest. They shouldn't push. Counselors should advise children, not boss them. They should never get impatient. They should give encouragement. That's important. But it's not necessary for them to know everything. It's more interesting for the children when the counselors are also learning.

Aspects of Camp Dramatics

Charlotte Perry, of the Perry-Mansfield Camp,[7] in a talk at the 1954 American Camping Convention in New York City, made a strong point of stressing the recall of sense impressions as an important part of dramatic training.

In order to refresh sense impressions, she suggested that the group be asked occasionally to return to real experience. "Listen for a moment to the noises you hear right in this room. . . . Now seem to hear imaginary noises—a mouse gnawing, a step, a door creaking."

Sense memories can be strengthened by exercises in recalling not only one's own real experiences but many from literature —such as seeing Mary Poppins out the window being blown through the gate, banging against the house, sliding up the banisters, taking out of her empty carpet-bag such things as a starched white apron which she ties around her waist, a box of throat lozenges, a small folding armchair, seven flannel nightgowns, a postcard album, and a folding camp-bedstead with blankets and eiderdown complete; tasting the medicine she pours into the spoon—anticipated with distaste but actually delicious; hearing her brusque, "I'll stay till the wind changes!"

With regard to characterization, Miss Perry suggested that the leader recall the story of Thurber's "Thirteen Clocks." The clocks might be children rather than painted scenery. For

[7] Steamboat Springs, Colorado.

example, one child might act a Grandfather Clock, another an Alarm Clock, first establishing movement and rhythm, then saying a word or a sentence that the clock might say.

She made the point, not often stressed, of showing *intentions,* saying that an actor has to act what isn't written whether he is speaking or listening. She suggested as an example that the player use the line, "Oh, come in!" welcoming a person after first making him feel unwelcome.

All of these things can be carried out in camps, using various materials and developing the ideas further. The awareness of sense impressions, especially, is something that contributes much to the enjoyment of living, whether a person ever plays in a dramatization or not; and camp is an especially good place to cultivate such awareness.

Recapturing an Experience

The recall of sense impressions plays a big part in the following exercise used with older girls in a dramatic club at camp.[8] The leader had illustrated unity, variety, and climax, by using concrete examples and bits of pantomime. Then, "What we are going to try to do now is some acting. This will require real concentration. You have to try to *feel* it—changes of action, feeling of unity, variety, and climax—the thing that is most exciting. I am going to tell you what is happening as we go along. You are going to try to forget you are in this room, make this an individual pantomime where you really forget each other." Then he began playing softly a record of music which established a mood for the exercise and continued throughout the pantomime. With this background, he told them what happened, his voice responding to the changing feelings they would have, and allowing time for the various parts of the action. His words are from a tape-recording.

[8] Camp Poyntelle, Pennsylvania, George New, director.

This overnight hike begins in the morning—starting from your cabin. We feel happy and glad to be going. Each of us has a pack on our back. It is bright and sunny and we are walking through a meadow. Now we come to a hill and begin climbing up the hill. The hill gets steeper, the going gets harder. Now we are climbing up a cliff, walking over rocks and it is very slow. We have to reach up, use our arms to help pull us up to the top. We rest. Then we notice that straight out before us in the valley below is a beautiful view, and we can see far across the meadows, and away over in the distance is a peaceful river. We can see so many things—we feel so peaceful!

Then we realize we have a long way to go, so we pick up our pack again, put it on, and then start down the hill—a gradual trip down the hill on the other side—this is easy going. Then we come to a marsh and our feet sink in and we have to wade through this marshland, and it is muddy and sticky, and it sticks to our feet and it is slow going and our shoes almost come off, and it gets darker. Clouds are gathering in the sky. We wonder if we should have come, after all. Now the rain begins to come down and we are cold and our packs so heavy! We are so discouraged, but finally we get through the marsh—with a sigh—and again we have a rest — we try to shake off the rain, get the mud off our shoes, and maybe we feel like having a drink from our canteen. This is a pause to refresh us, but then the leader says, "Come on, girls, we have a long way to go, we have to get through the woods." There are stickers and thorns, it is slow going, we have to push, sometimes we have to crawl. Then we come to a brook. We don't know how to get across, whether to jump, or walk across.

Now we are on the other side and at last we can put down our packs; but there is no fire yet. Some of us have to begin getting food ready, some of us have to gather sticks for franks and marshmallows, some of us have to get firewood. Everyone has a job of some sort—lots of busy activity. Now we have the fire built. We gather around the fire. We are going to have franks on sticks; the fire is getting hot. Watch the franks so they don't burn—maybe yours does burn—then we get it done, now we eat and we think it is the most delicious frank we ever had—so good! There is a great big piece of ash in that frank, but that is just one of the annoyances of having a campfire. Then we are going to get some corn roasted. The corn is so nice and juicy; we have to peel off all the corn silks; we peel the husks up over the corn and then we carefully put the corn in the hot ashes—don't burn yourself—the stick will help you get it all covered—don't burn yourself!

Now it is going to take a while for the corn to get done and we want something else, so we take the stick we had for the franks and we find a marshmallow and we are going to roast the marshmallow —be careful, they will catch fire—now we eat it and it tastes so good! We think it is such fun being here having these marshmallows and franks. In just a moment the corn is going to be done—but it looks black—it seems disappointing—gingerly we pull back the husks and there it is—put some butter on it and some salt and never mind if our hands do get sticky as it drips down—let's eat it right off, every bit of it—it is so succulent, so fresh from the garden—the best corn we ever had! It is so good—so good—so good! We throw the ears in the fire, our hands are sticky, we wipe them off. The counselor produces a surprise—a big basket of fruit, and gives each one an apple, a banana, an orange, or a pear, and now slowly we enjoy this fruit. Each one finds that her fruit is just right.

The fire is kind of going down now and we are so comfortable and feel so relaxed we pull up our blankets. We look up through the branches at the sky—it is late afternoon; the sun is just beginning to sink, we feel so happy to be out here with our friends. Our hike has been a success—pull the blankets over us—the first star, and there is the moon. Then we hear a strange sound—something such as we never heard before—listen—what can it be?—it is something out there in the dark, in the woods—we don't know what it is—we know something is happening—we get more excited —we are frightened—and then we see what it is—it is a mother deer and her little fawn and they are going down to the stream to have a drink of water. We watch them—they don't know we are watching them—they are having a drink. We watch them and then they go away and we understand they won't harm us—they are peaceful and comfortable just as we are, so we stretch out and again back to sleep—we get so quiet, so comfortable, so happy, and finally each one of us is dreaming a happy dream.

When the pantomime was finished, the leader was able to

tell them sincerely how real they had made it. One of the girls said, "The music helped a lot. It was much easier with the music."

"And we have had the real experience of an overnight hike," added another. "And even though this wasn't just like it, it did help me remember what I did and how I felt."

The group then discussed the points they had learned before the pantomime, and told what to them gave it unity and variety. The climax was not the same for every girl, some saying they had the strongest feeling when they were climbing the mountain, some when they were frightened at the noise in the night, and still others thought the high moment was when they reached the place where they were to camp.

Story Material for Camps

Whether for regular, eight-week camps or for shorter Scout or Campfire camps, the best material has an outdoor feeling. "The Elf and the Dormouse," "Fancy Dress," "The Three Bears," "Three Billy Goats Gruff," "Three Little Pigs," "Little Black Sambo," "Ask Mr. Bear," "The Little Pink Rose," "Peter Rabbit," "Why the Evergreen Tree Keeps Its Leaves in Winter," "The Rabbit Who Wanted Red Wings," "Little Duckling Tries His Voice," are some of the best for the youngest children.

"How the Robin's Breast Became Red," "A Legend of Spring," "Hansel and Gretel," "A Goblinade," "The Elf Singing," "The Old Market Woman," "The Peddler and His Caps," "Roads," "The Shepherd Boy and the Wolf," "Taper Tom," "How the Camel Got His Hump," "The Unhappy Echo," "Andy and the Lion," "The Magic Bed-Knob," "The Lion, the Witch, and the Wardrobe," are favorites for boys and girls a little older.

For children of ten and eleven "Johnny Appleseed," "The

Hurdy-Gurdy Man," "The Conjure Wives," "The Stone in
the Road," "The Wise People of Gotham," "Tom Sawyer,"
"Stone Soup"—and most especially "Robin Hood"—are among
the best.

Children older than this like: "The Old Woman and the
Tramp," "The Quest of the Hammer," "Ali Baba and the
Forty Thieves," "To Your Good Health," "Rip Van Winkle,"
Tree of Freedom, and perhaps even some Shakespeare stories
—*A Midsummer Night's Dream, As You Like It, The Taming
of the Shrew.*

Sunday Afternoon Programs

The Sunday afternoon program at some of the camps requires
careful selection of material. At Camp Holiday,[9] of which
Mary ("Kim") Farnum is director, they have used such stories
as Oscar Wilde's "The Young King," "The Happy Prince,"
and "The Selfish Giant," and Van Dyke's "The Story of
the Other Wise Man," and "The Lost Word." A narrator tells
or reads the story, with a cast to play the more dramatic incidents. Such presentations, even with few rehearsals and the
simplest of productions, can be beautiful and impressive if
the narrator reads or speaks extremely well.

Other fine stories that could be used for such a Sunday after-
noon program are "The Boy Who Found the King," "The
Rabbi and the Diadem," *The Boy Knight of Reims,* "Our
Lady's Juggler," "The Bishop's Candlesticks," and "Where
Love Is, There God Is Also."

Some Bible stories which can be very effective when played
in this way—and often the details have to be added for dramatization—are "Pharaoh's Daughter Finds Little Moses," the
story of Joseph, certain stories of David (see Chapter 10),
"Zacchaeus," "The Good Samaritan," "The Prodigal Son,"

---

[9] Hackensack, Minnesota.

"The Talents," and "The Lost Coin." Sometimes the *idea* of a parable is used, the parable being read from the Bible but the play being a scene from modern life.

Though dramatics, as a rule, is not a major activity in camp—the swimming, canoeing, riding, and other sports being naturally of highest importance as camp activities—yet with a capable dramatic counselor, it can play a significant part in realizing the objectives sought by every camp: creative education, social growth, and recreation. Certainly, with all its other values to the boy or girl at camp, it has wonderful power in providing wholesome fun.

CHAPTER 12

Therapy in Playmaking

WHOEVER HAS READ MARGUERITE DE ANGELI'S STORY *The
Door in the Wall* [1] will long remember Brother Luke's reply
when Robin asks him if he thinks his paralyzed legs will ever
straighten:

"I know not what to think about that," said Brother Luke gently.
"God alone knows whether thou'lt straighten or no. But this I tell
thee. A fine and beautiful life lies before thee because thou hast a
lively mind and a good wit. Thine arms are very strong and sturdy.
Swimming hath helped to make them so, but only because thou hast
had the will to do it. Fret not, my son. None of us is perfect. It is
better to have crooked legs than a crooked spirit. We can only do
the best we can with what we have. That, after all, is the measure
of success: what we do with what we have."

"None of us is perfect." Even we who are the so-called
normal people are full of imperfections. And some are handicapped physically like the boy in the medieval tale who was
stricken with infantile paralysis, some are mentally handicapped, some emotionally.

There are so many things that a handicapped child cannot
do that his self-respect almost inevitably suffers. Like every
other child he is hungry to express himself in some way. He

[1] (Copyright, 1949, by Marguerite de Angeli, reprinted by permission of
Doubleday & Company, Inc.).

wants to do things that are recognized as worthy. He needs to achieve a feeling of adequacy. To find the right way to make him feel adequate in *something* is the school's responsibility. One of the many ways is playmaking. As an eminent leader in child development expressed it, "Creative dramatics is magnificent therapy. It is used in mental institutions, it is used by psychiatrists. But why wait? Since it really has therapeutic value, why not use it as a preventive measure?"

PHYSICALLY HANDICAPPED CHILDREN

Few physically handicapped children ever have a chance to be in a play. If they see any plays they must always be audience. Yet they long to be *doers* like the other boys and girls. Here, with a kind of drama which is for the player, not the audience, is a real opportunity for playmaking *with* children. For in creative dramatics children can realize their heart's desire to be a part of it all. A play—the magic of it! The fun!

In a certain public school orthopedic room[2] the children molded very simple puppet heads on sticks, painted them painstakingly and, in some cases, with great difficulty. Their mothers then dressed the puppets to represent various characters from Mother Goose.

At the program for parents which was the climax of the puppet project, the children spoke the rhymes while their puppets acted them out. Children who could not speak well enough to be understood merely moved their puppets while someone else spoke the words. Sometimes a child could do nothing except hold his puppet up on the stage. But though the program was extremely simple, those fifteen crippled boys and girls were the proudest, happiest children imaginable as, in groups of twos and threes, they came back to their mothers from the color-

[2] Haven School, Evanston, Illinois. Jessie Crothers, teacher of puppetry.

ful little puppet stage in the front of the room. They had had their first chance to be part of a gay, glamorous show—a show replete with curtained stage, music, and lighting—and it was an experience which, one can be sure, will remain in their memory as one of the highlights of their childhood.

Though children like these are very limited as to action, adults have found many ways for them to have a part in dramatic play. Even those in hospital beds are sometimes given a chance for a bit of make-believe. One group of boys in a Seattle hospital ward were wheeled so that their beds formed a kind of circle around what they played was a lake. With a teacher of creative drama[3] to help them plan, they went on a wonderful fishing expedition, casting, waiting for nibbles, finally pulling in their catch. "The biggest fish I ever caught," exclaimed one of the boys. "Boy, will that taste good for supper!"

Imaginary surprise packages have delighted both children and adults in hospital beds. "What could they be?" Admiring them, shaking the boxes, opening them one at a time so that everyone can see what the gifts are, each child unwraps one, takes it out, and uses it so that everyone else can guess what it is.

Make-believe such as this can brighten the day and lift the spirits of many a boy or girl who has to spend long weeks in a hospital. Any kind of easy participation with hands and mind, whether in situations such as these or in stories can make them forget pain or boredom for a time and thus prove a happy interlude in the day.

A mother, too, with a fretful child in bed, has sometimes found that making a "party" of medicine-taking worked beautifully. Using the best tea-service, with tablets dissolved in cambric tea, and lollipops made of frozen orange-juice on sticks, she finds medicine time easy, even anticipated with pleasure.

Two of the *Let's Play* records of musical-action stories in

[3] Margaret Woods, University of Washington.

the Kay Ortmans series, described in the Record List in the Appendix, are so designed that they may be done by children in their beds. By listening to the gay music and the charming storyteller, the children are drawn into the playing with arms and, if possible, with the whole upper part of the body. "Farmland," "At the Edge of the Field," "Caves, Crabs, and Sand," and "Down by the River," will arouse the imagination of any child and, if he is physically able, will do much to free his body, mind, and spirit.

Children who are deaf often do the most expressive pantomime—better than most normal children. In a class with children who have their hearing they can play parts in stories that do not require speech. Many can even speak as a character and read the lips of the others in order to respond. If a hearing child plays with a deaf one, it spurs him on to do careful pantomime and correct lip movement in order to make the other child understand.

Boys and girls with little or no vision play simple stories which are either individual (such as Mother Goose may be) or with seeing children who can help them. Needless to say, this may do the seeing child as much good as the one who is blind. Because the other senses are sharpened, dramatic situations which require their use have much therapeutic value.

SPEECH HANDICAPPED CHILDREN

It is a common experience for children who stutter to take part in dramatics without giving any indication of their handicap. In fact, if they study with a special teacher of dramatics instead of their classroom teacher, she may not even know of the defect. When they take part in class discussion it is, of course, very evident. But such children usually say little except when they are assuming a character, and then they are lifted out of themselves and speak almost as fluently as the other

234 PLAYMAKING WITH CHILDREN

children. This is true, at least, when the defect is not too serious.

One speech teacher,[4] in working with sixth-, seventh-, and eighth-grade children, found that if she began by giving the handicapped child a part that was entirely pantomime (such as being the peddler in the ballad "The Old Market Woman"), he would often gain enough confidence so that he would be willing the next time to read the ballad as other children played it. Since the eyes of the group were upon the peddler and the old woman, he was not the center of attention, and he gained confidence to speak out. Later he worked with the speech teacher on the sounds which were difficult for him. At times, two of the speech handicapped children read the ballad together during the miming, one occasionally taking a phrase alone until he gained confidence to read the whole poem.

Marie was a homely little girl of six with several kinds of speech substitutions. She was in the first grade, and few people noticed her for she seldom spoke. She sat back, timid and unhappy because the other children could not understand her if she did say anything.

When the children dramatized stories Marie watched them eagerly but refused to take part though she wanted so much to play! The speech teacher worked with her all year and she improved noticeably. As soon as she thought she was good enough so that she was sure the children would not ridicule her, she ventured to try a small bit.

To her great joy she found that she could do it. That was all she needed. After this she volunteered regularly. And because she had a strong sense of the dramatic, the other children began to count on her for important parts. From now on her speech improved rapidly, and by the time she was in the second

[4] Madeline Bowers, Public Schools, Lake Forest, Illinois.

grade it was entirely normal, and she had taken her place as a leader.

THE MENTALLY HANDICAPPED

The children with high I.Q.'s have no monopoly on playmaking. In fact, they are sometimes surpassed by boys and girls with intelligence half as high. What is true in music and the graphic and plastic arts is true also in creative drama. The grammar would never pass any test, and the language is sometimes picturesque, even astonishing! But there is often a reality about the feeling in it that is truly striking.

Tommy was a second-grade boy who could not learn to read. One day he was chosen to be a rooster in the dramatization of a barnyard story his group was doing. The class never expected much from Tommy so they could scarcely believe their ears when at just the right moment a perfectly magnificent crowing came from the heart and soul of the rooster! In fact, they were so startled and thrilled that the dramatization almost went to pieces; and when it was over they were loud in their praise of him. Tommy himself was dazed. It was almost as if he thought the wonderful sound had come from somebody else.

"Great guns, Miz Taylor!" he exclaimed when he recovered a little, "wasn't I *wonderful?!!*"

"If Tommy never gets recognition again," said the teacher afterwards, "he has had *one big moment!*"

An "opportunity room" in a certain grade school was an indiscriminate mixture of fourteen boys and four girls, with I.Q.'s from 51 to 92. There was a man-sized Negro boy, Douglas, who sat half asleep and mumbling to himself much of the time; a small Negro boy, Clarence, a bully and a boss, whom the others were afraid to have as an enemy; Joseph, a psychopathic white boy of nine with pitiful home conditions, who hated everyone and expected everyone to hate him; and fifteen others of varying degrees of laziness, instability, and trouble-making propensities.

Their teacher[5] had attempted to use dramatics, but knowing little about it, had made the mistake of choosing material that was lacking in dramatic possibilities, and of expecting results that were too formal. While taking a course in creative dramatics, she saw demonstrations by expert teachers and learned more about technique and choice of material. Being an understanding and sympathetic teacher, she knew at once how to apply the method to her children; and she introduced it in the following very effective way:

The pupils in this opportunity room had been reading a simple story about a boy, Johnny, who dreamed that he took a fascinating trip to a strange land and was entertained by a king and a princess. As the children seemed to like it very much, she introduced the idea of dramatizing it by asking them about dreams they had had. This awakened such a lively response that she gave each one a chance to "act out" his dream. They were delighted, even big Douglas coming alive and surprising the others by the effectiveness of his dramatization. The next day the teacher asked them if they would like to play the story; and with elation born of the fun they had had with their own dreams, they were unanimous in wanting to dramatize Johnny's. What followed in the various periods in which they developed the dramatization was a revelation even to the teacher who knew them so well. Douglas was alert every minute, giving opinions and making suggestions. When the girls tried playing the mother who was making pies in the kitchen, he criticized them for "not making a thing!" Later, he volunteered to do the part himself, and he gave so perfect

[5] Mrs. Irene DeWolf, Noyes School, Evanston, Illinois.

a pantomime of mixing dough, peeling apples, and putting pies in the oven, that the whole group praised him highly. There-after, he was unwilling to relinquish the mother's part to any-one else!

Joseph, who thought everyone hated him, had actually been applauded by the other children for his dream-acting. And when the teacher chose the cast for the first playing of the story, they asked that he be the brownie because he was so light on his feet and so like a brownie in his movements. The effect on the boy was touching. He stayed after school of his own accord, and even though all the other children had left, he whispered to the teacher, "Mrs. DeWolf, I think the kids like me now, and I'm going to try to be a good boy."

In order to use Clarence's desire for leadership, she gave him special responsibility for the scene in which the king entertained Johnny in the palace. He himself acted as butler, moving among the guests with hands spread out as if passing a huge golden tray filled with sandwiches and cakes. No slightest indication did he give of what he was feeling until the scene had been played through once. Then it was that he burst out in tragic indignation, "Miz DeWolf, we're goin' to stop right now and have some lessons in manners and bein' clean! When I was serving those cakes, three of the kids almost knocked the tray out of my hands, they was so rude. And Norwood's hands was so dirty that he got germs all over the sandwiches! And then some of the kids tried to grab extra helpings. You gotta have good manners at a party!"

Poor Clarence, erstwhile problem himself, was glaring all the time at the culprits. And this accusation from one of their peers, followed by a group discussion on cleanliness and cour-tesy, did more good, according to the teacher, than all the ad-monitions she had given them the entire year!

Therapeutic possibilities in creative dramatics are limited

only by the teacher's understanding and ability to make use of them. In the case of the little dream-play, Douglas was so awakened that he never lapsed back into his former apathy. He had had no self-respect. He knew he was "dumb," and it was not until he had the opportunity to do something on which he was an authority that he dared to express himself. Along with the other children, Douglas had first acted out his own dream. Because this was a novel and amusing kind of show, the children applauded each player when he had finished. The applause did something for those boys and girls who so seldom received any kind of praise.

Now that the feeling of success was in the air, their teacher capitalized on it by bringing them a step further, using one experience to help them in the next. When Douglas saw the poor attempt of the girls in the pantomime, he knew he could do it better. Whether it was from observation or experience, he gave such a good demonstration of pie-making that he won the wholehearted approval of all the children in the room, and, as a result, some confidence in himself.

Joseph's problem was insecurity. He was ashamed of his home conditions; and having seen his father beat his mother, he knew his family didn't amount to much. He was sure they hated him, and he said he hated everybody else. But when the other children actually requested that the teacher choose him as the brownie because he was so nimble and so light on his feet, he had a feeling somehow of *belonging*. For the moment, at least, tensions were released and his view of the world was a little less warped.

As for Clarence, his father was a rough character and a braggart; and Clarence had to be tough in order to hold his own. Most of the time he used his ability as a leader to bully and frighten the other children. But when given a chance for serious leadership, he proved that he had some sense of the fitness of things. He carried through his responsibility and even managed to teach the other children a lesson in cleanliness and courtesy!

EMOTIONAL TENSIONS

Natalie Cole, of the Los Angeles elementary schools, author of *The Arts in the Classroom*,[6] has been one of the outstanding teachers in the country in the use of therapy in the arts. In creative writing she has freed her pupils to write about their innermost difficulties even when they were things that made them feel ashamed.

Beginning with her own childhood, she told them about experiences which had made her feel inferior. Then she went on to say, "I'm glad to tell you about these things because some people say that when you're brave and dig down under and tell about things that hurt, they don't hurt so much any more."

The outpouring of real bits of writing that came to her from a group of children of mixed races—not alone, of course, from one talk with the children, but from her whole association with them—was almost unbelievable. They knew that she had confidence in them, that she considered them "all right people" no matter what their families were like, no matter what happened at home.

"Children have spent years building defenses," she writes. "We must establish a rapport through kindliness and sympathetic interest and be patient. We can't expect children to give us their best until we prove that we deserve it."

What Natalie Cole has done with art, dance, and writing can also be done with dramatic play. Hartley, Frank, and Goldenson, who have made an intensive study of children's play devote two chapters of their book *Understanding Children's Play*[7] to dramatic play, considering it a significant factor in their

[6] (The John Day Co., Inc., 1940).
[7] (Columbia University Press, 1952).

development. "By permitting a child to play freely in a setting of security and acceptance," they write, "we enable him to deal satisfactorily and healthfully with his most urgent problems." And Erik Erikson[8] writes, ". . . to *play it out* is the most natural autotherapeutic measure childhood affords."

It is this playing out of difficulties which is the basis of the following kinds of therapeutic drama.

PSYCHODRAMA AND SOCIODRAMA

The words *psychodrama* and *sociodrama* were coined early in this century by Dr. J. L. Moreno[9] an Austrian psychiatrist who later established a clinic in New York City. *Psychodrama* is the use of drama as psychiatric treatment for the individual. *Sociodrama* means the use of drama as therapy for the group.

If a person responds inadequately to a life situation that troubles him, the situation may be developed into a scene with him as a character. He plays himself, with members of a clinic playing the other necessary roles. A great deal of study and discussion is behind this playing, and the discussion which follows it is even more significant. It is being much used in mental hospitals for veterans, and in clinics for psychiatric treatment of difficulties in marriage relations.

In a school situation, a group of problem children may play together when all have certain unfortunate attitudes in common even though each has character difficulties of his own. A psychodrama monograph called *Psychodrama in the Schools*,[10] by Nahum Shoobs, describes an experiment with eighteen maladjusted boys. Ten were confirmed truants and four were infantile. Some were petty thieves or pickpockets, others were merely overaggressive. All felt inadequate in school, and, too

[8] *Studies in the Interpretation of Play* (Genetic Psychology Monographs, 1940).
[9] *Psychodrama* (Beacon House, 1946) and other books.
[10] (Beacon House, 1944).

discouraged to keep on trying, they lost their tempers, fought, stole, played truant. "They wanted to be significant," he says, "without earning the position."

In the beginning he used a warming-up period to ask them to act out a situation concerning a test in arithmetic. It was to concern a boy "who finds it too hard, gets angry. He is not a boy who ever works too hard. Suppose you were the boy," said the teacher. "Show us what you would do."

One of the boys took the part of the teacher, another (a boy with an especially bad temper) was the pupil. But in spite of the fact that he could not do the problem, he kept on working as an average child would. Four others followed in the part, each repeating the model behavior. A fifth boy volunteered, and after looking at an example and attempting to do it, he threw down the pencil and sulked.

"Whose act did you like the best?" asked the teacher. The answer was unanimously for the last boy.

"But he quit, didn't he? He wouldn't even try."

The boys said, "yes he was yellow because he quit trying, but he was honest enough to show that he quit while the others faked it."

The teacher made no attempt to point a moral to the playing (which the boys greatly enjoyed) but he hoped to spoil the satisfaction they found in trouble-making as a compensation to a feeling of inadequacy, and ultimately to develop such objective reactions as gradual lack of respect for the disturber, and more and more self-restraint for preventing outbursts. The next time a boy lost his temper he might recall the class decision on such acts: "Yeh, he's yellow. He couldn't take it. He quit trying."

Through all the ensuing sessions there was a development of attitude through the acting out of more and more personal situations. The teacher always avoided driving home the point of the lesson, knowing this would arouse resistance. He even took care that it was not treated too seriously. Often it was humorous. After a time, during the discussion of the teacher's question, "Sometimes you have done something . . . you weren't so sure it was such a swell thing . . . did you have a funny feeling then?" the boys introduced Conscience as a character. When a boy did some negative act to attract attention, Conscience would say such things as "Want to be a big shot, don't you!"

In these improvised scenes and the discussions which precede and follow the acting, the psychiatrist gets an insight into the way the children would act in life situations. And because every phase of a child's performance is open to correction from the other participants, such playing may save him from trouble and sorrow in actual life.

From even this small preliminary situation, it can readily be seen that psychodrama is a technique for the psychiatrist, not the regular teacher. Mr. Shoobs, a psychiatrist, had known each pupil in the classroom for over a year, having worked with them in shop projects and given them remedial work, and the classroom teacher was aware of what he was doing.

When one probes into a child's inner feelings it is easy to find oneself on dangerous ground. One risks getting into situations where he does more harm than good. Therefore, the most the classroom teacher can do is to co-operate with the psychiatrist who is trying to help a child to meet difficult situations.

Sociodrama, on the contrary, or at least *role-playing,* can be used in any classroom. Role-playing is an aspect of sociodrama in which a real problem situation is acted out by a group of people. As a rule, the roles are reversed after one playing and the scene is played again. Its purpose is to change the attitude or the behavior of individuals or groups. It is a technique much used in human relations problems in such crucial areas as management and labor, parent and child, racial and religious groups.

Every classroom teacher experiences the arguments that arise on the playground, in which one faction blames the other until it is a very difficult thing to get to the bottom of the trouble.

"Let's play it out," she may say; and each child plays his own role as they re-enact the situation. Sometimes the whole trouble is ended with one playing. At other times they need to reverse roles and try again.

Aside from its value in clearing up confused issues, role-playing tends to lessen tensions. Like the Aristotelian theory of catharsis, it has more than a little value in cleansing the system of anger, and bringing reason to bear on a problem which concerns the whole group.

A fourth-grade group of city children, for instance, most of whom had no place to play except at a club run by a community chest agency, dramatized a situation which had made them very angry the day before. A ball with which some of them had been playing was accidentally thrown into a neighbor's garden. and the irate lady had ended the game by keeping the ball.

The children had come to school next day vowing to get even with "that old killjoy." Because their feelings were so stirred up their teacher[11] asked them if they would like to play out what happened. So they re-enacted the scene, one of the children playing the neighbor, four others being themselves playing with an imaginary ball. When the ball landed in the garden, the neighbor appeared, picked it up, and gave the children a piece of her mind.

"We didn't mean to throw it into your yard," they protested.

"Well, I can't help what you *meant*," she retorted. "You're just spoiling my garden and I'm going to keep your ball!"

"We won't do it again," the children said.

[11] Emily Pribble, dramatic teacher, Noyes School, Evanston, Illinois.

"That's what you always say," replied the neighbor, and she started back into her house with the ball.

"Go get Miss Smith" (the name of the real head of the club), said one of the children.

"Miss Smith," in the person of another little girl, was brought, and in a very mature, polite manner she told the neighbor how sorry they were, and how, if the neighbor would return the ball this time they would try to find a game that would be sure to keep the ball in their own narrow lot.

"I don't think the children know their own strength," she said apologetically! The ball was given back and the children went into a huddle to plan something different . . . By the time they had finished their playing, they had worked off their anger and probably had begun to recognize the fact that the neighbor had a point after all!

THE TIMID CHILD

Creative dramatics helps the timid child perhaps more easily than any other. Whether his timidity is caused by a dominant parent who makes decisions for him and gives him a feeling of inferiority or whether it comes from some other source, it makes him unhappy and very much inhibited. He sits silent in a class, seldom venturing an idea or trying a characterization.

Such a child has an image of himself which limits him in whatever he wants to do. Here is a plain little girl who has had many experiences in being unnoticed when others are recognized. She becomes more and more timid and mouse-like and unhappy, even though she retains a tremendous longing to express herself and have a place in the sun. She needs much encouragement to attempt even an easy part in playmaking. If a teacher can so stir her imagination about a character in a story that she feels an urge to play the part, a mild degree of success will induce her to volunteer for other roles.

Perhaps she wins the approval of the class for the way she individualized the character of Milk in the first episode of *The Blue Bird for Children*. The next time she may believe in her own ability enough to volunteer for the more difficult part of the Fairy Berylune. By the time she has played several parts successfully, the social image she had of herself may be sufficiently broken down for her to realize that she has possibilities she hadn't known were in her. If she can be these people satisfactorily, perhaps she could be a different sort of person from the one she is from day to day. And she is happier as she gains confidence in expressing freely the ideas and emotions that before she had kept hidden within herself.

THE SHOW-OFF

At the opposite extreme is the show-off or exhibitionist. He may be a petted child who is the center of attention in his family. More often, perhaps, he fails to get the recognition he wants so badly and so he resorts to any means he can think of to be noticed. Some children ask questions, others resort to buffoonery on the stage or off. This girl will volunteer for every kind of part, regardless of whether she has put any thought on the interpretation. That child will punch the boy next to him; and when he is on the stage, he will overplay his part with an eye on the audience to see how his acting is being received.

Playmaking should serve as a *legitimate* means of getting attention. Here is a chance for exhibition which satisfies his desire without bringing any blame upon him for trying to assert himself. But he has to learn to take his turn instead of playing all the time. He sees other children volunteering for small parts and he begins to understand that he should sometimes do the same. His ideas are not always accepted by the group. He has to give up his own way often if he expects to get along with other children.

The child who is inclined to be a show-off may be helped by a teacher who praises him sincerely for any honest effort in his playmaking. So far as possible she ignores his tendencies to overdo until she has attempted to help him by encouragement for what he does well. But if he insists on spoiling a scene by drawing all attention to himself, she will find it necessary to stop the playing and ask him to take his seat while someone else goes into his part. Without any reproof and in perfect good nature she will show him that clowning is not legitimate, and he will not be likely to do it again. By this procedure she is helping him to see a better and more satisfactory way to win recognition.

THE CHILD WHO LACKS SENSITIVITY

Then there is the child who wants very badly to have friends but doesn't know how to win them. He lacks the sensitivity to know what others are thinking by the way they look and act; therefore he persists in doing things which are unacceptable to them.

Since it is futile to try to make friends when one has no understanding of people, such a child needs to be made aware of the way other boys and girls show how they feel. If he were at all sensitive, he would realize that his clowning and bullying make him unpopular instead of winning friends for him.

In dramatization of any kind the characters show their feelings. They react to one another; and in creative dramatics if the players fail to do so, they are criticized by the rest of the group. In the attempt to project himself into another personality, the child has to think hard about how that other person feels and how he shows his feelings. The nature of drama demands that attention be constantly focused on the very thing of which he needs to be made aware. Thus, the child is gradually made more sensitive to what other children are thinking and, consequently, understands them better.

EMOTIONAL CONTROL

Everyday life gives a child little opportunity to express his emotions in a satisfying way. Feelings overflow happily in the play of small boys and girls, and they find expression in temper tantrums or other uncontrolled outbursts when children are frustrated. But older boys and girls are supposed to keep their feelings in check if they are well-behaved, though they have one outlet in their games. Opportunities are fewer as they grow older, however; and unless they go in for sports or drama they are forced to be satisfied most of the time by vicarious experiences with books, radio, television, and motion pictures.

Young people who develop satisfactorily grow steadily in *control* of emotions. Repression is worse than useless. Rather, the emotions should be directed into avenues where they will bring satisfaction to the children themselves and to others. Reason and emotion do not seriously conflict in a balanced individual; and though few people achieve an ideal blending, they would more nearly approximate it if home and school would give intelligent attention to this important aspect of a child's education.

ATTITUDES

No matter what children are studying they are constantly forming attitudes—attitudes toward the teacher, toward one another, toward the subject, toward school, and toward many other things. And what people *feel* about anything is more important than what they *think* about it. For attitudes are the moving force of life.

One does not have to look far for proof of this. We see people who are supposedly intelligent betraying their emotional immaturity by acting from a childish prejudice against people of other races and religions. We have witnessed the spectacle of thousands upon thousands following a demagogue who appealed to their fears and narrow self-interest; and again and again we are astonished at the way in which Wall Street reacts to feelings instead of cool reasoning. In fact, there is so much evidence on all sides that action is caused by attitudes that no teacher ought to ignore the grave responsibility of helping our children to develop emotional as well as mental maturity. If we are to have citizens worthy of a democracy, this is of greatest consequence.

Drama has to do with emotion—emotion concerning living situations, for it involves people and human actions. Dramatic expression "lets one step out of one's own personality into that of another. It lets one transcend one's own limitations and frees one from many of the taboos and inhibitions that circumscribe daily life." [12] In dramatizations children identify themselves with many characters and, according to their degree of maturity, they understand different points of view.

In the discussion of these characters, if a wise teacher, entirely by indirection, guides a child in forming fine attitudes toward the things most worth seeking in life, she may be doing a more significant thing for his future than she does in teaching mathematics, spelling, and natural science.

What people value in life is an indication of their degree of maturity. Home, school, books, experience, all have a part in teaching values. There are many opportunities for the children to discuss spiritual values as they plan a dramatization, play it, and evaluate their work. If a young person suspects that he

[12] Carleton Washburne, *A Living Philosophy of Education* (The John Day Co., 1940).

himself is the object of any such discussion, he hardens himself against what is said. But if he knows it is impersonal he is frank in expressing himself and quite open to suggestion. He is more likely, also, to make a personal application of a principle than he would be if he thought that an adult had started a discussion concerning him personally. Enduring likes and dislikes which will help to mature him emotionally and will strongly influence his future may result from such discussions. The leader must always remember, however, that *whatever guidance she gives should be limited to an occasional question.* But how important one's choice of a question can be!

A boy who plays a fine, upstanding part like Jean in *The Boy Knight of Reims*[13] cannot help growing a little in his sense of spiritual values. He does this not only because of Jean's fine character, but also by virtue of Jean's relationship to all the other people in the story and the sympathy that is built for him by the author. On the other hand, if he plays Master Anton, the corrupt goldsmith, he still gains; for he sees Anton in *his* relationship to the whole story. There is no sympathy for cheating and no sympathy for Anton when he is put out of the guild. So, far from developing a wish to be like the goldsmith, the playing of such a part strengthens a boy's dislike for that kind of a person.

If a child has conflicts with himself, or emotional tensions because of experiences at home or at school, it is a satisfaction and a release to act such a part as the cruel Master Anton—a part which gives him a chance to "let off steam," as it were, and to get out of his system the pent-up emotions which are tormenting him. The same may be said of playing Scrooge in *A Christmas Carol,* Cinderella's stepmother, the witch in "Hansel and Gretel."

[13] Eloise Lownsbery (Houghton Mifflin Co., 1927).

THE BUILDING OF SELF-RESPECT

The teacher who gives serious consideration to everything that is sincerely offered in playmaking or in any other subject helps to build the self-respect so vitally needed by both normal and handicapped children. No one who has read Natalie Cole's book could have failed to be moved by this educational gem written by one of the most limited children in her room:

"In the other school I could not learn and in this school I know all right all the time. I have more fun in school than in the other I used to go to, because I know how more times." Such an expression as this bears out what Viktor Lowenfeld [14] writes, "Since it is an established fact that nearly every emotional or mental disturbance is connected with a lack of self-confidence, it is easily understood that the proper stimulation of the child's creative abilities will be a safeguard against such disturbances."

If a person really learns self-respect, he comes gradually to care more for his own evaluation of himself than for what anyone else says to him. He can be satisfied without praise if he knows he has done something worthy; and no amount of praise can please him if he himself is dissatisfied. Many a person says, "I have to live with myself, and that can be mightily uncomfortable if I let down on standards." This self-respect is indispensable for a truly mature person and it should be a challenge to every teacher to instill it in all the children whose lives she touches.

THE FUN ELEMENT

Whenever we work in playmaking with children who are handicapped in body, mind, or spirit, the fun element should be uppermost. The magic of make-believe needs to come in

[14] *Creative and Mental Growth* (The Macmillan Co., rev., 1952).

greater measure to them than to normal children. For one reason or another they are cut off from so many joys that normal
children experience that all the brightness and charm possible
should be brought into their dramatic play. Suffering should
be lightened by laughter, dramatization should be within their
ability to do with satisfaction, and encouragement should spur
them on to do things they have not dreamed they could do.
Confidence comes from the memory of past successes; therefore, we should see to it that whatever we ask them to do
should be entirely within their power to do successfully. Our
minds should constantly be seeking ways to give them courage
and self-respect. Though we may not say it, we need always to
make them feel the truth and the reassurance in Brother Luke's
words to Robin:

"None of us is perfect . . . We can only do the best we can
with what we have. That, after all, is the measure of success:
what we do with what we have."

CHAPTER 13

Speech Improvement and Playmaking

"A DELIGHTFUL CREATIVE PLAY—IF ONE COULD HAVE UNDER-stood what the players said!" It happens often. The children are creative, the action is free, the characters well played, but the communication is bad. The children do not articulate their words clearly nor make their characterizations strong enough to project fifteen feet away.

This is a fault of many a class in creative drama. Nor is it a surprising one. When children improvise their dialogue, they have as much as most of them can do to think of *what* to say. Their words just have to come out the best way they can. Since each child must have in mind his particular character and try to say what *he* would say in the way he would say it, at the same time helping to make the story move, he must not be required to think about voice nor grammar nor enunciation. That must be automatic unless he has the chance to play one role enough times to feel confident in it. This may happen if the children play for an audience, and the cast is chosen long enough in advance so that the dialogue is partially set.

It is unthinkable to stop a child's playing to correct his grammar, pronunciation, or enunciation. Nothing so surely inhibits creative thinking or fluent speech as this, to say nothing of the embarrassment caused by being corrected in public.

Somehow his speech must be corrected though, and it is a question whether it can best be done (a) in connection with the material the class is working on; (b) by speech drills and games at the beginning of the period; or (c) by choral speaking.

RELATING EVERY TECHNIQUE TO THE
SAME MATERIAL

Some story material can be used beautifully for bodily movement, rhythm, and speech training, as well as for creative drama. For instance, the little poem "The Squirrel," in Chapter 2, which was used for rhythm and dramatic play, is perfectly adapted to speech training. "Whisky, frisky" has the "*wh*" sound so slighted by many children, and it can be stressed as they say the poem with the teacher. The final consonants *ky*, *p*, *d*, *ty*, can be made crisp and strong as they repeat it together and as they hippity-hop to the rhythm of the poem. By this means we are tying speech into the rhythm and dramatic play —the most direct way to incorporate correct speech into their playing.

Whenever we can see opportunities of getting needed voice and diction drill into the playing we should do so—as we can in "Little pig, little pig, let me come in!" of "The Three Pigs"; "It's pretty, it's lots of fun, and it makes you feel good from the inside out," from "Paddy's Christmas," and, from *A Christmas Carol*, "Oh! but he was a tight-fisted hand at the grindstone, Scrooge! a squeezing, wrenching, grasping, scraping, clutching, covetous old sinner!" Wonderful consonant sounds in the middle of words! Such phrases, repeated often in a story, or at least led by us with zest and repeated all together can be a kind of drill the repetition of which is enjoyable. When they can be combined with rhythmical action of some kind, they are the more valuable. This drill can come whenever it fits in—when reviewing the story or even in the middle of the playing. It can make for pleasing variety in the class hour and insure the participation of everyone.

SPEECH DRILLS

Drills and games designed to correct faults in voice and articulation are used either in classes separate from those in creative drama or for a few minutes at the beginning of the dramatic class. They are less directly—often not at all—concerned with any literature the class is using in creative drama. It is hoped that the good habits formed by such drills will carry over into the everyday speech of the children.

These drills must be intrinsically interesting enough to be enjoyed for themselves, for unless a child has a pronounced defect in speech the motivation for speech improvement is usually not strong enough to cause him to work hard at them. Boys and girls who do have such defects need to have private classes with a specialist, or at least work in small groups. The number of schools that have speech correctionists on their staffs is increasing year by year, though there are seldom enough specialists to do adequate work.

Carrie Rasmussen, in her *Speech Methods in the Elementary School*,[1] gives many excellent drills which the classroom teacher can use for improving both voice and articulation. It would be a very great asset if all teachers were required to take a course in voice and diction in order not only to help the children they teach but their own voices as well.

For imitation is a child's best way of learning speech, so that the example set by the teacher is of high importance. There is no excuse for a teacher's having an unpleasant voice, for almost

[1] (The Ronald Press Co., 1949).

any voice can be improved by the right kind of exercises. The unfortunate part of it is that most teachers who have strident or nasal voices do not realize it. Yet unquestionably they have a disturbing and irritating effect on their pupils.

A relaxed, low-pitched voice, with carefully articulated consonants, good grammatical sentence structure and, of course, correct pronunciation of words, characterize speech to which it is pleasant to listen. There is such a thing as being meticulous to the point of sounding stilted, but this is so uncommon among teachers that it is scarcely worth mentioning.

CHORAL SPEAKING

When Marjorie Gullan[2] led the revival of interest in choral speaking some years ago, she brought back an ancient art that we were acquainted with mainly through the choruses of the great plays of the Greeks. In the years since this dynamic teacher came from England to teach short courses in a number of American colleges, the use of choral speaking has spread widely over the country until now it is taught in a very large number of elementary and high schools.

The purposes of choral speaking or reading are several. If well taught it can build appreciation of poetry by participation in the motivated study and speaking of poems. It can give confidence in one's own ability to recite it, since there is no self-consciousness when a person is carried along with others as one is in community singing. It can be of great value in achieving pleasing voice quality, since relaxation is of high importance in its use and no one voice is allowed to stand out from the others. Clear-cut speech is stressed, for if words are to be understood by anyone else, each person needs to say them carefully.

Many exponents of choral speech insist that for normal chil-

[2] Author of several books on choral speaking, some of which are listed in the Bibliography.

dren it supplies all that is needed for good speech. No drills in speech sounds are necessary, they say, if they have good train-in this group work. Speech-handicapped children need a correctionist and sometimes even surgery. But the speech of most children can be improved immensely by regular work in choric speaking.

A further purpose of choral speaking is as a means of entertaining an audience by a verse choir. This may be of real value to those who participate but the emphasis in choirs must be on perfection. It is like formal drama in that one is always looking ahead to the *performance*, whereas for elementary children the other values are far more important.

The Need of Training

As in creative dramatics, a teacher needs specific training in choral speaking in order to do it acceptably. With a speech supervisor who can help her, the classroom teacher may be entirely capable of teaching it well. But there are so many pitfalls that she may do much more harm than good if she attempts it without training, especially if she is not a speech-trained person. Because it is so often done badly, the whole subject is a controversial one, many educators believing it to be a set, imitative thing in which the teacher, who may not be a good reader herself, stamps her speech pattern on all her pupils.

Too often the teacher begins with unison speaking, which is by far the most difficult phase of choral speaking and should be used only when the children have had plenty of experience in the other phases. Too often she begins with the aspects which should be achieved as a result of appreciating the *meaning*: inflection, stress, pitch, and the rest. Some teachers have even been known to drill pupils on making their voices "go up or down" with no understanding of why they do it!

The difficulties involved in avoiding the heavy pounding on words, of the sing-song monotony which results from reading all lines alike, and of overemphasizing the important words, is discouraging to a teacher who does not know how to cope with them.

Though the specialists in this field make it plain that the meaning of the poem must be thoroughly discussed by the group and the interpretation agreed upon, imitation of the leader is almost sure to be the case with younger children and less experienced older ones because she reads the poem to them a number of times. When the leader has fine sensitivity, a good voice, and thorough understanding of the poem, this is not a serious fault, since good speech is largely a matter of imitation anyhow. But in modern education, when we are trying to teach children to think for themselves, there is sure to be some suspicion of a type of speech work in which each child must conform to either the teacher's or the group's interpretation even if it does not seem right to him.

Most of these pitfalls, however, concern unison speaking. The earlier phases of choral speaking—the only phases used in some schools—are much easier and can be done with far less risk. The following are the progressive phases more or less agreed upon by authorities in choral speech.

1. THE RHYTHMIC OR ACTIVITY PHASE. In the beginning the children do not speak at all. The teacher or leader says a jingle with pronounced rhythm, the children only listening to the first reading. The second time she says it they often mark the rhythm by tapping or clapping, or they think of what action they could do to this rhythm: walking, skipping, hopping, swaying, and the like. The next time they *do* whatever action they feel. Many of the youngest children will not choose action that fits at all, but it is better to disregard it and wait for a child to sense this himself. He may see that some other child

has discovered a better kind of action and change to it. But if he doesn't, the teacher gives no indication that he is wrong, knowing that though he may be less sensitive to rhythm he will doubtless get it in time.

Mother Goose rhymes are most commonly used for this purpose. These good old rhymes can survive any kind of treatment and come up as hardy as ever! Marching or walking is the easiest action, so a leader might use not only the standbys "The Grand Old Duke of York" and "Hot Cross Buns," but "Galoshes" (from Chapter 2, which is made to order for this purpose), "Policemen," by Marjorie Seymour Watts,[3] and "Buckingham Palace," by A. A. Milne.[4] Another that they always enjoy in the first or second grade is

> Elephants walk like this and like that,
> They are terribly big and terribly fat.
> They have no hands and they have no toes,
> But goodness gracious, what a nose!

This is fun because by bending over, clasping their hands, and swinging their arms, they can be the big old elephants themselves!

"Hickory, Dickory Dock," "Jack Be Nimble," and "Whisky, Frisky" are excellent for skipping; "I Saw a Ship A-Sailing" from Mother Goose, and "Sweet and Low" by Tennyson have a swaying rhythm; and "The Popcorn Man"[5] (author unknown) is a delightful poem for hopping:

> The popcorn man gave a popcorn ball,
> The popcorn cart was the dancing hall,
> The popcorn dancers hopped and hopped
> And danced until their hats all popped!

[3] Haaga, Agnes, and Randles, Patricia, *Supplementary Materials* (University of Washington, 1952).
[4] *When We Were Very Young* (E. P. Dutton & Co., Inc., 1924).
[5] Haaga and Randles, *op. cit.*

Many other poems are suggested for all the phases of choral work in the various books on choral speaking. This phase has as its purpose the feeling of the rhythm through the whole body. Also, it shows the leader which of the children sense the rhythm.

2. THE REFRAIN. In this phase of choric speaking the children have their first chance to speak. The material chosen consists of poems and jingles with natural refrains. The leader says the stanza and the children give the refrain in the manner of the solo and chorus in singing. No action is used with this step except that in leading up to the speaking, there is often tapping or finger-tipping to help in sensing the rhythm as the teacher says the poem.

The leader first reads or speaks the jingle, poem, or ballad, and then repeats very slowly and accurately the refrain which the children are to learn. The aim is to secure the same pronunciation, rhythm, pace, and mood in the refrain as is used in the stanza. In the following delightful little poem,[6] it is chiefly the changes of mood that are important. It is fun for the children to change their voices to fit the mood suggested by the stanza.

> Who's that ringing at the front door bell?
>   Miau! Miau! Miau!
> I'm a little black cat and I'm not very well.
>   Miau! Miau! Miau!
> Then put your nose in this bowl of mutton fat,
>   Miau! Miau! Miau!
> For that's the way to cure a little pussy cat.
>   Miau! Miau! Miau!

"Refrains are valuable to train the speech-mechanism of speech-timid children," writes Elizabeth Keppie.[7] The child

---

[6] Anonymous.
[7] *Choric Speech* (Expression Co., 1935).

becomes used to speaking in concert, and not only gains confidence by being one of many, but grows in understanding of timing. For the leader gives only a slight signal for the children to begin speaking, and after they are accustomed to the refrain, they will need no signal at all.

Many jingles and poems are used for refrain speaking, beginning with Mother Goose: "Baa, Baa, Black Sheep," "Ding-Dong Bell," "Who Killed Cock Robin," "A Farmer Went Riding," and "John Cook's Little Grey Mare," and going on to such poems as Stevenson's "The Wind," Vachel Lindsay's "The Mysterious Cat," and, later, to some of the old ballads.

3. TWO-PART POEMS. For the first time, in this phase of choric speaking, the children do all the speaking of the poetry. Usually they are divided into groups—sometimes boys and girls, sometimes children on the two sides of the room. Now it is their responsibility to give the meaning of the poem and maintain the rhythm, each group speaking as nearly as possible as one person.

The teacher needs to give some visible signal for the beginning, and often after that the children take up their own cues, trying to make a clear-cut attack on the first word. In a rhyme such as "Pussy Cat, Pussy Cat, where have you been?" one group asks the question, the other answers it. One good poem for the younger children to use in this way is the following,

> What does the hail say?
> "Knock! Knock!"
> What does the rain say?
> "Pit! Pat!"
> What does the sleet say?
> "Sh! Sh!"
> What does the wind say?
> "Whoo! Whoo!"

The little poems "The Swallow," and "What Is Pink?" both

by Christina Rossetti (in Chapter 1) are good material for this phase of choric speaking. So is "Jonathan Bing" by B. Curtis Brown, "The Swing" by Stevenson, "Disobedience" by A. A. Milne, and a long list of others suggested in the various choral speaking books.

4. GROUPS AND SOLO PARTS. The poem is spoken partly by a group, partly by individual children in this phase of verse speaking. It should be said by way of warning that the dividing of poems into parts for groups and individual children can easily be overdone, requiring so much concentration on coming in on time that the meaning is lost.

There must always be a *reason* for the division. Unfortunately, there are books of poems divided arbitrarily into line-a-child parts with no possible justification. The subject-matter of the poem has not been taken into consideration, and the whole effect is choppy and meaningless.

Now in a poem such as "Bad Sir Brian Botany," by A. A. Milne, it is a natural division, with a group speaking the stanzas and a single person doing Sir Brian. This is true with Rose Fyleman's "Mice" and the delightful poem "Who's In?" by Elizabeth Fleming, in which the dog, the cat, the fly on the wall, and ever so many other live things resent someone's saying, "everyone's out." May Hill Arbuthnot's *Children and Books* contains an especially good poem for "line-a-child." It is Ivy Eastwick's "Where's Mary?" and is divided into parts for nine children, with the final two lines spoken by all. Also, in this book is the delightful nonsense poem "Godfrey Gordon Gustavus Gore," [8] which has good possibilities for group and solo parts.

> Godfrey Gordon Gustavus Gore—
> No doubt you have heard the name before—
> Was a boy who never would shut a door!

[8] William Brighty Rands.

The wind might whistle, the wind might roar,
And teeth be aching and throats be sore,
But still he never would shut the door.

His father would beg, his mother implore,
"Godfrey Gordon Gustavus Gore,
We really *do* wish you would shut the door!"

Their hands they wrung, their hair they tore;
But Godfrey Gordon Gustavus Gore
Was deaf as the buoy out at the Nore.

When he walked forth the folks would roar,
"Godfrey Gordon Gustavus Gore
Why don't you think to shut the door?"

They rigged out a Shutter with sail and oar,
And threatened to pack off Gustavus Gore
On a voyage of penance to Singapore.

But he begged for mercy, and said, "No more!
Pray do not send me to Singapore
On a Shutter, and then I will shut the door!"

"You will?" said his parents; "then keep on shore!
But mind you do! For the plague is sore
Of a fellow that never will shut the door,
Godfrey Gordon Gustavus Gore!"

The poem divides very naturally into solo and group parts,
with all or most of the children saying the descriptive and nar-
rative parts, the father and mother talking to their exasperating
son, a group "roaring" at Gustavus to shut the door, and one
child speaking as Gustavus. It can be good fun as well as an
excellent speech drill.

This phase of choric speaking is, of course, far more difficult
to weave into anything like a smooth rendition of the poem.
An instant of delay in beginning any part of it destroys the
rhythm, and any lack of appreciation of the mood detracts from

the interpretation of the whole. Nevertheless, if divided into natural parts, the children enjoy it very much.

5. UNISON. The last to be undertaken and the most difficult is unison speaking. All the preceding steps should be mastered before this is attempted, especially when the poem is to be spoken for an audience. Since this aspect of choral speaking becomes a formal project for exhibition, a discussion of it does not belong here. It is enough to say that such an experience may be very valuable and enjoyable to the participants when directed by a leader who has had training in this work.

Choral Speaking as a Part of Playmaking

Choral speaking becomes a part of playmaking when one group says the verse while the other pantomimes it, as described in Chapter 2. Children like to say the nonsense poem from *Alice in Wonderland*, "Tweedledum and Tweedledee" while three of their number pantomime it:

> Tweedledum and Tweedledee
>   Agreed to have a battle;
> For Tweedledum said Tweedledee
>   Had spoiled his nice new rattle.
>
> Just then flew down a monstrous crow,
>   As black as a tar-barrel;
> Which frightened both the heroes so,
>   They quite forgot their quarrel.

"A Goblinade," by Florence Page Jaques, is another poem easy to use in this way, and so also is Milne's "The King's Breakfast." Many of the Mother Goose rhymes are usable for this since they are short and full of action. All of the poems spoken by children together should be short. They should be impersonal also except when a line is spoken by a single child.

This use of action is of much greater value to the speech aspect than to that of creative play, due to the fact that the time element limits the children's creative ideas. However, it is definitely worth using occasionally to add interest.

PLAYMAKING'S GREATEST VALUE
IN SPEECH TRAINING

What the children's experience in playmaking contributes to their speech is only indirectly in voice and diction. There is an incentive to make themselves understood and to speak correctly when they are playing characters who would naturally be careful of their speech. But in itself it is a creative experience—something entirely different from a drill subject.

What it does contribute to their speech is the ability to think on their feet and express ideas readily. This means that if a child has a good deal of experience in creative drama, he acquires a considerable degree of poise in speaking. The thing that is likely to happen when children are given freedom in speech and dramatics is illustrated by a certain brother and sister who had attended private schools all their lives. The sister was being educated in a formal school of high scholastic standards, the brother in a much more informal country-day school.

The daughter, Marjorie, came home from high school one afternoon to find a visitor having tea with her mother. Having been trained in good manners, she came in as a matter of course and met the visitor, though she excused herself at once. It was easy to see that she was not at ease; and when she had left, her mother remarked that Marjorie was disappointed that she could not go in for a certain activity because her grades were too low.

"They tell me that her I.Q. is high enough," her mother said, "but she doesn't get high grades because she can't express herself well. They've had her since kindergarten," she added, "and it does seem as if they could have *taught* her to express herself!"

Shortly after, Jim, the younger brother came in from his

school. With a ready smile and outstretched hand, he greeted the caller with all the poise in the world.

"Your mother tells me you have been chosen to play Scrooge in the Christmas play," said the caller. "Congratulations! That's wonderful!"

"We recorded the first scene today," the boy replied with a kind of friendly ease. "It was a lot of fun!" And as the visitor took her leave, the thought came into her mind, "I wonder what would have happened if Marjorie and Jim had exchanged schools!"

INCENTIVES FOR GOOD SPEECH

Children's incentive for good speech must of necessity be the intrinsic interest which the exercises, the games, the choric speaking, and the playmaking hold for them. For little value is placed upon correct speech habits in this country, and many well educated people set so low a standard in their speech that they are poor examples for boys and girls to follow.

If it is a requisite for being in plays, or for radio or television, it means something to them. They hear many more speech-trained people nowadays because of the mass media, and this may awaken an interest in some of them; but in general our children's speech will continue to be poor unless the attitude of parents toward the need for speech training causes it to be made a part of the public school curriculum.

Schools in which the language arts are well taught stress not only creative drama but good speech habits in every subject taught. There is need in most elementary schools, however, for speech-trained teachers who can set a good example and supply incentives for better speech habits in their children.

CHAPTER 14

The Teacher's Role in Playmaking

WHO WILL BE THE CHILDREN'S GUIDE IN PLAYMAKING: THE classroom teacher or the specialist? Will drama be a part of the curriculum like music and art? Will it be used simply as "a way of teaching?" Will it be offered only in extracurricular classes? As a recreational activity on the city playgrounds? Which way *should* it be taught?

THE CLASSROOM TEACHER

A classroom teacher who has the ability and the training is in a position to make the best use of creative drama. She knows her children and the special needs of each one. She is there when the children are in the mood for playing a certain seasonal poem or a dramatic story which they find in their reader. She can fit it into their program. In a word, she can make use of the dramatic method whenever the time is right.

Aside from teachers of kindergarten, however, only a small proportion of classroom teachers *are* making any considerable use of it. Most of them have not been trained in creative drama, and those who are trained have no supervisor to encourage them to take time in their school program for this creative work.

Though increasing numbers of teachers are now being educated in the colleges and universities offering courses in creative dramatics (some of which require it of all elementary majors), it is safe to say that such training will never be universal. Even if it were, schools would still need supervisors or consultants as they do in the other arts. At present, a supervisor in drama is needed in every community to train teachers who do not know how to make use of creative dramatics, to give special help when it is needed, and to keep standards high. Until such a person is a part of the staff, the use of creative dramatics in the schools will inevitably be haphazard.

The teacher's own feeling about creative dramatics is the biggest single factor in the extent to which she uses it in her teaching. If she considers it a frill, the most she will do with it, probably, is to allow a group of children to go out of the room occasionally to prepare in a few minutes a dramatization of some story they have liked. She may do this either to satisfy the desire that children always have for the dramatic, or as busy work for some of the brighter children while she is laboring with her slow pupils.

Such an experience is of little value unless the children have learned *how* to dramatize a story, how to use their imaginations in seeing its possibilities. Natalie Cole's classic pronouncement, "Children cannot create out of a vacuum," [1] is usually exemplified in the outcome of such an experience. For even when a capable child is in charge of the group, the children rarely do more than put the synopsis of the story into dialogue form. As well expect them to set a poem to music when they have had no experience in composing music.

On the other hand, if a teacher believes that creative dramatics has real value, she will take advantage of a summer course in the subject, or at least attend a workshop for elemen-

[1] *The Arts in the Classroom* (The John Day Co., Inc., 1940).

tary teachers. She will read books on creative dramatics and experiment until she can guide her children successfully. If she already teaches other creative subjects such as writing or arts and crafts, it will be easier, for the underlying principles are the same. She has had experience in getting children to think creatively, and if she has been successful in one such subject, she is more likely to be in another.

Problems of Numbers, Space, Time

Aside from the question of training, her problems are likely to be (a) too many children for an ideal group; (b) too little space; and (c) an already crowded schedule. These are very real problems, too, and will prevent her from the fullest use of this creative work. But within certain limits she can use it effectively to enrich her school program.

As for the number of children—though twenty is an ideal number for such a class, there are many aspects of creative dramatics which can be done very satisfactorily with a much larger group. Pantomime and creative movement with music are only limited by space, and even these can usually be done by a part of the class at a time in aisles and the front of the room.

Third- or fourth-graders, for instance, can all be the people in "Doorbells," [2] each walking along the street as a character and ringing a doorbell. Fifth-grade children can be Midas, touching the objects in his bedroom and feeling disappointed that they do not turn to gold—until the first rays of the sun bring him the Golden Touch! Most of the pantomimes used for sense training (Chapters 2 and 3) can be used by many children at the same time. So can all the activity pantomimes.

Even without leaving their seats, the children can all be the tailor (in "The Tailor and the Bear") busily cutting out and sewing a suit of clothes. If older children were playing the

[2] See Story List in the Appendix for all stories mentioned in this chapter.

Roger Williams episode described in Chapter 8, all who were not the chief characters in the front of the room could be the townspeople reacting and occasionally voicing their feelings.

In place of dramatizing entire stories, the children may use *elements* of the stories they read, one group playing at a time and enacting only a short scene, thus giving the opportunity for several different groups to give their interpretation in succession. Once in a while it may be practicable to dramatize an entire story; but since this requires a good deal of time, incidents from stories or interesting characterizations may have to suffice. By making dramatization a part of literature or social studies in this way, and utilizing occasional free periods, the problem of finding time for dramatics is not too difficult.

The Environment for Creativity

How does one get children to be creative? What does it require from the teacher?

In the first place, the feeling in the room must give the children a sense of freedom—freedom with control, of course, rather than license. They need to be sure that the teacher has confidence in them, that her standards are not beyond their reach, that no sincere effort or idea will be rebuffed by her or ridiculed by the other children. A critical, demanding teacher gets no really creative work from her pupils.

Sometimes the spirited reading of a story is enough to fire their imagination, but very often a good introduction linking it with their own experience helps the children to get more from the reading. Then a build-up by discussion brings out creative ideas, and soon the children are ready to begin developing a play.

For little children there is nothing better than actual experiences to stir imagination for dramatic play. A trip to a lake, a short ride on a train, a walk in the woods, a children's theatre play—any one of many new experiences will offer food for their imagination; and the teacher who sees to it that her children *notice* things helps them build a rich store of material on which to draw. Vicarious experiences read or heard about are sufficient to motivate older children.

The Teacher as Guide

Always the teacher must keep in mind her role: that of a guide who, from her wider experience will help the children to read between the lines and see the possibilities in a story. She is not a director, as she would be if she were producing a formal play. This she must never forget.

It is easier to tell children what to think than to draw out ideas from them; easier to suggest what the characters would say than leave it to the children with their halting dialogue. But if it is to be *their* play, the teacher must accept the children's immature work and remember that perfection is an adult requirement, that *product* is of less consequence than process. It is far more important that *each child* be made to feel the joy of achievement than that a good play be developed for an audience.

For when a creative play is to be given as a performance, it is inevitable that the teacher must do more than guide it. Few children are skillful enough to make it effective for an audience without some direction; and in so far as she directs it, it becomes more her play than theirs. It is thus better that the only audience for most of the children's playing be the part of the class not in the cast at the time. An occasional sharing of a creative play that has turned out well with another home room of the same age or younger is satisfying so long as its development has not been hurried to meet a deadline, and so long as it is done simply and without special costumes. What is important is that children shall not think it is the *object* of playmaking.

A Dramatic Way of Teaching

It is possible to have a dramatic *way* of teaching without ever doing a play. The classroom of such a teacher is never dull because she gives children an outlet for feelings as well as for thought. It would be well if there were more such teachers, for there are so few opportunities for emotional release in our schools.

Kindergarteners, however, have many outlets. The playhouse, the boats and trains and stores they construct, the preparation for new experiences, and reliving of past ones—all of these mean that make-believe is inevitable.

Teachers of older children do not usually realize that the love of the dramatic goes far beyond kindergarten. "Tell your parents goodbye before you come to school tomorrow," says the fourth grade teacher, "because we start for Hawaii at ten o'clock!" How much more exciting, more real, than if she had said, "Locate Hawaii on the map and read what it says on page 56 about the formation of the islands!"

One teacher whose children always have a sense of reality about the countries they study—a sense of actually going there —took the occasion one day when they had visitors to say, "Since you are just back from a trip to Australia and I have a chance to go there next winter suppose you give me some advice as to what I should wear and what I should see."

Many hands were in the air immediately, and the first piece of advice, given by Janet, was, "Be sure to take your summer clothes."

"You're kidding," laughed the teacher. "I said I was going next *winter*."

"But the seasons are different there," insisted Janet with authority, and she went on to explain what kind of a climate her teacher might expect.

In the meantime another member of the class was anxiously waiting to tell her that she wouldn't have to worry about understanding the language because they spoke English. Others were full of information about the cities, the crops, the natural resources, the animals, and about as many other aspects of Australia as there were children in the room.

A former group taught by the same teacher[3] had written letters of appreciation to the children's theatre director, and one after another of the letters asked if "Heidi" couldn't be given the following season "because we went to Switzerland this year and I would like to see a play about it." When the director read the first letter she thought the child's visit was an actual one; but on reading the others she decided that their study of Switzerland had simply made it very real to them.

It seems safe to say that children who experience vicariously the countries they study will retain far more factual knowledge about them than do the ones who try to memorize these facts. Furthermore, they get much more than facts. One group who "went to Holland" became so interested in the Dutch people that when, a short time later, Holland was visited by terrible floods, they voted to send towards its relief all the money they had collected from selling paper. It is not likely that the usual way of studying geography would have brought about such warm human sympathy as was evidenced by these children's action.

A classroom teacher need never apologize for using a dramatic approach in her teaching. She may not see its effect at first because of her lack of experience in using it skillfully. If she is sincere in trying it, however, she will be surprised at the enthusiastic way in which her children will respond. For she will be appealing to a universal interest, and both she and her children will learn more than is written in their books.

[3] Ruth Hadden, Haven School, Evanston, Illinois.

THE SPECIAL TEACHER

The specialist in creative drama is or should be a speech-trained person, skillful in teaching his—or generally her—subject. With experience she should grow to be an artist-teacher, capable of teaching both children and teachers, as well as supervising the work in elementary schools.

Her advantage over the classroom teacher is that her education for teaching the subject consists of far more than a college course in creative dramatics. To be a special teacher in this field she should be a graduate of a school or department of speech in a college or university, with a broad education in liberal arts, and courses in child psychology, children's literature, storytelling, creative dramatics, and probably children's theatre and dance, in addition to general speech and drama. She should have done student-teaching with children, preferably both in classroom subjects and in drama; and she would be a much better teacher of dramatics if she had a year or more of general teaching before specializing.

Just as a specialist in medicine is advised to be a general practitioner first, so the experience under a classroom teacher, especially if supplemented by a year of general teaching, prepares one to be a much better specialist—one who will understand the school curriculum, the problems of the classroom, and the children themselves. Experience with boys and girls in all kinds of situations is helpful, and because of having been a classroom teacher herself, she will be better able to work with other teachers in correlating material.

A leader should be skilled enough so that she is an excellent example to the children in posture and grace, in pleasing voice and clean-cut diction. And she would not be a specialist in creative drama if she did not have a strong belief in the power it can be in the lives of children, and confidence in her ability to teach it. That she enjoys boys and girls and gets on well with them has no doubt been the strongest influence in her decision to teach the subject.

Like all teachers, however, she has much to learn about teaching children. Therefore, this part of our discussion will concern the problems of the specialist as she *begins* her teaching. The experienced specialist has no need of help.

Problems of the Beginning Teacher

Youth and attractiveness in a beginning teacher have both advantages and disadvantages. Because she is nearer the age of her pupils than is the older teacher, they accept her with greater pleasure; and if they erect any barriers against her, they are lower than if she were older.

One earnest young student-teacher of creative dramatics, having planned every step of her first lesson, introduced it with great care and at some length to a seventh-grade class that for some reason seemed uncannily quiet. She felt highly successful until the time came for them to take over the discussion and planning. To her dismay they seemed to have taken in nothing at all of her careful introduction. It was a labored and uninspired participation and she was almost in tears by the end of the period. Only the smiling supervisor in the back of the room knew the cause: the children were so hypnotized by the young teacher's beauty and exquisite grooming that they had not heard a word she said!

Though such overpowering good looks are not commonly the cause of a teacher's failure, her youth makes it harder for her to win the children's respect, and they often take advantage of her. In a class where a good deal of freedom is essential for creative thinking, when hands are not needed for books or paint-brushes, there is more than the usual temptation for distractions. This means not only that *something of real interest*

should always get under way at once, but also that the teacher
should compel the feeling from the very first meeting that she
is a leader, firm and assured, for all her youth and friendliness.

The Planning

The planning of the first sessions with children always demands prayerful consideration! Whether or not this is an extracurricular group, it is important that the children enjoy it so
much that they will look forward to coming again. No good
teacher depends on the inspiration of the moment for either the
first or any other session. She will doubtless discard half a
dozen ideas before she settles on the one she likes best for the
beginning lesson. From there on she will try to think of fresh
ideas for each meeting, knowing how much variety helps in
sustaining interest.

If she is fortunate enough to have a classroom of her own,
she will always be on the lookout for pictures and properties
that will be pleasing and stimulating to the imagination. She
will be constantly searching for records to use as mood music
and accompaniment for rhythms. Most certainly she will want
a bookshelf for her favorite stories and poems.

Definite objectives for the whole course and specifically for
each meeting with the children are absolutely necessary. Th
general objectives mentioned in Chapter 1 are the ones m
widely accepted by experienced leaders in creative drama.
a teacher also needs, of course, to know what she wants t
complish at each session.

The First Session

If the class is extracurricular the children will not b
in together, so that the leader will be able to greet
individually. For classes that do enter all at once t
greeting will be followed, no doubt, by some sort o

introductions that will be warm and cordial and perhaps even jolly. Such informality will not, of course, be possible if the class is large; but a feeling of friendliness can be established no matter what the size of the group.

Every child wants recognition, wants to be considered a person of worth. A good teacher, therefore, loses no time in getting to know the names and the children who answer to them. When the class is small and some already know one another, they like to introduce a friend to the teacher.

"Miss Black, this is Sally," one child may say. The teacher shakes hands with Sally, greeting her with a smile and making her feel that she is a person of consequence. Perhaps she will make a little personal comment as she acknowledges the introduction. Sally may be able to introduce several other children, and they in turn may present the rest. If some of the children are not acquainted with anyone else in the group, they will have to introduce themselves. The leader, knowing this, will make it a point to see that they make friends very soon.

A more informal way of getting acquainted is by the teacher's asking each in the semicircle to tell her his first name. She does her best to concentrate hard enough to memorize the names, and the second time around she tries to name the children herself. The boys and girls consider it great fun to watch her struggle to remember them all, and they chuckle gleefully if she hesitates and says, "Don't tell me! Just give me the first letter." For a group of not more than fifteen, it is a jolly introduction, and is one of the best ways to associate the various names with the children to whom they belong.

How to begin the actual work of the class in the most natural way is something each teacher has to decide for herself. Immediate experiences are usually the surest approach to dramatic play with the very young children. The season of the year offers many possibilities. If it is fall—the time when most classes

begin—one could not do better than to use the type of lesson recorded in Chapter 2 by a kindergarten class. This synthesis of dramatic play, rhythm, and sense training shows what one may expect from five-year-old children.

If it were winter, there would be just as many opportunities in cold winds, snowflakes, Jack Frost, snow men, and all the other accompaniments of that season. Spring and summer, too, are rich in possibilities for sense training and imaginary play. Whatever one uses, she will get the best results by capitalizing on something that is of special interest at the moment.

Familiar activities, often seasonal, are also natural beginnings for children of third, fourth, fifth, and sixth grades. After the get-acquainted period, they may enjoy a guessing game in which they pantomime something they like best of anything to do. Some of the miming will be so simple that the class guesses in an instant that it is reading, skating, playing football, dancing. But those who like best to collect stamps, make airplanes, or go to the movies will have a succession of actions which are more complicated.

This kind of pantomime at the outset helps to show the interests of the children, giving the teacher a better chance to know them, and perhaps suggesting further pantomime. The poem "Imaginings," quoted in Chapter 3, is a more novel way of introducing creative drama to children of these age levels, and whether or not used at the first meeting, is wonderfully good as an incentive for creative thinking, especially in the third and fourth grades. The exercises in sense impressions, too, are very successful both for finer sensitivity and for careful bodily action.

Seventh and Eighth Grades

The problems involved in beginning classes for seventh, and especially for eighth grade, are less simple than for younger children. Self-consciousness combined with fast-growing bodies not well under control make it difficult for adolescents to forget themselves in pantomime. This often causes cover-up tactics which come out in clowning in the boys and colorless, unimaginative playing in the girls. Both boys and girls are so afraid to show real feeling, particularly in front of the opposite sex, that they are a distinct problem to the teacher of drama.

One of the pitfalls of an inexperienced teacher is making such indefinite assignments to these older children that before she realizes her mistake the class gets entirely out of hand. "Next time, bring in an interesting pantomime—anything you choose," she says, and then is appalled to find that what they choose is a collection of hold-ups, murders, and kidnapings! These from really decent young people who, without guidance, simply got their ideas of what was "interesting" from newspaper headlines, television shows, and movies.

Once they have vied with one another in crime pantomimes it is not easy to win them over to less lurid scenes. How much better to have taken more care in making assignments than to have to try to bring them back to sane situations after exciting melodrama! The teacher could easily have avoided such a predicament if she had assigned specific types of pantomimes such as are suggested in Chapter 4—pantomimes which give the pupils plenty of freedom but limit them to ideas which are worth dramatizing. The junior high school students who worked out the situation of the lost purse could not have been more deeply interested, yet they brought into it nothing at all of crime.

A beginning eighth-grade class can be very enjoyable when it is made up of all girls or all boys. The majority of extracurricular dramatic classes, as well as electives in school, are likely to have a minority of boys; but the boys who do elect such a class often have special ability and are therefore leaders in the group. Seventh-grade children usually have less fear of one another than eighth-graders and are therefore more natural and forthright.

If all children had a good background in creative bodily movement, much of the problem of handling an eighth-grade class would disappear. Their experience in pantomime when they have had creative drama in the lower grades helps greatly; and many an eighth-grade class, playing one of the witches' scenes from *Macbeth* on a half-darkened stage, has been able to forget its individual fears and enact the strange, unearthly creatures of Macbeth's imagination with surprising abandon.

Discipline Problems

"It would be such fun to teach children if only there weren't any discipline problems," sighs a young teacher. "Why is it that I who teach a subject the children like so much can't have a nice, well-behaved class like Mrs. Moore's?"

Perhaps, if she were to ask Mrs. Moore, the classroom teacher would tell her that the children in her first class were not angels either; that she has simply learned from experience how to handle children until now it is a joy to teach them.

When successful teachers of playmaking are asked for advice concerning the handling of children, they will give various answers. One teacher in a private school says: "I have established a ritual that the children always follow from the time they come into the room. No matter how they race up the stairs, from the time I greet them at the door they observe a special way of taking their seats and making ready for the beginning of the class. There never is any confusion in coming in so that I no longer have to wait for them to get quiet. I used to have to wait sometimes as long as ten minutes—and I *waited*."

Many teachers who have large classes in auditoriums give the children permanent seats, with an empty seat between each one and his neighbors in order to remove temptation for private conversations.

All teachers need to have some signal which means quiet. It is explained carefully the first day and quiet is *insisted* upon whenever the signal is given. It soon becomes such a habit that the children automatically become silent when they hear it. The signal may be a piano chord, a gong, chimes, or even some special word spoken incisively.

If, when the children are quieted by the signal, the leader asks them to come back to their seats rather than try to talk to them scattered over the room, she finds it much easier to hold their attention. She must constantly watch herself, however, to see that she doesn't talk too much—a common fault of teachers!

The leader who speaks with relaxed voice, never raising it in annoyance when there is confusion but saying something worth hearing when she does speak, is always listened to by the children. It is sometimes necessary to wait for silence before speaking, and most good teachers refuse to try to speak until their class is quiet no matter how long it takes. Sometimes a glance at the clock reminds the children that they are wasting precious time—and as a rule they enjoy dramatics enough so that the time is all too quickly spent.

One likes to have the children eager to volunteer for parts, but in many classes they will clamor for a role they want until they cause much noise and confusion. So, many teachers simply refuse to assign parts to those who try to attract attention by asking, "May I be Caddie?" "May Marge and I be customers?" She is very sure, too, to give *everyone* a chance, not just the ones whose hands are always waving.

No teacher should permit a scene to continue when it is being spoiled by silliness or burlesque. If she stops the playing and either calls the cast to their seats or makes a substitution if only one child is overplaying, the class will soon understand that creative drama is to be respected at all times even when the material is humorous. It will not be necessary to reprimand anyone.

Some leaders find it effective to spend a short time on a discussion of professionals and amateurs if they have a class with a tendency to regard dramatics as not worthy of great respect. They ask what the difference is between the two, bringing out the idea from the children's experience with sports that the professional has a serious attitude toward what he does because it is his livelihood whereas an amateur does something because he enjoys doing it.

"Which do you like more—to throw a ball around or play a game?" The reply is always that the game is more fun. And if one then asks, "Which is more fun—to do just any kind of a skit or work out a really good play?" they are unanimous for the play.

"Then, from the first, let's be amateurs with a professional attitude in whatever we do here," says the leader, "and I'll promise you that it will be far more fun than if we just 'played around' with dramatics."

One of the perplexing problems is what to do about a child who is a delight as long as he is playing and a pest when he is not. After he has had a turn and is not likely to have another he loses interest and is a distraction to the other children.

This is one of the strongest arguments against a large class. Even the most co-operative children prefer to play rather than watch. It also is a reason for playing small units of the story and in alternating individual playing with the "trying on" of characters, with all or a number of the class active at the same time. By so doing, a leader can give several chances to each child.

When the teacher is annoyed by one or two children she

does not reprimand them in front of the class, thus utterly spoiling its spirit. If one or two good-natured warnings do not get results she speaks softly on the side to the offenders or talks to them separately afterwards. By scolding she loses her rapport with all her pupils. If she finds it impossible to interest a certain child who continually interferes with the other children she excludes him from the class. It is not fair to the others to allow him to spoil the feeling in the group.

Though of course she likes some of the children better than the others, she never lets it be evident by any favoritism or comparison; and she sincerely tries to find the good qualities in the ones who attract her least.

She is careful not to let her personality dominate the class, for she knows she will get much more creative thinking, more concentration, and less imitation if she can avoid doing so.

She knows that she must never moralize or seem to disapprove of anything she thinks unethical in the playing or the discussion if she wants the children to feel free to be honest with her. At the same time, it is just as important not to give the impression of putting a stamp of approval on it. If a pupil introduces something questionable into a scene and the other children laugh, she usually ignores it unless it is commented upon, in which case she is likely to ask the opinion of the class.

Very often a question of standards or values comes out of the story or the playing and there is a wonderful opportunity for discussion. The leader who, without taking sides, can ask the right questions to bring out the best thinking of the children does much more for her class than the one who gives her own opinion. We have unusual opportunity in drama to help boys and girls in the building of a worthy life philosophy. With our guidance they are enacting characters and evaluating them. When stories they dramatize concern ethical questions, the way they are handled is largely the responsibility of the teacher.

If by indirection we open their eyes to see more clearly what is worthy and what is cheap we are doing for them something of lasting value.

A teacher who appreciates what every child in her group contributes, and sincerely tries to help him believe in his own best self will in time have a class with few behavior problems. The sensitivity to know which child is most in need of praise and which works best when challenged by criticism is one of the assets of a valuable teacher. The appeal to a child's best self—her confidence in him as a person and as a creative thinker—will make him dissatisfied to give her anything less than his best. "Whoever believes in me may lead me." [4]

The beginning teacher of dramatics who never meets difficult problems is exceptional. When they do confront her she should not be discouraged but she needs to do some creative thinking in order to find the solutions to them! For she never can be really successful until she does solve them.

QUALIFICATIONS OF A TEACHER OF PLAYMAKING

If we try to catalogue all the qualifications of an ideal woman teacher of creative drama we shall find her to be discouragingly perfect, with all the finest qualities of women in general, all the assets of the best teachers in any field, besides all the special qualifications needed for her work in creative dramatics. These in addition to her educational background, which has already been discussed.

Let us take heart, however. No one has them all! Remember what Brother Luke told Robin in *The Door in the Wall*—that, after all, the measure of success is "what we do with what we have."

"What we have." One public school supervisor said: "If I am considering two teachers and know that one is more highly

[4] Hughes Mearns, *The Creative Adult* (Doubleday & Co., Inc., 1940).

skilled than the other but not quite so fine a person, I always engage the finer person, feeling sure she will learn. And in the meantime it is a privilege for the children to be associated with her. If a person is lacking in personal stature and sensitivity her skill is of little value."

Integrity in character and art comes first, of course. The honesty, the sincerity that characterizes a person is recognized by children and adults alike. It shines through everything she does, and builds respect for her even if she is lacking in some other important qualities.

One such quality is *sensitivity*. Without it one cannot go far in any art, cannot even be an understanding friend. It is the quality that enables us to move imaginatively inside the lives of others and experience vicariously what they are feeling. Fortunately, it can be cultivated to some extent, so that a sensitive teacher can develop a degree of awareness in many of the children she teaches.

Before anyone can help boys and girls with their very real problems she needs to be *emotionally mature.* She is never petty, and she is able to be objective about herself and her pupils. Further, she can be counted on to be unprejudiced against races or religions, realizing that each individual must be judged on his own merits.

Judgment and *taste,* indispensable companions, are near the top of the list of requisites. Good judgment—a sense of the fitness of things—must be learned by experience though home background counts greatly. Good taste goes hand in hand with good judgment and leads one to do the things which are fine and suitable.

As a teacher of creative dramatics she would be handicapped indeed without a *sense of humor!* Especially is there hope for her if she can be amused at herself when enjoying martyrdom because people do not appreciate her! Children like a teacher who smiles, who enjoys the fun both in stories and in situations that arise in class. Though they always react to a young and pretty teacher, they would exchange her any time for an older, less attractive person with a grand sense of humor. Personal appearance does count, but careful grooming, pretty colors, and a radiant personality more than make up for beauty of face and figure.

Whoever would be a successful teacher of lively youngsters, no matter what she teaches, needs plenty of *vitality!* One must be gloriously alive to teach playmaking for, as Ruth Sawyer writes in that fine book *The Way of the Storyteller* "it is not possible to kindle fresh fires from burned-out embers." Good health makes it easier for her to be vital but it is less important than qualities of mind and spirit.

Boys and girls sense almost at once whether a leader really likes children, whether she takes a sincere interest in them as individuals. If she does she will be friendly to all and at the same time she will be firm enough to inspire their respect. And this respect comes from her leadership in handling a class, from her knowledge and skill in teaching her subject, and from the fact that they can look up to her as a person.

A Creative Personality

Hughes Mearns, in his notable book *The Creative Adult* [5] writes, "Before anything significant can be done in the creative education of youth by adults, they themselves must learn to be creative personalities."

Such a statement from no less an authority than Mearns may be discouraging to those of us who have doubts about our own creative gifts unless we can be reassured by Mearns' definition of creative personalities. For, he says, they are "individualists, those who come daily to original judgment, who respect their

[5] (Doubleday & Co., Inc., 1940).

own sense of what is true and good and beautiful, who are unafraid of the imputation either of ignorance or of low taste, but
only of the accusation of untruthfulness."

The teacher with individuality has a horizon far wider than
her classroom. Books and travel can do much to make her a
more interesting person both in and out of the classroom. She
may know much about gardening, about birds, boats, art, or
music. She has strong social consciousness, is a part of the
community life, is concerned about the national scene and willing to take the trouble to write her congressmen on crucial issues. She has a global point of view, knowing that she is edu-
cating boys and girls who must be creative thinkers, able to
adjust to change and to expanding opportunities. For half of
them may choose life work unheard of today just as a large proportion of present adults are working at jobs which did not
exist when they were children.

For the challenging situations youth will meet in business,
industry, science, politics, in the arts, and in living itself, the
need for creative thinking will be great. What education has
done in the past is far, far short of what it must do now if our
world is to be saved from destroying itself. Home, church, and
school must somehow build leaders who are more foresighted,
more understanding, more courageous in speaking and acting
according to their convictions. They must develop people who
think independently, who can live peaceably with others.

It is a grave responsibility, yet a thrilling opportunity for the
teacher. Whether she is a specialist or a classroom teacher she
needs to *believe* in her calling, have faith in its value. She must
have a strong sense of the direction in which she is guiding
children, and know *why* she is guiding them that way. One
small classroom can influence the world. Let her remember this
when she reflects on her role as a teacher.

Bibliography

THE BOOKS FOR THIS LIST HAVE BEEN CAREFULLY CHOSEN AS THOSE most directly helpful to the teacher who is to guide children in playmaking. The brief annotations should make the list more useful to the inexperienced leader. A few of the very valuable books are out of print and will need to be read in libraries.

Some of the following books concern playmaking exclusively, some have chapters concerning it, while many others offer the leader valuable background for deepening her understanding of creative teaching.

Whoever guides informal drama should also understand formal plays. A limited list of good books on this subject, with chapters on the construction of plays, has therefore been included. Those who wish to read further will discover in many of these books bibliographies which supply a wider list for each specific subject.

EDUCATION AND MENTAL HEALTH

Applegate, Mauree, *Everybody's Business—Our Children* (Row, Peterson & Co., 1952).

This is probably the most informal and refreshing book in all of education. Full of valuable ideas for teachers and parents.

Axline, Virginia, *Play Therapy* (Houghton Mifflin Co., 1947).

A method of treatment for disturbed children in play activities.

Dewey, John, *Experience and Education* (The Macmillan Co., 1938).

An authoritative book on the vital place of experience in education.

Dixon, C. Madeleine, *High, Wide, and Deep* (The John Day Co., Inc., 1938).

Creative heights, social widths, and the depths of wonder give the author her title. Dramatic play is stressed for nursery-school children because of the important social adjustments which it brings about.

Gesell, Arnold, and Ilg, Frances L., *The Child from Five to Ten* (Harper and Brothers, 1946).

Interesting information about the child's concern with dramatic play at various ages, and its values.

Glover, Katherine, *Children of the New Day* (Appleton-Century-Crofts, Inc., 1934).

A parent or teacher who feels a responsibility in guiding children toward emotional maturity will do well to read this book.

Huizinga, Johan, *Homo Ludens: A Study of the Play Element in Culture* (The Beacon Press, 1950).

A significant work in which the author interprets one of the most fundamental elements of human culture: the instinct for play.

Hartley, Ruth E.; Frank, Lawrence K.; Goldenson, Robert M., *Understanding Children's Play* (Columbia University Press, 1952).

An exploratory study of play in the fostering of healthy personality development in young children. Two chapters are devoted to dramatic play.

Jersild, Arthur T., *Child Psychology* (Prentice-Hall, rev. 1947).

A standard work on child psychology.

Moreno, J. L., *Psychodrama* (Beacon House, 1945).

There are chapters in this three-volume work by the originator of the terms *psychodrama* and *sociodrama* which apply specifically to the therapeutic use of drama with children.

Morgan, John J. B., *The Psychology of the Unadjusted School Child* (The Macmillan Co., 1936).

The author's discussion of how to discover the presence of conflict in a child, and how to help him adjust will be of value to any teacher.

Osborn, Alex F., *Applied Imagination* (Charles Scribner's Sons, 1953).

This and an earlier publication *Your Creative Power* are stimulating books concerned with waking up the imagination of adults. It has implications for cultivating the imagination of children.

Plant, J. S., *The Envelope* (The Commonwealth Fund, 1950).

A psychiatrist tells how important it is that children are afforded a constructive emotional outlet.

Prescott, Daniel, *Emotion and the Educative Process* (American Council on Education, Washington, D.C., 1938).

This book proposes that the schools pay as much attention to children's emotions as to the three R's.

Slavson, S. R., *Creative Group Education* (Association Press, 1937).

Socializing the self-centered and aggressive drives of the child is the main theme of this book.

Slavson, S. R., *An Introduction to Group Therapy* (The Commonwealth Fund, 1943).

The method of psychotherapy used in a New York social-service agency in guiding children with personality problems is described in this book.

Travis, Lee E., and Baruch, Dorothy W., *Personal Problems of Everyday Life* (Appleton-Century-Crofts, Inc., 1941).

This very helpful book on mental hygiene deals with the everyday mental and emotional ills which beset both children and adults.

Washburne, Carleton, *A Living Philosophy of Education* (The John Day Co., 1940).

The chapter on "Dramatic Expression" is particularly good, but the whole book is valuable to a teacher.

Wilson, Gertrude, and Ryland, Gladys, *Social Group Work Practice* (Houghton, Mifflin Co., 1949).

The authors say, "This book describes the knowledge and skill that the social worker needs to acquire in order to make creative use of the social process in the group."

Witty, Paul A., and Skinner, C. E., *Mental Hygiene in Education* (Farrar & Rinehart, Inc., 1939).

An elementary teacher will find this book helpful in understanding the problems of children and how to deal with them.

PLAYMAKING AND THE RELATED ARTS

Andrews, Gladys, *Creative Rhythmic Movement for Children* (Prentice-Hall, Inc., 1954).

If all children could have the kind of creative experiences described in this book they would gain wonderful freedom for playmaking.

The Athletic Institute, *The Recreation Program* (The Athletic Institute, Chicago, 1954).

A useful handbook on all phases of recreation, with chapters on the various arts.

Burger, Isabel, *Creative Play Acting* (A. S. Barnes & Co., Inc., 1950).

Very practical procedures in pantomime and in developing creative plays; with several examples.

Brown, Corinne, *Creative Drama in the Lower School* (Appleton-Century-Crofts, Inc., 1929).

Worth reading although more emphasis is placed on producing plays for *audiences* than many teachers and psychologists believe is wise.

Cole, Natalie, *The Arts in the Classroom* (The John Day Co., Inc., 1940).

A fascinating book which no teacher of playmaking can afford to miss. The essence of creative teaching.

Dewey, John, *Art as Experience* (Minton, Balch & Co., 1934).

Here is a stimulating work by the leader in modern education, with many implications for the teacher of creative drama.

Dixon, C. Madeleine, *The Power of Dance* (The John Day Co., Inc., 1939).

Using the data of children's classes, the author "gives accounts of ways and means for making the arts clear channels for communication."

Durland, Frances Caldwell, *Creative Dramatics for Children* (The Antioch Press, 1952).

This book concerns the developing of a creative play for an audience.

Fisk, Margaret Palmer, *The Art of the Rhythmic Choir* (Harper & Bros., 1950).

An inspirational book on worship and symbolic movement.

Haaga, Agnes, and Randles, Patricia, *Supplementary Materials for Use in Creative Dramatics with Younger Children* (University of Washington, 1952).

A résumé of 27 sessions with 5-6-year-old children, together with book and record references. A helpful guide for the inexperienced teacher.

Lease, Ruth Gonser, and Siks, Geraldine Brain, *Creative Dramatics for Home, School, and Community* (Harper and Bros., 1952).

A very fine and practical book on the guiding of children in creative dramatics, whether at home, school, or in community programs.

Lowenfeld, Viktor, *Creative and Mental Growth* (Macmillan Co., rev. 1952).

An important book on what education in art contributes to the development of a child.

Mearns, Hughes, *Creative Youth, Creative Power, The Creative Adult* (Doubleday and Co., 1928, 1929, 1940).

It seems safe to say that most of the creative teachers in the country have received their greatest inspiration from these three books, especially from *Creative Power*. They are a striking contribution to the field of creative education, and though concerned specifically with writing, are quite as important for teachers in any other field.

Merrill, John, and Fleming, Martha, *Play-making and Plays* (The Macmillan Co., 1930).

Based on the dramatic work done at the Francis Parker School in Chicago, this book contains an especially good chapter on the importance of drama in education.

Pethybridge, David C., *Directed Drama* (The University of London Press, Ltd. 1951).

The experiments described here begin with improvised drama by elementary children, but end with a script which the teacher writes.

Slade, Peter, *Child Drama* (The University of London Press, Ltd. 1954).

An important book from a leader of creative drama in England. Whether or not one agrees entirely with his arguments and the way in which they are expressed, he will find it well worth reading.

Ward, Winifred, *Creative Dramatics* (Appleton-Century-Crofts, Inc. 1930).

The author's first book on creative drama. For teachers of the upper grades and directors of plays.

BACKGROUNDS OF LITERATURE AND LIFE

Arbuthnot, May Hill, *Children and Books* (Scott, Foresman and Co., 1947).

A complete course in children's literature. An invaluable book. On pages 587-589 is an especially good list of poems for use in choral speaking with elementary-school children.

Chute, Marchette. *An Introduction to Shakespeare* (E. P. Dutton & Co., 1953).

A simple and interesting little book which is good background for both teacher and pupils.

Dalgliesh, Alice, *First Experiences With Literature* (Charles Scribner's Sons, 1937).

A practical guide for parent or teacher in giving children their first taste of literature.

Duff, Annis, *Bequest of Wings* (The Viking Press, 1945).

An inspiring book telling how a mother guided her children to a love for fine literature.

Eaton, Anne T., *Reading With Children* (The Viking Press, 1940).

So delightfully does the author write about all the really good books for children that one is impelled to begin at once to broaden his acquaintance with them.

Eaton, Anne T., *Treasure for the Taking* (The Viking Press, 1946).

A basic annotated list of books for boys and girls by a nationally known critic.

Foster, Genevieve, *George Washington's World, Abraham Lincoln's World, Augustus Caesar's World* (Charles Scribner's Sons, 1941, 1944, 1947).

A rich source of information concerning these eras.

Hartman, Gertrude, *Medieval Days and Ways* (The Macmillan Co., 1937).

Excellent background material for teacher and pupils who develop medieval plays. Authentic illustrations.

Huber, Miriam Blanton, *Story and Verse for Children* (The Macmillan Co., 1940).

An exceptionally good anthology of children's literature.

Johnson, Edna; Scott, Charles E.; Sickels, Evelyn R., *Anthology of Children's Literature* (Houghton Mifflin Co., rev., 1948).

An extensive collection of prose and poetry for children.

McLeod, Mary, *The Shakespeare Story Book* (A. S. Barnes & Co. No date indicated).

The stories of Shakespeare's plays told in an interesting style. These versions may be readily dramatized.

Meigs, Cornelia; Nesbitt, Elizabeth; Eaton, Anne; Viguers, Ruth Hill, *A Critical History of Children's Literature* (The Macmillan Co., 1953).

A survey of children's books in English from earliest times to the present. By four experts in the field of children's literature.

Quennell, Marjorie and C. H. B., *A History of Everyday Things in England.* 3 volumes. (Charles Scribner's Sons, 1918-35).

Information concerning customs from 1066 to 1934. Many pictures.

Sawyer, Ruth, *The Way of the Storyteller* (The Viking Press, 1942).

A beautifully written book on the art of storytelling—the best in the field. Eleven of the author's stories are included.

Shedlock, Marie, *The Art of the Story-Teller* (Dover Publications, 1951).

Written by one of the great storytellers of years ago, this book was recently reprinted.

Ward, Winifred, ed., *Stories to Dramatize* (Children's Theatre Press, 1952).

A collection of stories which have proved favorites for creative plays. For every age level up to high school.

Wilson, J. Dover, *Through Elizabethan Eyes: An Abridgment of Life in Shakespeare's England, for Junior Readers* (The Macmillan Co., 1939).

Rich material to be used for better understanding of life in Shakespeare's day.

GOOD REFERENCE BOOKS FOR LEADERS OF CREATIVE DRAMA IN RELIGIOUS EDUCATION

Adult Education Association of the U.S.A., *How to Use Role Playing* (This pamphlet may be ordered from the Service Dept.,

General Board of Education of the Methodist Church, Nashville, Tenn.).

A description, with case examples, of the use of role-playing and other tools of learning.

Applegarth, Margaret, *Right Here, Right Now!* (Harper & Bros., 1950).

Twenty-eight interesting worship services, most of them requiring a reading choir.

Bailey, Albert Edward, *Daily Life in Bible Times* (Scribner's, 1943).

A good source of informational background for a church school teacher.

Barton, Lucy, *Costuming the Biblical Play* (Walter H. Baker Co., 1937).

Authentic drawings and descriptions of Biblical costumes by a leader in her field.

Brown, Jeanette Perkins, *The Storyteller in Religious Education* (The Pilgrim Press, 1951).

A valuable little book on how and what to tell. It includes fifteen complete stories.

De Jong, Meindert, *Bible Days* (The Fideler Co., Grand Rapids, Mich., 1948).

Beautiful and authentic pictures and descriptions of life and customs of ancient Palestine.

Ehrensperger, Harold A., *Conscience on Stage* (Abingdon Press, 1947).

A discussion by an outstanding authority of the educational approach to drama in its use in the church. It concerns the relation of drama to religion as it applies to all ages.

Farjeon, Eleanor, *Ten Saints* (The Oxford University Press, 1936).

Beautifully told stories of St. Francis, St. Christopher, and other saints.

Niebuhr, Hulda, *Ventures in Dramatics* (Charles Scribners Sons, 1935).

An interesting account of a series of dramatic projects with the older boys and girls of a church school. A very specific help for the leader.

Smither, Ethel L., *The Use of the Bible With Children* (Abingdon Press, 1937).

A very helpful guide in learning how to make the Bible effective in the lives of children.

Smither, Ethel L., *A Picture Book of Palestine* (Abingdon Press, 1947).

Useful information and illustrations concerning Palestine.

Willcox, Helen L., *Bible Study Through Educational Dramatics* (Abingdon Press, 1924).

Though long out of print, this book should be read in libraries for it is very superior.

PUPPETS AND MARIONETTES

Ackley, Edith Flack, *Marionettes* (Frederick H. Stokes Co., 1929).

A charmingly written book which is of great help to those who wish to make simple marionettes. Clear designs and instructions.

Batchelder, Marjorie, *The Puppet Theatre Handbook* (Harper & Brothers, 1947).

A practical guide by one of the authorities in the field.

Bufano, Remo, *Book of Puppetry*. Edited by Arthur Richmond (Macmillan Co., 1950). A revision of Bufano's earlier work, *Be a Puppet Showman*.

Ficklen, Alexander, *A Handbook of Fist Puppets* (Frederick H. Stokes Co., 1935).

Careful instructions on how to make and use fist puppets. Information about producing a puppet play.

Joseph, Helen Haiman, *A Book of Marionettes* (The Viking Press, 1920).

One of the earliest and best histories of puppets in this country.

McPharlin, Paul, *The Puppet Theatre in America* (Harper and Brothers, 1949).

An authoritative history by a leader in the field.

Mills, Winifred H. and Dunn, Louise M., *Marionettes, Masks and Shadows* (Doubleday & Co., Inc. 1927).

A standard book on all aspects of puppetry.

Sarg, Tony, *The Marionette Book* (The Viking Press, 1935).

A valuable book by a master showman.

Warner, Frances Lester, *The Ragamuffin Marionettes* (Houghton Mifflin Co., 1932).

A description of homemade puppets and how to use them. Contains three plays.

CHORAL SPEAKING AND SPEECH IMPROVEMENT

Gullan, Marjorie. *Spoken Poetry in the Schools, Choral Speaking* (Methuen and Co., 1926, 1933. Also Expression Co.).

The leader and highest authority in modern choral speaking has also written a number of other good books on her subject.

Hamm, Agnes Curren, *Choral Speaking Technique* (The Tower Press, 1946).

A good discussion of choral speaking, with chapters on teaching voice and diction, rhythmic movement, etc.

Rasmussen, Carrie, *Choral Speaking for Speech Improvement* (Expression Co., 1939).

The emphasis is on improving speech through choral speaking. For junior high school.

Rasmussen, Carrie, *Speech Methods in the Elementary School* (The Ronald Press Co., 1949).

A standard book on elementary speech methods, including creative dramatics. Comprehensive and practical.

Strickland, Ruth G., *The Language Arts in the Elementary School* (D. C. Heath and Co., 1951).

One of the best of the books on language arts. It contains a good chapter on "Dramatic Interpretation."

REFERENCES IN FORMAL DRAMA FOR THE TEACHER IN PLAYMAKING

Alberti, Madame Eva, *A Handbook of Acting* (Samuel French, 1932).

This book is especially helpful in pantomime.

Albright, H. D.; Halstead, William P.; Mitchell, Lee, *Principles of Theatre Art* (Houghton Mifflin Co., 1955).

An introduction to all aspects of the theatre for the beginner.

Barton, Lucy, *Historic Costume for the Stage* (Walter H. Baker Company, 1935).

A valuable single-volume costume book extending in scope from ancient Egypt to 1914.

Chorpenning, Charlotte B., *Twenty-One Years With Children's Theatre* (Children's Theatre Press, 1954).

An account by a remarkably creative woman of the experience of writing and directing plays.

Corson, Richard, *Stage Makeup* (Appleton-Century-Crofts, Inc., 1942).

Though makeup is not generally used in creative dramatics, a teacher sometimes needs to know the principles given in this book.

Fisher, Caroline, and Robertson, Hazel, *Children and the Theater* (Stanford University Press, 1940).

Based on the work of the Palo Alto Children's Theatre, this book discusses formal theatre as it benefits the participants.

Healy, Daty, *Dress the Show* (Row, Peterson & Co., 1948).

An extremely helpful book in costuming plays for children and young people. Large illustrations and patterns for both realistic and fanciful costumes.

Mitchell, Roy, *Creative Theatre* (The John Day Company, Inc., 1929).

One of the most inspiring and thought-provoking books on the theatre.

Ward, Winifred, *Theatre for Children* (Children's Theatre Press, rev., 1952).

The history and philosophy of children's theatre, together with the writing and staging of a children's play. An annotated list of plays for child audiences.

APPENDIX II

Story List

THESE STORIES ARE SUGGESTED AS GOOD MATERIAL FOR CREATIVE plays. Most of them have been tested and many are favorites of the children. It is far from an exhaustive list, but inexperienced teachers and leaders will have a greater chance of success if they choose stories such as these which have proved popular with children as material for playmaking.

No story can be placed absolutely in one age level. Two eight-year-old children may be as unlike as a child of five and one of nine. Furthermore, the selfsame material may appeal to a group of seven-year-olds and another of ten years. Each will do a different thing with the story and have a delightful experience in doing it.

Certain story interests can be counted on in the various age levels, however, and these considerations (discussed in Chapter 5) have led to the placing of the following stories. When children have had little or no experience in story dramatization it will be wise for them to choose material for creative drama from a younger group at first because they need to feel very sure of it. Experience has proved that children can understand and appreciate many stories which are too difficult for them to play successfully.

The numbers refer to one or more books in the Sources of Stories list (p. 323) where the individual stories may be found. Most of the traditional tales are included in many more collections.

GROUP I

For Children of Five and Six Years

THE ADVENTURE OF THREE LITTLE RABBITS 111

They are in real danger when their feet stick in the treacle—until the Little Old Woman builds a fire!

ASK MR. BEAR 9(b), 40, 57, 111

Danny can't think what to give his mother for her birthday and so he asks some animals to help him. Finally the bear whispers an idea to him and he goes home and gives her a great big bear hug!

THE BREMEN TOWN MUSICIANS 32, 50, 57, 61, 95, 111

The familiar old folk tale about the donkey, the dog, the cat, and the rooster, who found a home where their music frightened away some robbers.

THE BUTTERBEAN TENT 9(a), 90

A poem with good possibilities for dramatic play. It needs music when all the wee creatures come past the child in the tent.

THE CAP THAT MOTHER MADE 10, 78

The Swedish tale of how everyone tries unsuccessfully to trade Anders something for the cap his mother has made for him.

CHOOSING SHOES 9(a)

All children like to choose shoes and so they enjoy playing this little poem about a shoe store.

THE CRIMSON BALLOON 18

The poem about the headstrong balloon is quoted in Chapter 2.

THE ELF AND THE DORMOUSE 15, 109, 111

How we came to have umbrellas is explained in this poem which tells of an elf who used a toadstool for an umbrella.

THE ELVES AND THE SHOEMAKER 25(b), 32, 50, 57, 78, 111

The fun of playing the little elves who make wonderful shoes every night, and the sympathy for the kind old couple make this story a favorite.

FANCY DRESS 111, 112

A charming little poem about a fairy who decided to make herself "a dress of apple-blossom frills to dance in at the ball," and a gnome who thought the apple-tree belonged to him.

GALOSHES 44, 110

A little poem (quoted in Chapter 2) that is excellent for dramatic rhythm.

A GOBLINADE 15, 111

A little girl is not frightened of this goblin, and so he decides to be an elf. Music is an asset.

GOLDILOCKS AND THE THREE BEARS 57, 61, 95, 111

That this is the perfect story for dramatization by little children is proved by the fact that it is used more than any other. It has a simple and beautiful pattern, delightful characters, and a dramatic climax.

THE GOOD SHEPHERD 20(a)

The story of the shepherd who leaves his flock to search for the one lamb that is lost.

HICKORY DICKORY DOCK 81

This nursery rhyme has many possibilities for dramatization with or without music. It can be a simple rhythm or a creative play, with a clock shop containing various kinds of clocks, customers to buy them, and a mouse to run up one of them.

HIDING 4, 9(a)

Benny's parents look in very strange places for him—and the children can think up others!

THE LARKS IN THE CORNFIELD 25(b)

Only when the farmer decides to attend to the reaping himself does the mother lark think it is time to move her young.

LITTLE BLACK SAMBO 13, 57, 111

Children always love to play this story of the little boy who meets the tigers.

THE LITTLE BLUE DISHES 111

A Christmas story which tells of Gretchen's longing for a set of little blue dishes and how it is that she gets them.

LITTLE DUCKLING TRIES HIS VOICE 9(b)

A fat little duckling tries to talk like the cat, the puppy, the bird, and the cow. But he finally decides that his own mother has the prettiest voice of all.

THE LITTLE ENGINE THAT COULD 78

A favorite story with children from three to six, and good for dramatization.

LITTLE MISS MUFFET 61, 81

There can be many Miss Muffets and as many spiders. Other characters may be added if desired.

THE LITTLE PINK ROSE 25(b), 111

When at last the Pink Rose lets the Wind and the Rain come into her underground home, they bring her up into the lovely garden. Music sets the mood for the playing of this attractive little story.

THE LITTLE RABBIT THAT WANTED RED WINGS 10, 78

But when he gets them his mammy doesn't know him and so he is glad enough to wish them off.

THE LITTLE RED HEN 25(b), 111

Children like to play the story of the industrious little red hen who plants the wheat, takes it to the mill, makes the bread, and feeds her chicks.

MY LADY WIND 81, 111

A tiny poem which is charming for pantomime with music.

THE NIGHT WAS CREEPING 57

This lovely poem by James Stephens inspires children of any age to imaginative pantomime.

OLD KING COLE 57, 81

Music is needed for the kind of play which this rhyme inspires, with its court processional, its fat, jolly king, and its fiddlers three.

THE PIG BROTHER 25(a)

Though this story of an untidy little boy is decidedly didactic, the children like it for the humor lent by the pig. It plays well.

THE QUEEN OF HEARTS 81

This has more possibilities for a complete play than almost any other Mother Goose rhyme.

A RIDDLE 110, 111

A four-line verse, quoted in Chapter 2, that can inspire endless dramatic play.

SING A SONG OF SIXPENCE 81

This rhyme can be used in various ways. See Chapter 2.

THE SNOW MAN 111

A delightful poem for little children to play. It can be used for rhythm work, for dramatic play, or for story dramatization.

THE SQUIRREL 9(a), 57, 110

"Whisky, frisky"—quoted in Chapter 2. A good poem for dramatic play.

THE SWALLOW 91, 110

The children bid the swallow to fly away over the sea when summer has gone, and to come again in the spring.

THE TALE OF PETER RABBIT 57, 86, 111

Little children are so fond of Peter Rabbit's adventures that they love to play them.

TEENY TINY 59, 61, 78, 111

The teeny tiny woman who takes the clothes off a scarecrow hears a teeny tiny voice in the night saying, "I want my clothes!" The surprise ending is always fun!

THE THREE BILLY GOATS GRUFF 32, 57, 61, 111

One of the most popular of all stories for the dramatizations of little children.

THREE LITTLE KITTENS 57, 111

Understandable to the youngest children. Good for dramatic play.

THREE LITTLE MICE 81, 111

Venturing out to find something dainty for tea, they are sent scampering by Pussy's eyes "so big and bright." (Quoted in Chapter 2.)

THE THREE PIGS 57, 59, 116

Though this story is less simple to play than "The Three Bears," children know and like it so well that it is a possibility.

THE TOWN MOUSE AND THE COUNTRY MOUSE 32, 50, 57, 61, 111

"Better beans and bacon in peace than cakes and ale in fear." Plenty of implications for any age.

WHY THE EVERGREEN TREES KEEP THEIR LEAVES IN WINTER 25(a), 111

Only the spruce, the pine, and the juniper trees will shelter the little bird with the broken wing, and so the Frost King forbids the North Wind ever to blow off their leaves.

THE WONDERFUL TAR-BABY STORY 51, 111

Children will drop the dialect of this inimitable Uncle Remus story, but the situation is a merry one to play.

GROUP II
For Children of Seven and Eight Years

BEHIND THE WATERFALL 8, 111, 113

A delicate poem which stirs the imagination to create either a story or a dance-pantomime.

BRER RABBIT FRIGHTENS HIS NEIGHBORS 51

One of the most humorous of the Uncle Remus stories, and very playable.

THE CHILDREN'S BLUE BIRD 75

Episodes from Madame Maeterlinck's lovely story about the search for happiness can be used very effectively by children with imagination.

CINDERELLA 32, 54, 57, 61, 77, 78, 85, 111

This best loved among the fairy tales is beautifully suited for informal plays.

THE CLOWN WHO FORGOT HOW TO LAUGH 111

A usable little story about how he remembered as soon as he began to make a little girl forget her troubles.

DOORBELLS 15, 39, 111

All kinds of people can come to the door, and the children have fun weaving them into a story.

EEYORE'S BIRTHDAY 79(a)

One of the very clever Winnie-the-Pooh stories which an occasional superior group will enjoy playing.

THE ELF SINGING 57, 111

A dramatic little poem which can be used for choric speaking and pantomime.

THE DWARF AND THE COBBLER'S SONS 46, 111

How Franz, Friedrich, and Fritz were tested by the cross little dwarf and won a Merry Christmas for the family.

Feet. Hands 44

When children lie on their backs in the gymnasium, the action in these Dorothy Aldis poems is not only enjoyable but valuable for the recall of sense impressions.

The 500 Hats of Bartholomew Cubbins 97

Every time Bartholomew takes off one hat another appears in its place. Opportunity for much comedy in characterizations.

The Good Samaritan 20(b), 111

This finest of all the parables for a creative play may be used at this and higher age levels.

The Great Quillow 103

A little toymaker puts to rout the giant Hunder and saves his village.

Hansel and Gretel 50, 57, 78

Both in informal drama and in opera, this story is enjoyed.

How the Robin's Breast Became Red 31, 111

An Indian myth which may be used effectively either for an informal play or as an idea for a dance pantomime.

The Hundred Dresses 38

Children at school tease and ridicule Wanda because she is "different." A charming story which makes children think.

Imaginings 84, 110

Behind the little red door is a world of imagined beings and things, different for every child. Quoted in Chapter 3.

Jack and the Beanstalk 32, 57, 58, 61, 78

One of the hardy fairy tales which keeps its popularity generation after generation.

Mrs. Mallaby's Birthday 45, 111

A charming story about a little old lady who longed for one special gift. After the neighbors brought her other presents, the longed-for gift came to her at last.

A LEGEND OF SPRING 111

An Indian legend which has fine possibilities both for dramatization and for creative rhythmic movement.

MANY MOONS 104

A delightful tale in which a princess asks for the moon and a
jester gets it for her.

THE MYSTERIOUS BOX 110

Story in Chapter 3.

NATHAN'S FRIEND 23

Nathan, a boy in north Judea, has heard so many stories about
Samaritans that he thinks they must be monsters. What he dis-
covers when he ventures to climb the hills to look over is a friend.
Best for children of eight or nine.

THE NATIVITY STORY 20(c), 111

Many beautiful creative plays based on the Nativity story are
given in churches and schools all over the land each Christmas
season.

OF A TAILOR AND A BEAR 110

Described in Chapter 3. Story in RCA Record Album Listening
Activities, Vol. 2 for Primary Grades.

OLD MAN RABBIT'S THANKSGIVING DINNER 10

A humorous little story in which Old Man Rabbit entertains all
the other creatures at a delicious dinner without realizing it is
Thanksgiving.

THE OLD MARKET WOMAN 81, 111

The simple old soul falls asleep on the King's highway; and after
a practical joker comes along and cuts her petticoats off up to her
knees, she doesn't know whether or not she is she!

PADDY'S CHRISTMAS 80, 111

A loved story about how a brown, bouncing bear cub found out
the meaning of Christmas. Children younger and older than this
age level also enjoy playing it.

THE PEDDLER AND HIS CAPS 111

One of the "sure-fire" stories to play. The monkey episode is great fun for very young children, and the village scene is excellent for older children.

PETER AND WENDY 14

Some of the episodes from this priceless book are delightful to use for dramatization.

PHARAOH'S DAUGHTER FINDS LITTLE MOSES 20(d), 111

The story is dramatic and full of action. The sister Miriam, "the little girl who could be trusted," is sometimes made the heroine.

PINOCCHIO 69

Many incidents of this famous story are suitable for dramatic use.

THE PLAIN PRINCESS 74

After the princess has lived for a time with a poor family, and learned the joy of working and sharing, she is no longer plain.

THE PRINCESS WHO COULD NOT CRY 42, 111

If the princess can be made to cry just once she will be a normal child. After all the wise men fail to cure her, little Marigold finds a clever way to make her cry.

THE REAL PRINCESS 5, 32, 61

Andersen's satirical tale about the princess with such exquisite sensitivity that she cannot sleep because there is a pea under her twenty mattresses.

ROADS 39, 57, 111

"A road might lead to anywhere," and the tiny poem leads the imagination to all sorts of interesting places.

RUMPELSTILTSKIN 32, 57, 61, 111

The popular fairy tale of the miller's daughter who has to spin straw into gold and of the dwarf who does it for her.

THE SELFISH GIANT 78, 117

The Oscar Wilde story of the giant and the little boy has many possibilities for playing.

THE SHEPHERD BOY WHO CRIED WOLF 1, 32, 61, 111

This old fable is one of the simple stories which can be used for any age. Various types of villagers will come into it.

THE SLEEPING BEAUTY 50, 54, 57, 111

A favorite for playmaking with children of this age level.

SNOW WHITE AND THE SEVEN DWARFS 43, 54, 57, 111

One of the top favorites among fairy tales. Wonderfully good situations for creative scenes.

SOME ONE 34, 57, 61

The music and the mystery in this poem have a strong appeal to children. The recall of night sounds is fine sense training.

A SUMMER MORNING 39, 44

An exquisite little poem for dance-pantomime.

TAPER TOM 102, 111

Humorous folk tale in which Tom makes the princess laugh by parading before her with a long line of people attached to his goose.

THE THREE WISHES 50, 59, 78, 111, 116

A Spanish story in which a man and his wife are given three wishes which they use so foolishly that the third has to be used to undo the damage.

TIGGER HAS BREAKFAST 79(b), 111

Though the charm of the Winnie-the-Pooh stories is principally in dialogue this is one that has very good action.

TWIG 62

A gay little story about the dream of an imaginative child which takes place in the back yard of a city tenement.

THE UGLY DUCKLING 5, 32, 57, 61

Andersen's classic story about the duckling who became a swan is well worth dramatizing.

THE UNHAPPY ECHO 11, 111

A charming story of a little girl who comes upon the house of the funny little Echo who answers the shouts of the campers.

THE WEATHER FACTORY 9(a), 108

As soon as summer is gone the little weather-folk are all a-flutter with their big job of making frost and snow for winter.

WHO'S THERE? 87, 111

Mrs. Goose brings in her neighbors to help her catch whatever is making a strange noise in her closet.

THE WONDERFUL WEAVER 57, 111

A poem which lends itself to dance pantomime.

GROUP III

For Children of Nine, Ten, and Eleven Years

AMAHL AND THE NIGHT VISITORS 76

On their way to find the Christ Child, the three Kings stop at the home of a crippled boy and his mother. What happens there is a dramatic and beautiful story—wonderful for a Christmas play.

ANDY AND THE LION 33

Andy reads so many books about lions that he has a fantastic dream in which he is Androcles. Full of humor, and popular with fourth-graders.

THE BAD JOKE THAT ENDED WELL 37, 111

The Council of a badly run town in Switzerland learns the secret of good management from a practical joker.

THE BAILIFF'S WONDERFUL COAT 72

This interesting Swedish tale, which is found in dramatic form in *More Legends in Action,* may be told as a story if used for creative dramatics.

BEAUTY AND THE BEAST 50, 95

The many incidents in this story make it more difficult to play than most of the fairy tales. It is highly dramatic, however, and makes an interesting play.

A BELL FOR URSLI 28

A charming Swiss tale in verse; interesting not only because of its playable story but also for its information about Swiss customs.

BHIMSA, THE DANCING BEAR 111, 114

Incidents from this fine story of India can be used, or the entire book may be the center of an integrated project. One episode may be found in *Stories to Dramatize.*

THE BOY KNIGHT OF REIMS 70

A dramatic and beautiful story from which very fine scenes can be used. Children get much of cultural value as well as enjoyment from working on them. One scene is included in *Stories to Dramatize.*

CADDIE WOODLAWN 21

The story of a pioneer family in Wisconsin. Caddie is a tomboy and a friend to the Indians. Several adventures can be played.

THE CHRISTMAS NIGHTINGALE 65

A Polish story involving a little boy who sings, and a Christmas marionette play.

A CHRISTMAS PROMISE 93, 111

A lovely Spanish tale about three kings and a little boy on Christmas Eve.

THE CONJURE WIVES 111, 115

Fun for the Hallowe'en season comes with the playing of this weird old southern tale.

DAVID 20(e)

Several episodes from the story of David in the Bible are good possibilities for dramatization. (a) David the shepherd boy, (b) David summoned to play for Saul, (c) David and Jonathan, (d) David spares Saul's life in the cave, (e) David and Jonathan's son.

THE EMPEROR'S NEW CLOTHES 5, 50, 57, 111

The rare humor of the story appeals especially to the older children in this group. If the leader knows Charlotte Chorpenning's play of this name (Samuel French, publisher), she will guide the children into a more interesting interpretation of the rogues.

FRIGGA'S NECKLACE 96

An interesting and usable story from Norse mythology.

GABRIEL AND THE HOUR BOOK 98

Though not highly dramatic, this is a good story for an integrated project on medieval life. Gabriel is the young color-mixer for a monk who is making an illuminated manuscript.

THE GOLDEN TOUCH 32, 50, 52, 111

The dramatic story of King Midas is always a favorite for dramatization.

THE GREEN GINGER JAR 63, 111

This book about Chicago's Chinatown is most interesting as the center of an integrated project.

HOMER PRICE 73

The stories about this small-town boy are full of humor and wisdom.

HOW ARTHUR BECAME KING 50, 88

One of the most usable of the Arthur stories. He alone, among all the aspirants to the throne, is able to pull the sword from the stone.

THE HURDY-GURDY MAN 19, 111

A tale in which the music of the hurdy-gurdy man socializes an unsocial community.

In Clean Hay 65

A beautiful Polish story in which some children do a marionette play of the Nativity, and give the money they earn to a poor man and woman whose boy baby has just been born in a stable. Excellent for a group that can do marionette plays.

Indian Captive 67

The same true story on which Charlotte Chorpenning based her play of this name—the story of a child who was captured by Seneca Indians.

The Indians and the Quaker Family 54

When all the other settlers fled because of a rumored Indian attack, a Quaker family remained behind and gave the Indians food. In return, they fastened a white feather over the Quakers' door and the family never again had to fear an attack.

Johnnie Appleseed 36, 111

A dramatic incident from one of the books about this greatly loved frontier saint.

The Knights of the Silver Shield 2, 32, 78

A fine story which glorifies spiritual courage above physical bravery. Best liked by sixth and seventh grades.

The Lantern and the Fan 55, 111

A charming little nature myth from Japan which can be developed into an interesting play.

The Lion, the Witch and the Wardrobe 68

Four children, spending a holiday on an old English estate, find their way through the back of a huge wardrobe into the mysterious land of Narnia. They have many adventures in that strange country.

The Magic Bed-Knob 82

Miss Price, who is learning to be a witch, buys the children's silence by giving magic properties to Paul's bed-knob. This begins a series of adventures that land the children finally on a

South Sea isle complete with cannibals and Miss Price. A modern story with much action and fun.

THE MAID WHO DEFIED MINERVA 31, 111

The dramatic mythological tale of Arachne who was turned into a spider for boasting that she was a better weaver than Minerva.

MARY POPPINS 107

The priceless story of an English nursemaid who has magic powers. She gives Jane and Michael some wonderful adventures and then, with a brusqueness which makes them believe they must have been dreaming, she disclaims any part in them.

THE MISER AND HIS MONKEY 111

A fable with humor and plenty of action showing that money is of value only when it is put to use. Also found in *Forty Famous Stories* published by the Hall and McCreary Co.

THE NUREMBERG STOVE 89, 111

An especially fine story for a creative play, greatly liked by sixth and seventh grades.

THE NUTCRACKER OF NUREMBERG 30

See Chapter 7.

PETERKIN PAPERS 49, 111

The absurd doings of this impractical family are very amusing to children, especially the one in which Mrs. Peterkin puts salt in her coffee by mistake. This incident is in *Stories to Dramatize*.

OLD PIPES AND THE DRYAD 32, 100

A long but interesting story which is good material either for a creative play or a dance drama.

PANDORA 50, 52

The girl in Greek mythology who opens the chest and lets out the troubles of the world. It lends itself both to dramatization and to dance drama.

THE PIED PIPER 25(a), 50, 57

A story which is used as play material for children of nearly every age level.

THE QUEST OF THE HAMMER 22, 111

The very amusing episode from Norse mythology in which Thor and Loki dress like a bride and her handmaiden and go to the castle of Thrym, the giant king, to recover Thor's hammer.

ROBIN HOOD 88, 111

Various stories of this legendary hero have long been favorites for dramatization. How Robin became an outlaw, the episode with Little John on the bridge, with Midge, the miller, the Widow's three sons, and the shooting match at Nottingham are all favorites.

SAINT FRANCIS AND THE WOLF 16

A charmingly illustrated story telling how Saint Francis tamed the great wolf who had terrified the villagers. It shows the power of love and understanding, he says, to make peace between the most dangerous of enemies.

THE SORCERER'S APPRENTICE 92, 111

The famous story of the apprentice who reads his master's magic book and learns how to make the broomstick carry water but fails to learn how to stop it! The music record should be used to set the mood.

STONE SOUP 24

A good version of the folk tale "The Old Woman and the Tramp." Three soldiers take the place of the tramp and there are many villagers.

TO YOUR GOOD HEALTH 23, 66

A folk tale in which a shepherd refuses to obey the king's command to say "To your good health!" when he sneezes, unless he can have the princess for his wife.

TOM SAWYER 29, 111

"Sure-fire" material for sixth- and seventh-grade children, who never fail to respond to the whitewashing and graveyard episodes for dramatics.

The Tree in the Trail 56

A well-written book with superb illustrations of the Southwest. With imagination, children can use it for an excellent play.

Tyll Ulenspiegel's Merry Pranks 60

Several stories about Tyll, a legendary little fellow in Germany, tell of pranks which children like to dramatize.

The Voyage of the Wee Red Cap 93, 111

Ruth Sawyer's charming Christmas story of the stingy old Teig who is taken by the wee folk to see the spirit of giving in other lands. An Irish tale with fine possibilities for creative drama.

Why Four Men Tore Up a Roof 20(c)

The story of the four men who have such faith that Jesus can cure their friend that they let him down through the roof.

Why the Chimes Rang 2

Though this story may be had in play form, it is a fine experience for the children to make their own play.

William Tell 12, 111

Children like to play this story of the freedom-loving Swiss hero who was made to shoot the apple from his son's head. There is opportunity for good characterizations in the people of the crowd.

The Wind in the Willows 47, 111

An occasional class that appreciates this fine book will enjoy dramatizing one or two of the chapters. One episode, "Mr. Toad's Disguise" may be found in *Stories to Dramatize*.

The Wise People of Gotham 12, 111

The people of Gotham pretend to be simple so that the king will not think it worth while to have their noses cut off. A good humorous story which can be used both for this age level and the preceding one.

ZACCHAEUS 20(g)

An interesting telling of the story of the little man who climbed a tree to see Jesus, and whose whole life was changed thereby.

GROUP IV

For Children of Twelve, Thirteen, and Fourteen Years

ADAM OF THE ROAD 48

A rich story of England in the days of minstrelsy. "There is the pattern of a medieval tapestry, but the lines are not mellowed, they are sunny, warm, and alive."

ARABIAN NIGHTS TALES 7

Aladdin and Ali Baba, rich, adventurous stories, satisfy the craving of boys and girls of this age for color and excitement.

THE BIRTHDAY OF THE INFANTA 117

The Oscar Wilde story of the little hunchback who danced for the Infanta and then died of a broken heart when he discovered that she was only ridiculing him. For very superior groups.

THE BISHOP'S CANDLESTICKS 111

Only older children of exceptional appreciation should play this story from *Les Miserables*. Its wonderful spiritual quality will be inspirational if the teacher can help the children to appreciate it.

THE BOY WHO FOUND THE KING 2

A king has disappeared, leaving word that he needs to live among the people before he is worthy to be their ruler. What he does and how he is discovered makes a story which has a strong spiritual lift.

THE CHRISTMAS APPLE 93, 111

An unusually beautiful story of a little German clockmaker. An entertaining and inspiring Christmas play can be created from it.

A CHRISTMAS CAROL 35

No Christmas story is better liked by the older children for play-

making than is this story of old Scrooge. Two favorite scenes
are included in *Stories to Dramatize*.

COUNT HUGO'S SWORD 98

An interesting and dramatic story of a French boy who prevents
his benefactor from fighting a duel by hiding the sword of his
opponent, Count Hugo. Not easy but worth dramatizing.

THE ENCHANTED SHIRT 53, 111

A modern ballad telling of the king who could be cured of his
illness by sleeping one night in the shirt of a happy man. And
when at last a happy man is found he has not a shirt to his back.

THE FORGIVING FATHER 20(i)

This title suggests a truer meaning for the parable than does the
Prodigal Son. For it is the father's love and understanding of
both his sons that makes this a beautiful story.

GET UP AND BAR THE DOOR 50, 101, 111

A short, humorous ballad in which the good man and his wife
agree that "whoever should speak the foremost word would rise
and bar the door." The comedy should be stressed from beginning
to end.

HUNGRY HANS 64, 111

A very amusing "comic tragedy" in which a long, lean apprentice
devours a little pig which his mistress left him to roast for dinner.
Children of about twelve greatly enjoy playing this story.

JOSEPH AND HIS BROTHERS 20(h)

This adventurous story is one of the finest of all Bible stories
for a creative play. It can be used in either this or the preceding
period.

KING HENRY AND THE MILLER OF MANSFIELD 101

A good ballad with plenty of comedy. Henry so enjoys his adventure with the miller that he makes him a knight.

KING JOHN AND THE ABBOT OF CANTERBURY 32, 50, 61, 111

An old ballad which falls easily into dramatic form. If the Abbot cannot "answer questions three his head shall be smitten from his body!" Good also for the preceding age level.

THE LEGEND OF THE BLACK MADONNA 23

The unknown artist of a stained glass window works out a bitter grudge by making the Madonna of black glass. But the sun, pouring through it, changes it to dazzling brightness, so that the hearts of both artist and congregation are moved.

LITTLE WOMEN 3

Christmas at the March's, with the rehearsal and performance of Jo's play, is always popular with the older girls.

THE LOST VIOLIN 63

A dramatic story of Bohemian immigrants newly come to this country. Can be developed into an effective integrated play.

MASTER SKYLARK 17

A well-told story of Shakespeare's time based on fact. It concerns a boy singer who is kidnapped by a company of strolling players.

THE MOOR'S LEGACY 58, 111

A favorite story for twelve-year-olds. One of the legends which Washington Irving immortalized in *Tales of the Alhambra*. Full of mystery and adventure.

THE OLD WOMAN AND THE TRAMP 54, 111, 116

A clever tramp pretends to a stingy old woman that he can make broth out of a nail. It must be played in the spirit of fun, with no hint of seriousness.

OUR LADY'S JUGGLER 111

A beautiful legend about a little juggler who served in the way he knew best.

THE PAGE OF COUNT REYNAURD 98

An interesting and very usable story in which a certain page plagiarizes a ballad for his master to enter in a contest and is caught by a clever device.

THE PARABLE OF THE TALENTS 20(j)

This may be effectively played either in the setting Jesus used or as a modern story.

THE PEDDLER OF BALLAGHADEREEN 94

Ruth Sawyer's telling of the fine Irish story about the peddler who had an extraordinary dream—and of a landlord who helped to make the dream come true.

THE PRINCE AND THE PAUPER 29, 111

Many of the incidents in this novel make wonderfully fine material for playmaking.

THE PRINCESS AND THE VAGABOND 94

Ruth Sawyer's delightful Irish version of *The Taming of the Shrew*. Because it is more romantic than the Shakespeare play, it is more suitable for a group of older girls than for a mixed group.

THE RABBI AND THE DIADEM 32

A kind Rabbi finds in his garden the priceless diadem which the empress of Rome has lost. What he does with it makes a dramatic story.

RIP VAN WINKLE 58, 111

There is much opportunity for interesting characterizations in this story. Emphasis is put more on Rip's good nature and laziness than on his drinking.

THE STONE IN THE ROAD 111

One of the most useful of stories for teaching characterization. It never fails to interest children of this age level.

STORIES FROM SHAKESPEARE'S PLAYS 71, 111

Episodes from *The Comedy of Errors, Julius Caesar, King Lear, A Midsummer Night's Dream, Macbeth, The Merchant of Venice, The Taming of the Shrew,* and *Twelfth Night* have proved most suitable for eighth-grade boys and girls.

Preteens + Teens: A Stone In the Road
Winnie-the-Pooh, Anatole: The Cheese
Taster, Wizard of Oz, Alice in Wonderland,
Wind in the Willows. / Norton Juster
Roauld Dahl - The Fantastic Fox / The Phantom T

THREE MEALS A DAY 72

This merry Dutch legend, which has been dramatized in *More Legends in Action*, may be told as a story for informal dramatization.

THE THREE SILLIES 50, 59, 78, 116

A nonsense tale which is fun to play, and simple enough for inexperienced players.

TREASURE ISLAND 99

Incidents from this great story can be used for playmaking, though it is most successful as a formal children's theatre play.

TREE OF FREEDOM 26

An exciting story of pioneers in Kentucky during the French and Indian War.

THE VISITOR 110

Poem in Chapter 4.

WHAT MEN LIVE BY 106

Tolstoy's fine story of the angel who comes to the home of the humble Russian shoemaker and learns of the three things by which men live.

WHERE LOVE IS, THERE GOD IS ALSO 105

The theme of this story is "Inasmuch as ye have done it unto one of the least of these my brethren, ye have done it unto me."

WICKED JOHN AND THE DEVIL 27

A folk tale of the southern mountains telling about "the most ornery blacksmith in history and his outwitting of the devil." Richard Chase has collected his tales in the American communities where storytelling as a folk art still flourishes.

SOURCES OF STORIES

1. Aesop: *Fables* (The Viking Press and others).
2. Alden, Raymond MacDonald, *The Boy Who Found the King,*

Booth

The Knights of the Silver Shield, Why the Chimes Rang (The Bobbs-Merrill Co.).

3. Alcott, Louisa M., *Little Women* (Little Brown & Co.).

4. Aldis, Dorothy, *Everything and Anything* (Minton, Balch & Co.).

5. Andersen, Hans Christian, *Fairy Tales* (E. P. Dutton & Co. and others).

6. Applegarth, Margaret, *Right Here, Right Now!* (Harper & Bros.).

7. Arabian Nights: *Their Best Known Tales* (Charles Scribner's Sons).

8. Arbuthnot, May Hill, *Children and Books* (Scott, Foresman & Co.).

9. Association for Childhood Education, (a) *Sung Under the Silver Umbrella*, (b) *Told Under the Magic Umbrella* (The Macmillan Co.).

10. Bailey, Carolyn Sherwin, *For the Story Teller* (Milton Bradley Co.).

11. Bailey, Carolyn Sherwin, *The Story Telling Hour* (Dodd, Mead & Co.).

12. Baldwin, James, *Fifty Famous Stories Retold* (American Book Co.).

13. Bannerman, Helen, *Little Black Sambo* (Frederick Stokes Co.).

14. Barrie, James M., *Peter Pan and Wendy* (Charles Scribner's Sons).

15. Barrows, Marjorie, *One Hundred Best Poems for Boys and Girls* (Whitman Publishing Co.).

16. Beatty, Hetty Burlingame, *Saint Francis and the Wolf* (Houghton Mifflin Co.).

17. Bennett, John, *Master Skylark* (Appleton-Century-Crofts, Inc.).

18. Bennett, Rowena Bastin, *Around a Toadstool Table* (Thomas S. Rockwell Co.).

19. Bianco, Margery, *The Hurdy-Gurdy Man* (Oxford University Press).

20. The Bible, (a) Matthew 18, (b) Luke 10, (c) Luke 2, (d)

Exodus 2, (e) I. Samuel, II. Samuel, I. Kings, (f) Mark 2, (g) Luke 19, (h) Genesis 30, (i) Luke 15, (j) Luke 19.

21. Brink, Carol Ryrie, *Caddie Woodlawn* (The Macmillan Co.).

22. Brown, Abbie Farwell, *In the Days of Giants* (Houghton Mifflin Co.).

23. Brown, Jeanette Perkins, *The Storyteller in Religious Education* (The Pilgrim Press).

24. Brown, Marcia, *Stone Soup* (Charles Scribner's Sons).

25. Bryant, Sara Cone, (a) *How to Tell Stories to Children* (b) *Stories to Tell to Children* (Houghton Mifflin Co.).

26. Caudill, Rebecca, *Tree of Freedom* (The Viking Press).

27. Chase, Richard, *Grandfather Tales, Wicked John and the Devil* (Houghton Mifflin Co.).

28. Chonz, Selma, *A Bell for Ursli* (Oxford University Press).

29. Clemens, Samuel L., *The Prince and the Pauper, Tom Sawyer* (Harper & Bros.).

30. Cooke, Donald, *The Nutcracker of Nuremberg* (John C. Winston).

31. Cooke, Flora J., *Nature Myths and Stories* (A Flanagan).

32. Curry, C. M., and Clippinger, E. E., *Children's Literature* (Rand, McNally & Co.).

33. Daugherty, James, *Andy and the Lion* (The Viking Press).

34. De la Mare, Walter, *Peacock Pie* (Henry Holt & Co.).

35. Dickens, Charles, *A Christmas Carol* (Garden City Publishing Co.).

36. Douglas, Emily Taft, *Appleseed Farm* (Abingdon Press).

37. Duvoisin, Roger, *The Three Sneezes* (Alfred A. Knopf, Inc.).

38. Estes, Eleanor, *The Hundred Dresses* (Harcourt, Brace & Co.).

39. Field, Rachel, *Pointed People* (Yale University Press).

40. Flack, Marjorie, *Ask Mr. Bear* (The Macmillan Co.).

41. Forbes, Esther, *Johnny Tremain* (Houghton Mifflin Co.).

42. Fyleman, Rose, *The Rainbow Cat* (Doubleday & Co.).

43. Gag, Wanda, *Snow White* (Coward, McCann, Inc.).

44. Geismer, Barbara Peck, and Suter, Antoinette Brown, *Very*

Young Verses (Houghton Mifflin Co.). "Galoshes" also in Bacmeister, Rhoda W., *Stories to Begin On* (E. P. Dutton & Co.).

45. Gilbert, Helen Earle, *Mrs. Mallaby's Birthday* (Rand McNally Co.).

46. *The Golden Christmas Book* (Simon & Schuster).

47. Grahame, Kenneth, *The Wind in the Willows* (Charles Scribner's Sons).

48. Gray, Elizabeth Janet, *Adam of the Road* (The Viking Press).

49. Hale, Lucretia, *The Peterkin Papers* (Houghton Mifflin Co.).

50. Hallowell, Lillian, *A Book of Children's Literature* (Farrar & Rinehart, Inc.).

51. Harris, Joel Chandler, *Uncle Remus: His Songs and Sayings* (Appleton-Century-Crofts, Inc.).

52. Hawthorne, Nathaniel, *The Wonder Book* (Houghton Mifflin Co.).

53. Hay, John, *The Enchanted Shirt* (Houghton Mifflin Co.).

54. Hodgkins, Mary D. H., *The Atlantic Treasury of Childhood Stories* (Atlantic Monthly Press).

55. Holbrook, Florence, *Nature Myths and Stories* (Houghton Mifflin Co.).

56. Holling, Holling C., *The Tree in the Trail* (Houghton Mifflin Co.).

57. Huber, Miriam, *Story and Verse for Children* (The Macmillan Co.).

58. Irving, Washington, *Rip Van Winkle, Tales of the Alhambra* (Houghton Mifflin Co.).

59. Jacobs, Joseph, *English Fairy Tales* (G. P. Putnam's Sons).

60. Jagendorf, M. A., *Tyll Ulenspiegel's Merry Pranks* (The Vanguard Press, Inc.).

61. Johnson, Edna; Scott, Carrie E.; Sickels, Evelyn R., *Anthology of Children's Literature* (Houghton Mifflin Co.).

62. Jones, Elizabeth Orton, *Twig* (The Macmillan Co.).

63. Judson, Clara Ingram, *The Green Ginger Jar, The Lost Violin* (Houghton Mifflin Co.).

64. Keller, Gottfried, *The Fat of the Cat*, adapted by Louis Untermeyer (Harcourt, Brace & Co.).
65. Kelly, Eric, *In Clean Hay*, *The Christmas Nightingale* (The Macmillan Co.).
66. Lang, Andrew, *The Crimson Fairy Book* (Longmans, Green & Co.).
67. Lenski, Lois, *Indian Captive* (Frederick Stokes Co.).
68. Lewis, C. S., *The Lion, the Witch, and the Wardrobe* (The Macmillan Co.).
69. Lorenzini, Carlo, *The Adventures of Pinocchio* (Thomas Nelson & Sons).
70. Lownsbery, Eloise, *The Boy Knight of Reims* (Houghton Mifflin Co.).
71. MacLeod, Mary, *The Shakespeare Story Book* (A. S. Barnes & Co.).
72. McCaslin, Nellie, *More Legends in Action* (Row, Peterson & Co.).
73. McCloskey, Robert, *Homer Price* (The Viking Press).
74. McGinley, Phyllis, *The Plain Princess* (J. B. Lippincott Co.).
75. Maeterlinck, Mme. Maurice, *The Blue Bird for Children* (Silver Burdett Co.).
76. Menotti, Gian, *Amahl and the Night Visitors* (McGraw-Hill Book Co.).
77. Miller, Alice Duer, *Cinderella* (verse) (Coward-McCann, Inc.).
78. Miller, Olive Beaupre, *My Bookhouse* (The Bookhouse for Children).
79. Milne, A. A., (a) *Winnie-the-Pooh*; (b) *The House at Pooh Corner* (E. P. Dutton & Co., Inc.).
80. Monsell, Helen A., *Paddy's Christmas* (Alfred A. Knopf, Inc.).
81. *Mother Goose* (Many publishers).
82. Norton, Mary, *The Magic Bed-Knob* (G. P. Putnam's Sons).
83. Olcott, Frances, *Story Telling Ballads* (Houghton Mifflin Co.).
84. Paget-Fredericks, J. T., *Green Pipes* (The Macmillan Co.).
85. Perrault, Charles, *Old Time Stories* (Dodd, Mead & Co.).

86. Potter, Beatrix, *The Tale of Peter Rabbit* (Frederick Warne & Co.).

87. Potter, Miriam Clark, *Mrs. Goose of Animaltown* (J. B. Lippincott Co.).

88. Pyle, Howard, *The Merry Adventures of Robin Hood, The Story of King Arthur* (Charles Scribner's Sons).

89. Ramée, Louisa de la ("Ouida"), *The Nuremberg Stove* (J. B. Lippincott Co.).

90. Roberts, Elizabeth Madox, *Under the Tree* (The Viking Press).

91. Rossetti, Christina, *Sing Song* (The Macmillan Co.).

92. Rostron, Richard, *The Sorcerer's Apprentice* (William Morrow & Co., Inc.).

93. Sawyer, Ruth, *This Way to Christmas* (Harper & Bros.).

94. Sawyer, Ruth, *The Way of the Storyteller* (The Viking Press).

95. Scudder, Horace E., *The Children's Book* (The Macmillan Co.).

96. Sellew, Catherine F., *Adventures With the Giants* (Little, Brown & Co.).

97. Seuss, Dr., *The 500 Hats of Bartholomew Cubbins* (The Vanguard Press).

98. Stein, Evaleen, *Troubadour Tales* (Bobbs-Merrill Co.). *Gabriel and the Hour Book* (L. C. Page & Co.).

99. Stevenson, Robert Louis, *Treasure Island* (Charles Scribner's Sons).

100. Stockton, Frank, *Fanciful Tales* (Charles Scribner's Sons).

101. Tappan, Eva March, *Old Ballads in Prose* (Houghton Mifflin Co.).

102. Thorne-Thomsen, Gudrun, *East o' the Sun and West o' the Moon* (Row, Peterson & Co.).

103. Thurber, James, *The Great Quillow* (Harcourt, Brace & Co.).

104. Thurber, James, *Many Moods* (The Viking Press).

105. Tolstoy, Leo, *Twenty-Three Tales* (Oxford University Press).

106. Tolstoy, Leo, *What Men Live By* (Thomas Y. Crowell Co.).

107. Travers, Pamela, *Mary Poppins* (Reynal & Hitchcock).

108. Turner, Nancy Byrd, *Magpie Lane* (Harcourt, Brace & Co.).
109. Untermeyer, Louis, *This Singing World* (Harcourt, Brace & Co.).
110. Ward, Winifred, *Playmaking With Children*, rev. (Appleton-Century-Crofts, Inc.).
111. Ward, Winifred, *Stories to Dramatize* (Children's Theatre Press).
112. Webb, Marion St. John, *Orchard Fairies* (Medici Society Ltd., London).
113. Welles, Winifred, *Skipping Along Alone* (The Macmillan Co.).
114. Weston, Christine, *Bhimsa, the Dancing Bear* (Charles Scribner's Sons).
115. Wickes, Frances G., *Happy Holidays* (Rand McNally & Co.).
116. Wiggin, Kate Douglas, and Smith, Nora Archibald, *Tales of Laughter* (Garden City Publishing Co.).
117. Wilde, Oscar, *Fairy Tales* (G. P. Putnam's Sons).

APPENDIX III

Record List

THE CHOICE OF MUSICAL RECORDINGS TO STIR THE IMAGINATION AND set the mood for stories the children play is a delicate and difficult undertaking. Unless the leader has sensitivity and taste it would be better to use no music at all. Like lighting a children's theatre play, it requires much experimenting. But when it is right it can lift the whole activity into an imaginative and beautiful experience.

In the compilation of the following list, Ann Heekin was of very great help, discovering valuable records and experimenting with them in her classes. An effort was made to choose music which was not hackneyed by too much use, so that it would not be associated in the children's minds with other experiences.

The list is intended merely as a suggestion of a few good available records for various purposes. There is no end to such a search, and every leader will have her own favorites to add to this list.

The record numbers change so rapidly—some records being discontinued, others issued in a new form—that it would seem useless to indicate them except for the fact that dealers can locate the music more readily if a number is given.

I. FOR CHILDREN'S RHYTHMIC ACTIVITIES

    1. *"Let's Play" Series.* Musical-Action Stories, Kay Ortmans Productions, Ltd. 1644 West Broadway, Vancouver 9, B.C. Two sets of children's records of creative rhythms to Kay Ortmans' original music.

    Set No. 1 (2 records) (a) At the Edge of the Field, (b) Farm Land, (c) Caves, Crabs and Sand, (d) Down by the River.

Set No. 2 (3 records) (a) Friendly Animals, (b) Adventures in the Forest, (c) The Bear's Joke, (d) Up on the Hill, (e) Playing With the Wind, (f) Let's Have a Rest.

Here are two sets of records of creative rhythms for young children that are utterly captivating, and very easy to use because the teacher is on the records! Though doubtless planned for children below the fifth grade, older girls would enjoy and profit from using them also.

Set 1 is planned so that it is possible to play it sitting at desks or in beds. Set 2 is for large, free movements of the whole body. Both call forth the child's creative imagination.

2. *Childhood Rhythms.* Arranged and recorded by Ruth Evans, 326 Forest Park Ave., Springfield, Mass.

Four albums: Series I. Elementary Rhythms. Series II. Intermediate Rhythms. Series III. Advanced Rhythms. Series IV. Application of Rhythmic Patterns to Dance.

Beginning with basic rhythms, later records stimulate interest in dramatizing animals, toys, fairies, giants, swings, etc. The accompaniment is familiar music on the piano.

3. *Rhythmic Activities.* RCA Victor Record Library for Elementary Schools. Notes for teachers prepared by Lilla Belle Pitts and Gladys Tipton.

Basic Rhythm Program: Volumes I, II, III, Primary Grades. Volumes IV and V, Upper Grades.

Basic Listening Program: Volumes I, II, III for Primary Grades. Volumes IV, V, VI, Upper Grades.

With an orchestra playing classical music, all kinds of rhythms are given meaning by imagining dwarfs, birds, clowns, horses, etc. The notes for teachers are of much help in stirring children's imagination.

4. *Young People's Records.* Most of these records are songs or stories with music accompaniment, less usable for playmaking than are the Kay Ortman's "Let's Play" sets. Some, however, can be used satisfactorily. They are of good calibre.

5. The Children's Record Guild, 27 Thompson St., New York 13, N.Y. These records, too, have high standards. They are distributed regularly to subscribers. Prokofiev's "Cinderella" is an example of the outstanding records the subscribers sometimes receive from them.

II. MOOD MUSIC

Often played when children are planning their dramatizations, trying on characters, playing scenes in pantomime. On the rare occasions when they present their plays for other children, the music often sets the mood for the audience.

A. LIVELY, EXCITING:

1. *Carnival of Animals.* Charles Saint-Saëns. Other side: Young Person's Introduction to an Orchestra — Angel 35135

2. *Circus Time.* Ringling Brothers and Barnum and Bailey's Circus Band — Decca DL 5480

3. *The Comedians.* Dimitri Kabalevsky. Boston Pops Orchestra — RCA Victor, LM 1106

4. *Fireworks.* Igor Stravinsky. Fantasy for Orchestra — Camden CAL 162

5. *Miniature Viennese March.* Fritz Kreisler — G-HE 661

6. *La Boutique Fantasque Ballet.* Giocchino Rossini. (The Fantastic Toyshop) — Angel 30001

B. SMOOTH, BEAUTIFUL:

1. *Clouds.* In Nocturne No. 1. Claude Debussy — Mercury MG 50005

2. *Concerti Grossi.* For strings. No. 5 and 6. George Frederic Handel — London LPS 396

3. *Eight Dances for Harp* (one a minuet). Played by Carlos Sazedo — Mercury Classics MG 10144 B

4. *In a Monastery Garden*. Albert   Columbia 7523 M
Ketelby. Kostelanetz Orchestra

5. *Morning*. Edward Grieg. Phila-   Columbia 2037
delphia Orchestra

6. *Music for the Flute*. William   Columbia ML 4339
Kincaid. The Debussy number
has a haunting melody, fine for
shepherds' pipes

7. *Music of the Rococo*. Five minu-   Plymouth P 12-36
ets by Franz Schubert

8. *Premiere Rhapsody*. Claude De-   Decca ED 3505
bussy. Clarinet. Ethereal, imagi-
native

9. *The Swan of Tuonela*. Jean Sibe-   Columbia ML 2158
lius. Philadelphia Orchestra

C. STRANGE, WEIRD:

1. *Danse Macabre*. Charles Saint-   Capitol H-8169
Saëns. Eerie music for Hallow-   (Side 1)
e'en

2. *The Hall of the Mountain King*.   Columbia 2037
Edward Grieg. From the Peer
Gynt Suite

3. *Jungle Drums*. Drums exclusively   Decca DL 5426

4. *La Mer* (The Sea). Claude De-   Angel 35081
bussy. Philharmonic Orchestra

5. *A Night on Bald Mountain*.   Capitol H-8169
Modeste Moussorgsky. Meeting   (Side 2)
of Witches

6. *Scythian Suite*. Op. 20. Sergei   LPM 4142
Prokofiev. Splendidly barbaric
music

D. VARIOUS MOODS ON THE SAME RECORDS:

1. *Ballets Nos. 1, 2, 3*. Dmitri Shos-   CE 3012-A
takovitch. Short pieces of various
kinds: waltz, polka, romance, ga-
votte, etc. Usable for many stories

2. *Children's Corner Suite.* Claude   Angel 35172
Debussy. The Little Shepherd,
Serenade for a Doll, Snow is
Dancing, Golliwog's Cake Walk,
Jimbo's Lullaby

3. *Children's Suite.* The Villa-Lobos   VM 970
Album. Including Serenade for a
Doll, by Debussy; March of the
Dwarfs, by Grieg; The Tame
Bear, by Elgar; The Knight of the
Hobby-Horse, by Schumann

4. *Concert for Toys and Orchestra.*   Young People's
Walter Hendl   Records 432

5. *Dance of the Hours.* Amilcare   London LP 180
Ponchinelli. From La Gioconda

6. *Façade Suite.* William Walton.   Columbia Master-
Philadelphia Orchestra   works ML 4793

7. *Fall River Legend.* Ballet Suite.   Columbia ML 4616
Morton Gould. New York Sym-
phony Orchestra

8. *Folk Songs for Orchestra.* Anatol   Young People's
Liadov   Records 405

9. *Le Tombeau de Couperin.* Mau-   Capitol P 8244
rice Ravel. Italian Country
Dance, Minuet, etc.

10. *Rondos: Sonatina, for Children.*   Bartok Records
Bela Bartok Mood Studies,   BRS 917
rhythms

11. *The Walk to Paradise Gardens.*   Camden Cal 215
Frederick Delius. Five short
pieces by Khatchaturian, Franck,
Rimsky-Korsakov, Prokofiev, Cha-
brier

III. DIGNIFIED MARCHES

1. *Coronation March,* from *The*   Columbia 71287 D
Prophet. Giocomo Meyerbeer. CBS
Orchestra

2. *Festival March*, from *Tannhauser.*   RCA Listening Ac-
Richard Wagner. RCA Victor Or-   tivities, Vol. 5
chestra

3. *Gallop and Dance of the Parents.*   Angel 35004
Peter Ilich Tchaikovsky. From the   (and others)
complete *Nutcracker Suite*

4. *Lute Song.* Procession   Decca DA 445

5. *Triumphal March*, from *Aida.*   RCA Victor
Giuseppe Verdi. Boston Pops Orches-   49-4107
tra

6. *Royal Fireworks Music.* George Fred-   London LS 620
erick Handel. Amsterdam Concert-
gebouw Orchestra

IV. MUSIC OF OTHER PEOPLES

Folk music and folk songs are listed by countries in Schwann's
Long Playing Record catalogue.

1. *Caucasian Sketches.* Michael Ippo-   Angel 35145
litov-Ivanov. Philharmonia Orchestra   (and others)

2. *Folkways Records*—117 West 46th
St., New York. Many folk songs and
dances are available from this company.

3. *Imperial Court Music.* Cook Labora-   Cook 1132
tories, Stamford, Conn. Japanese
music. 16th, 17th, 18th centuries.
Other side, modern Japanese music

4. *Basic Indian Album.* RCA Victor   RCA Victor E-89
Orchestra. Ceremonials, chants,
dances, lullabies, of various tribes

5. *Music for the Nostalgic Traveler.*   RCA Victor
The George Melachrino Orchestra.   LPM 1053
Each band has a short piece typical
of a different country: British Isles,
France, Italy, Spain, Central Europe,
Tropics

6. *Music of India.* From the moving
picture, *The River.* Original musical
score recorded in India

7. *Music of the Orient.* China, Japan,   Decca DX 107
Bali, Indonesia, Persia, Egypt, Tunis,
etc.

8. *Nights in the Gardens of Spain.*   Angel 35134
Manuel de Falla. National Orches-
tra

9. *Ports of Call.* Jacques Ibert. Phila-   Columbia ML 4983
delphia Orchestra

V. RECORDS TO USE WITH SPECIFIC STORIES

1. *Amahl and the Night Visitors.* Gian   RCA Victor LM
Menotti. Much of the opera music   1701
can be used with the story played
creatively.

2. *Cinderella.* Sergei Prokofiev. The   CHS 1304
feeling for the fairy tale will be en-
hanced by listening to this lovely
music.

3. *Humoresque.* Peter Ilich Tchaikov-   Victor 14947
sky. For a grotesque character such as
the Cobbler in "Ali Baba"

4. *A Midsummer Night's Dream Over-   Victor DM 1280
ture.* Felix Mendelssohn. NBC Or-
chestra. Fairy dancing

5. *The Nutcracker.* Peter Ilich Tchai-   Angel 35004
kovsky. It would be well to decide   (and others)
which dances are desired, and find
the records which include them.

6. *Of a Tailor and a Bear.* Edward   RCA Record Li-
MacDowell. See Chapter 7   brary for Elemen-
                                             tary Schools. Lis-
                                             tening   Activities,
                                             Vol. 2

7. *Peter and the Wolf.* Sergei Prokofiev.   Victor LM 1761
   Op. 67. Alec Guinness, narrator
8. *Scheherazade.* Maurice Ravel. Suisse   London LL 1196
   Romande Orchestra. Wonderfully
   good for Arabian Nights tales
9. *Seven Jumps.* RCA Victor Folk   Educational Series
   Dance Orchestra. This is excellent   45-6172
   for one of the Hurdy-Gurdy man's
   tunes.
10. *The Sorcerer's Apprentice.* Paul Du-   RCA Victor LM
    kas. NBC Symphony Orchestra. The   1118
    children often hear the story and
    the record before dramatizing it.
    Parts of the record can be played
    during the creative play.

VI. SOUND-EFFECTS RECORDS

Two sound effects companies are:

Speedy-Q Sound Effects
Box 438 Foulke Station
Richmond, Indiana

Standard Radio Transcription Service
360 N. Michigan Ave.
Chicago, 1, Illinois

A good record of sea sounds is Voice of the Sea. Cook Labora-
tories 5011. Surf, tugboats, fog horn, etc.

Index

339